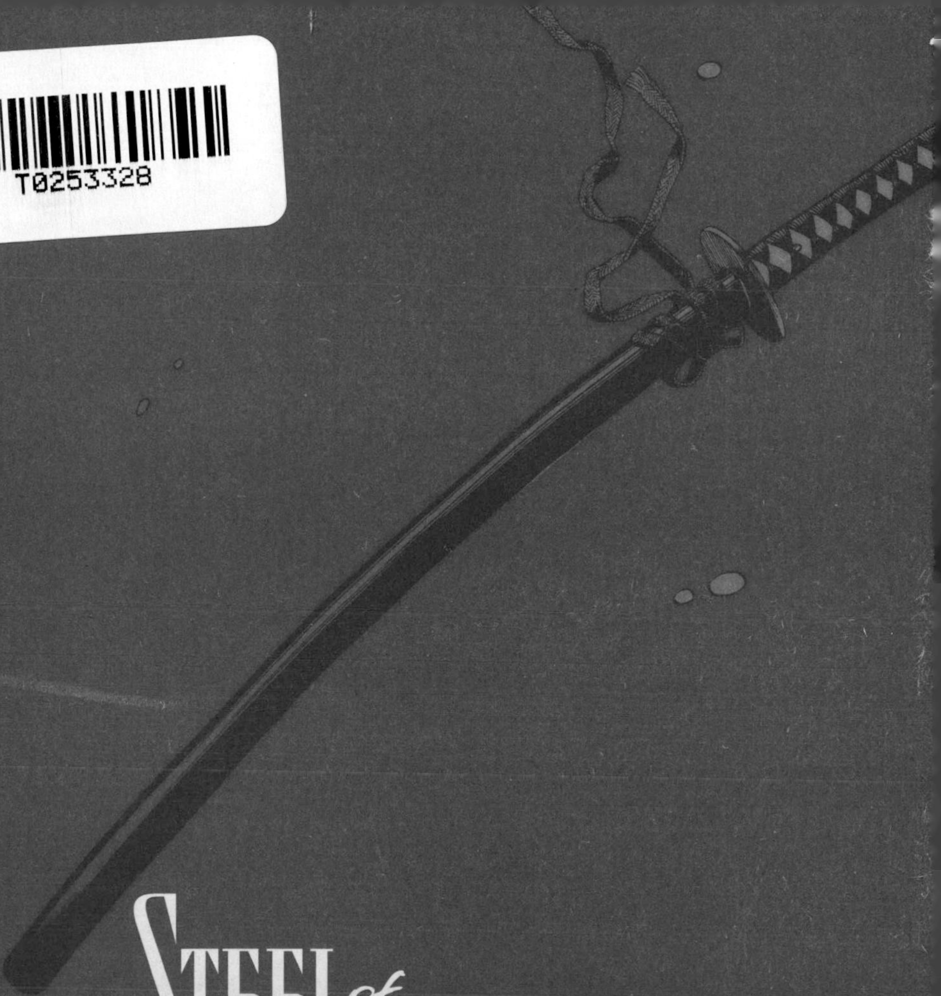

STEEL of the CELESTIAL SHADOWS 3

STORY & ART

DARUMA MATSUURA

SUPERVISION BY
TOSHIKI MIZUTANI
NOBORU HISAYAMA

MADARA	AKI	TSUKI	RYUDO KONOSUKE

A woman shunned by society for her ability. She stands in the way of Konosuke and Aki.

A bright and cheery traveling *ichiko* medium. She's arrived in Edo for reasons of her own.

An otherworldly beauty who mysteriously appeared from nowhere to wed Konosuke. Why does she adore him so?

A low-ranking samurai who can't seem to catch a break. Metal warps when he touches it or it gets near his body, so he can't wield a blade.

Ryudo Konosuke is a low-ranking samurai struggling

to survive abject poverty. He owes his destitution to

his seemingly cursed ability to warp any metal that

comes near him. One day, a beautiful woman named

Tsuki shows up at Konosuke's door and marries him.

Their happiness is short-lived, however, as Tsuki is

whisked away by a strange man with supernatural

powers. When Aki—a blind medium with the ability to

view a person's future—finds her way to Konosuke, he is

determined to use his new friend's power to save Tsuki.

But there are dark forces conspiring against him...

[CONTENTS]

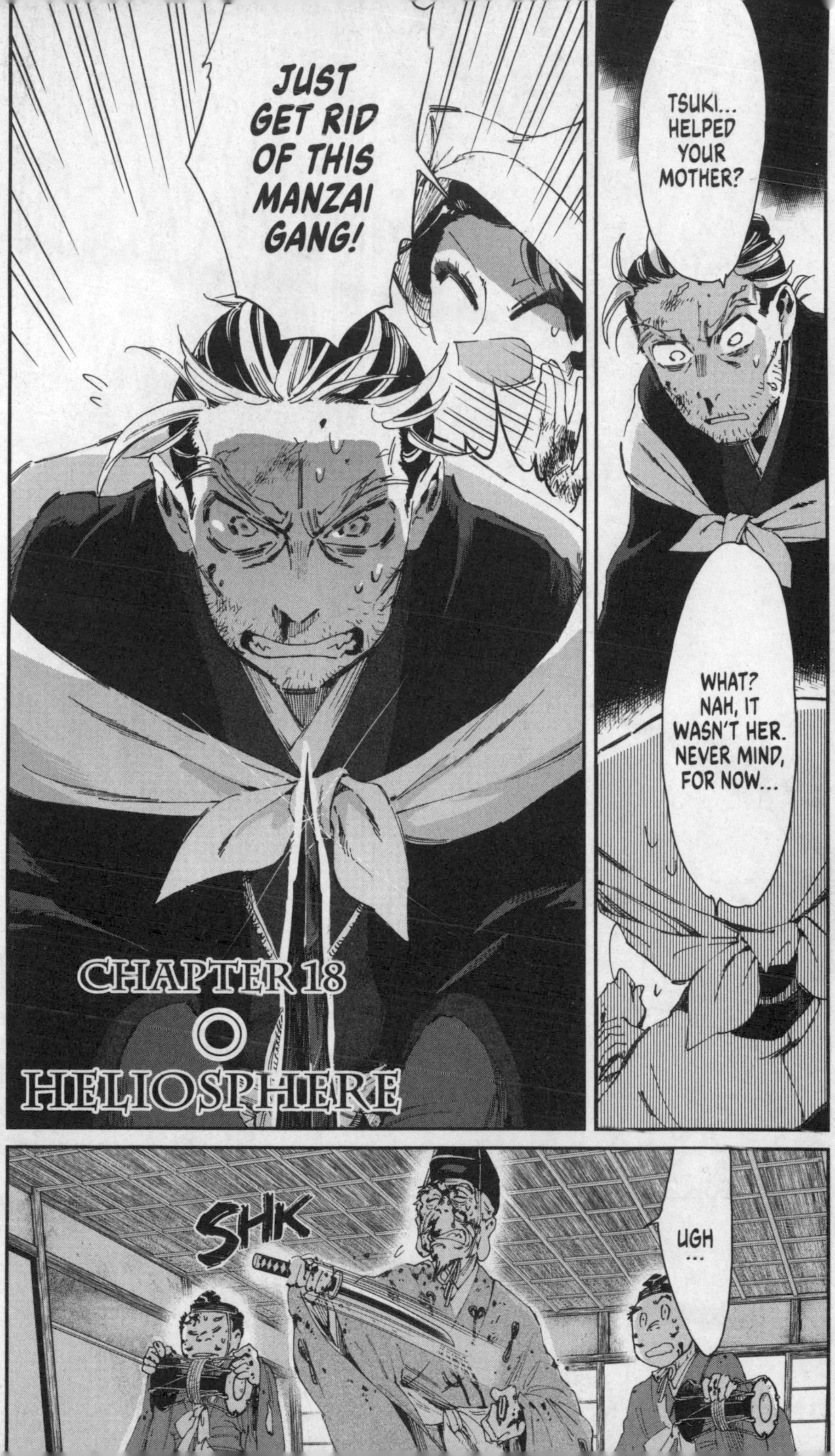
TSUKI... HELPED YOUR MOTHER?
WHAT? NAH, IT WASN'T HER. NEVER MIND, FOR NOW...
JUST GET RID OF THIS MANZAI GANG!
CHAPTER 18
O
HELIOSPHERE
UGH ...
SHK

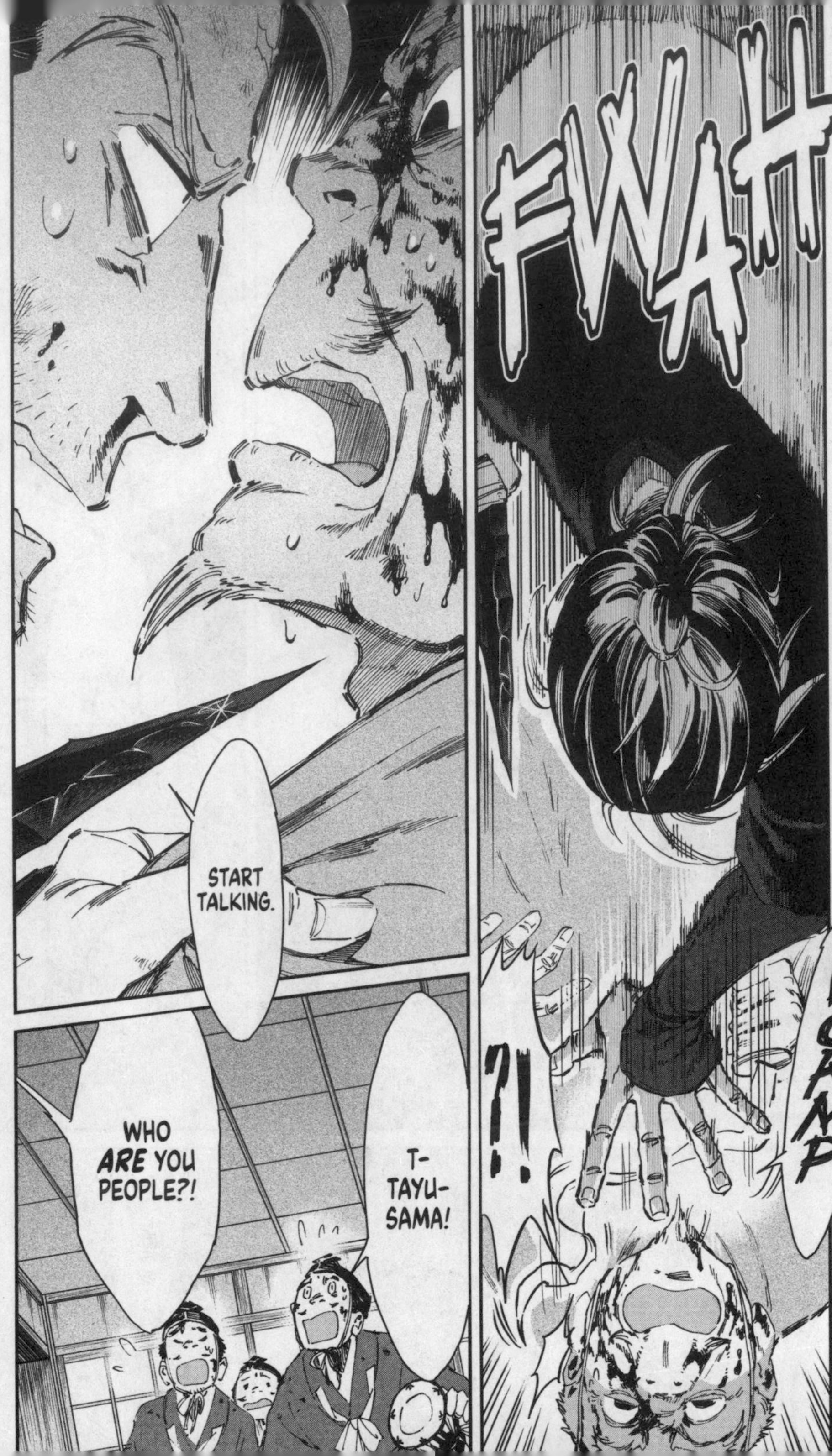
FWAH
WORMP
?!
START TALKING.
T-TAYU-SAMA!
WHO ARE YOU PEOPLE?!

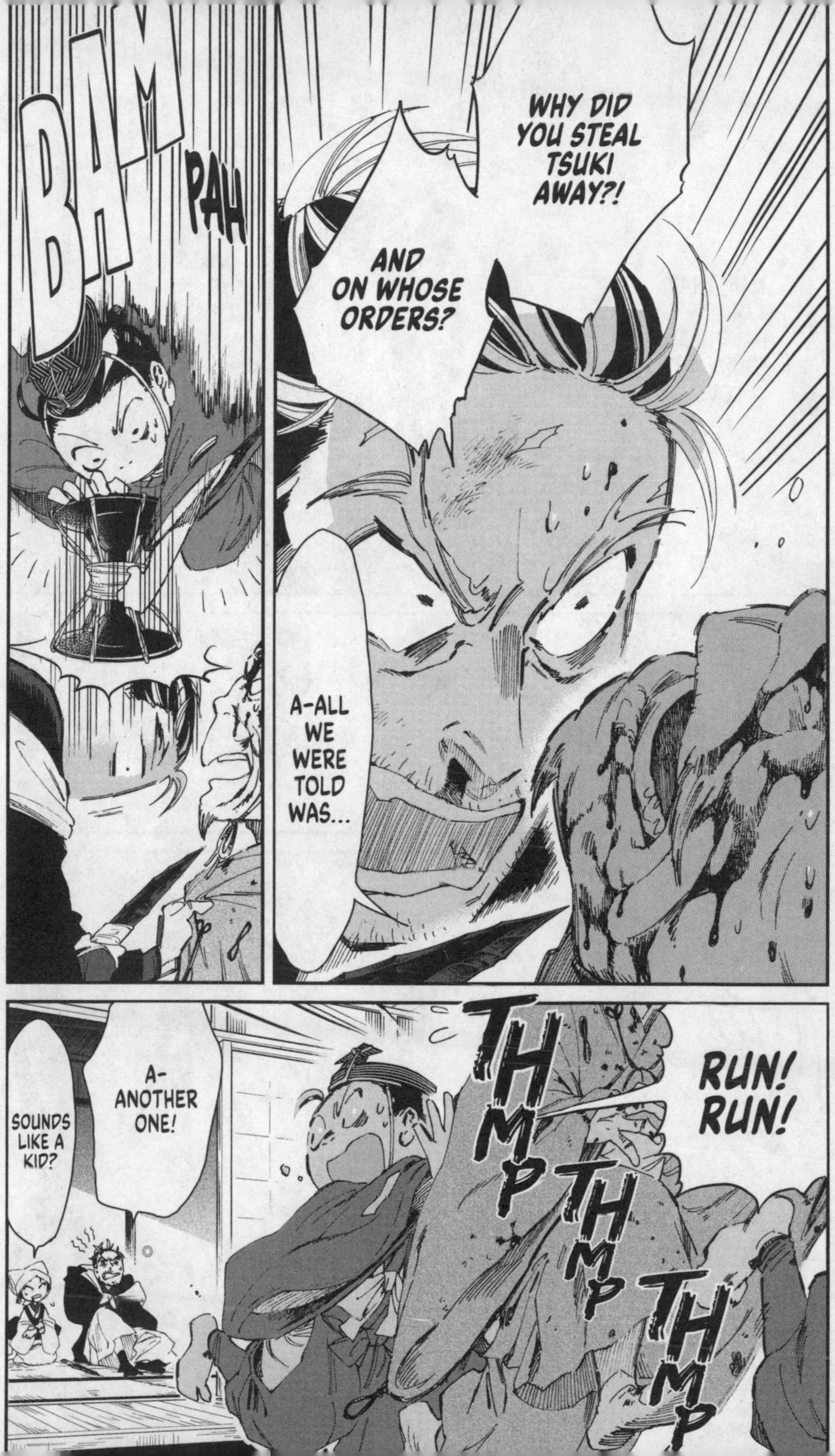
WHY DID YOU STEAL TSUKI AWAY?!
AND ON WHOSE ORDERS?
A-ALL WE WERE TOLD WAS...
BAM
PAH
RUN! RUN!
THMP
THMP
THMP
THMP
A- ANOTHER ONE!
SOUNDS LIKE A KID?

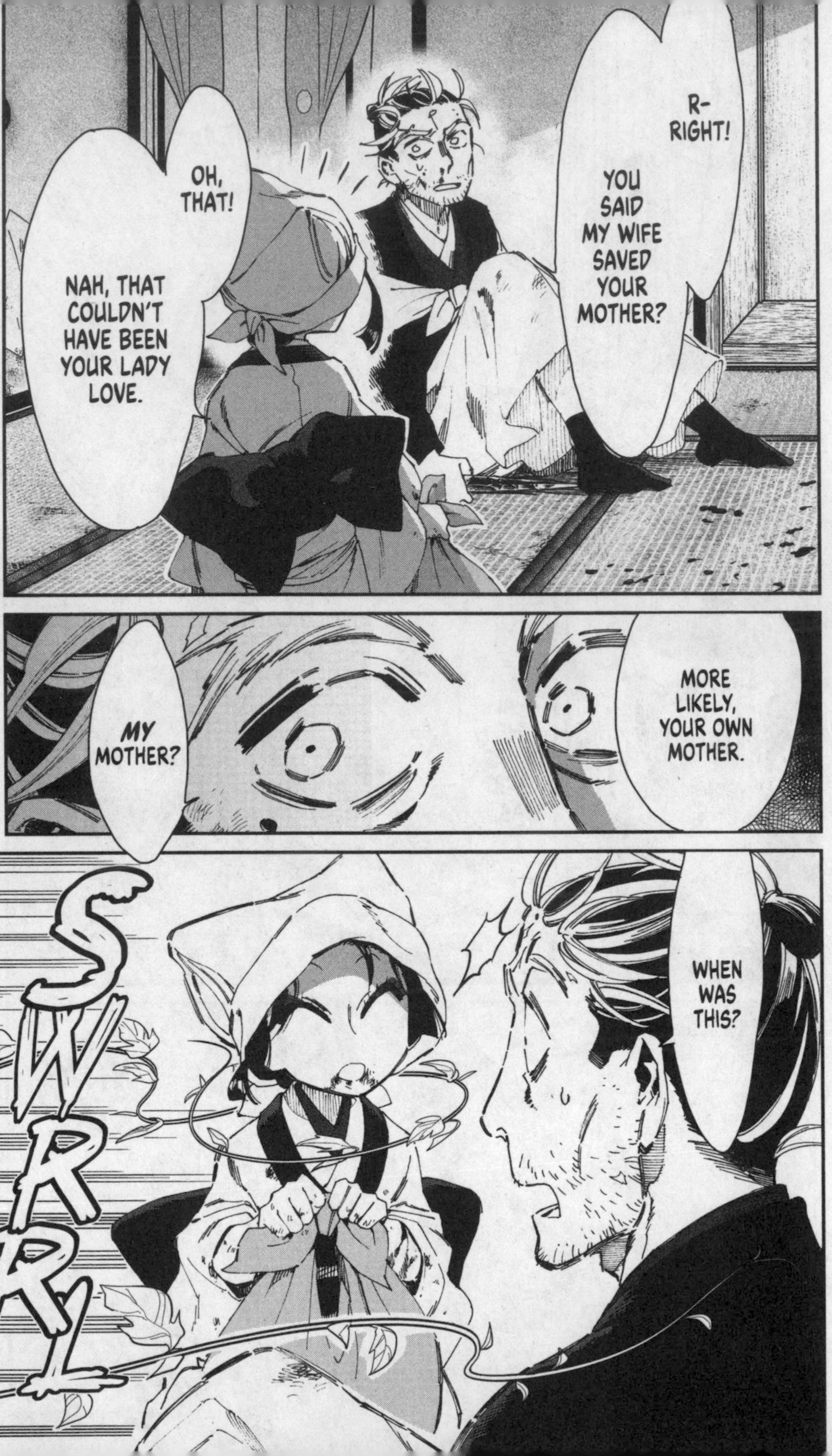
R-RIGHT!
YOU SAID MY WIFE SAVED YOUR MOTHER?
OH, THAT!
NAH, THAT COULDN'T HAVE BEEN YOUR LADY LOVE.
MORE LIKELY, YOUR OWN MOTHER.
MY MOTHER?
WHEN WAS THIS?
SWRRL

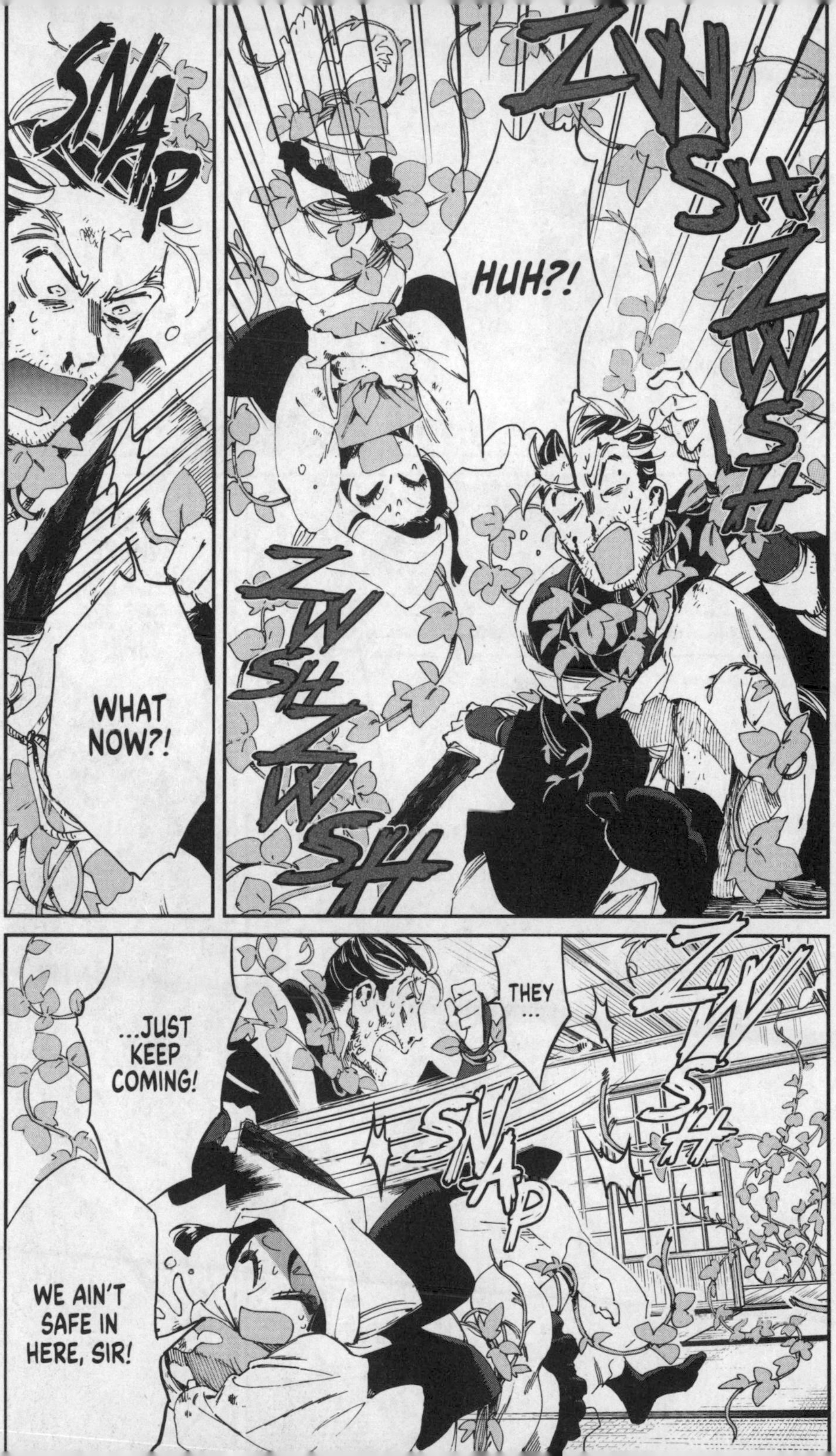
ZWSH
ZWSH
HUH?!
ZWSH
SNAP
WHAT NOW?!
ZWSH
SNAP
THEY...
...JUST KEEP COMING!
WE AIN'T SAFE IN HERE, SIR!

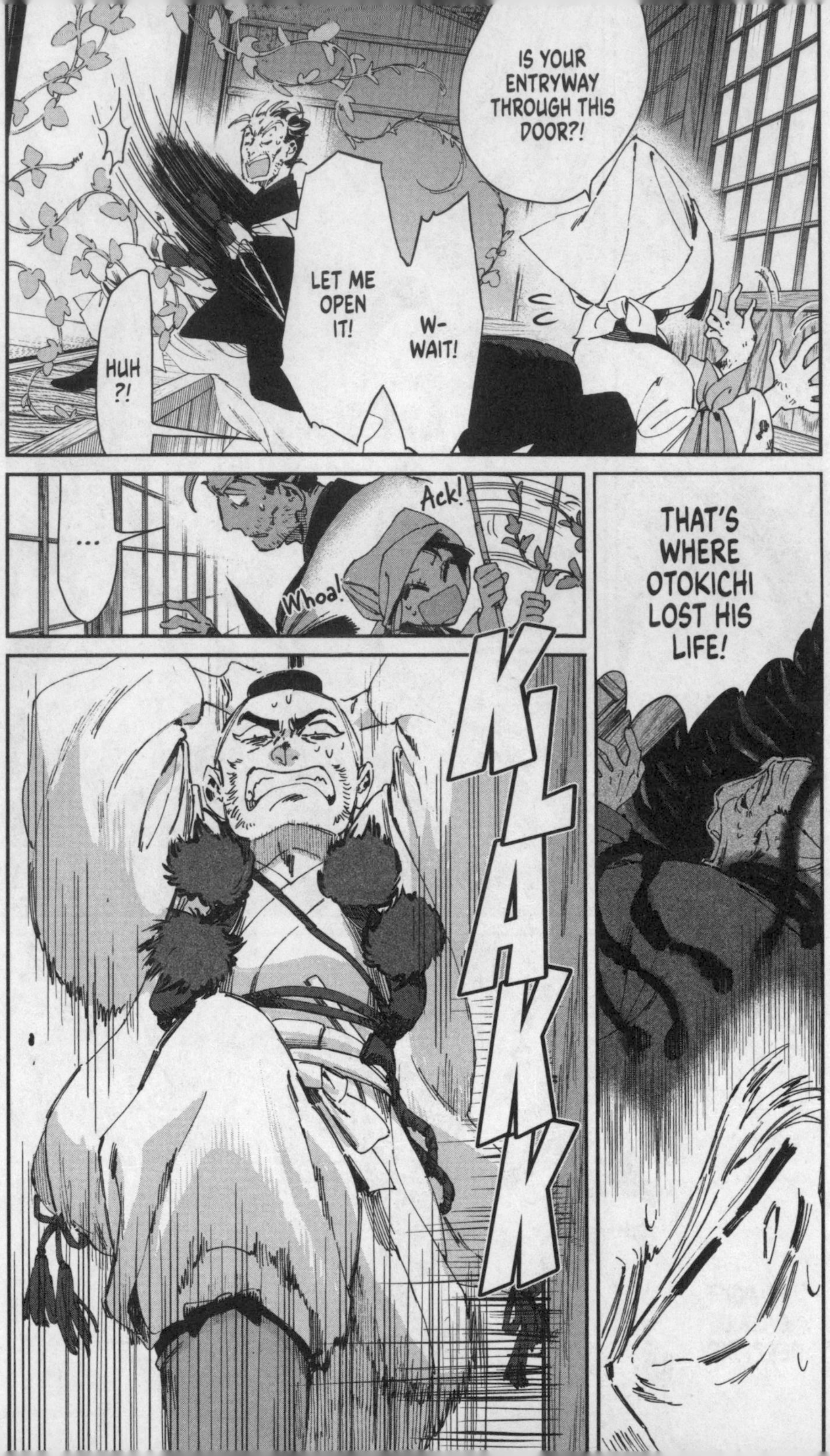
IS YOUR ENTRYWAY THROUGH THIS DOOR?!
W-WAIT!
LET ME OPEN IT!
HUH?!
Ack!
Whoa!
...
THAT'S WHERE OTOKICHI LOST HIS LIFE!
KLAKK

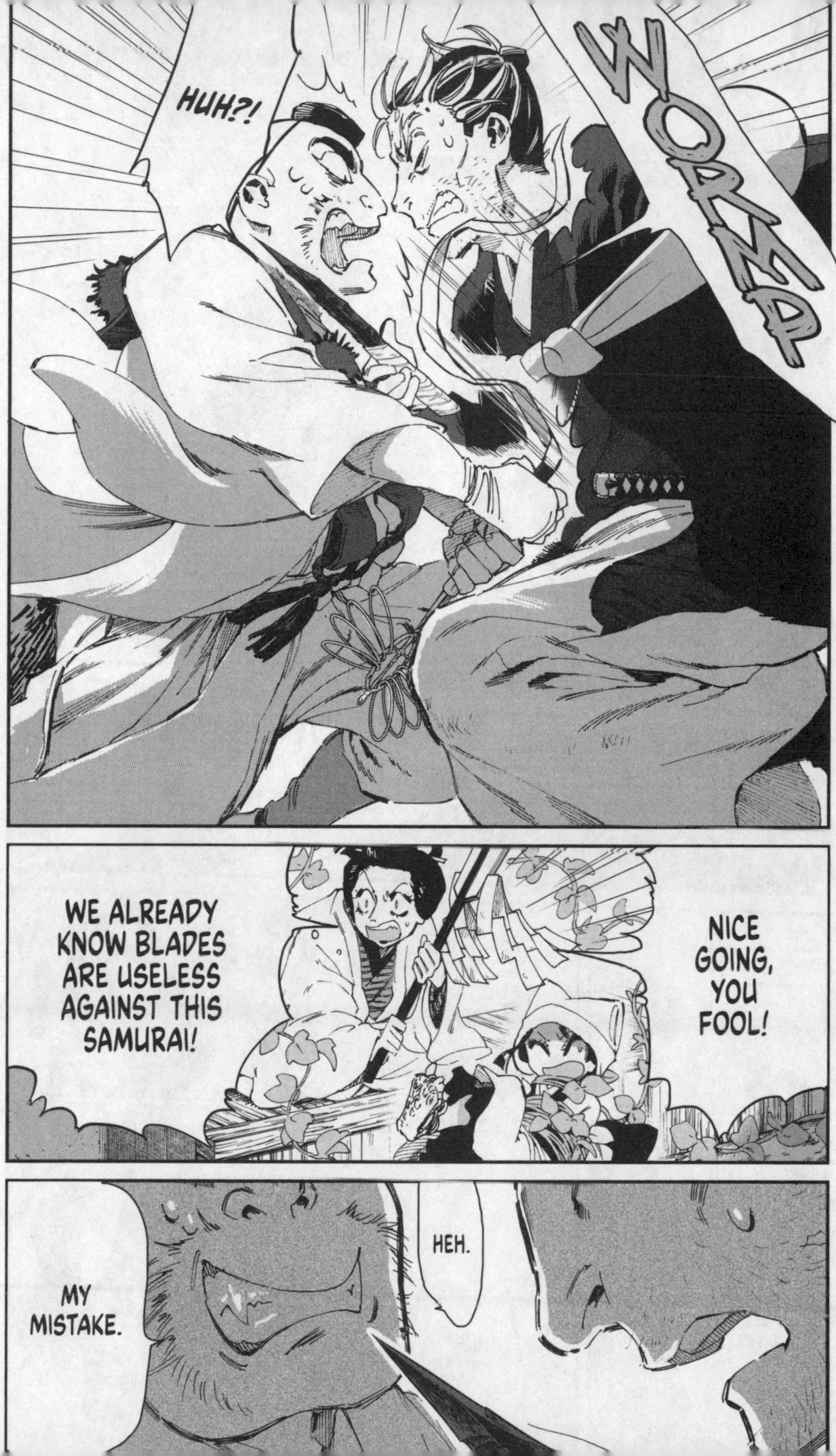
WORMP
HUH?!
NICE GOING, YOU FOOL!
WE ALREADY KNOW BLADES ARE USELESS AGAINST THIS SAMURAI!
HEH.
MY MISTAKE.

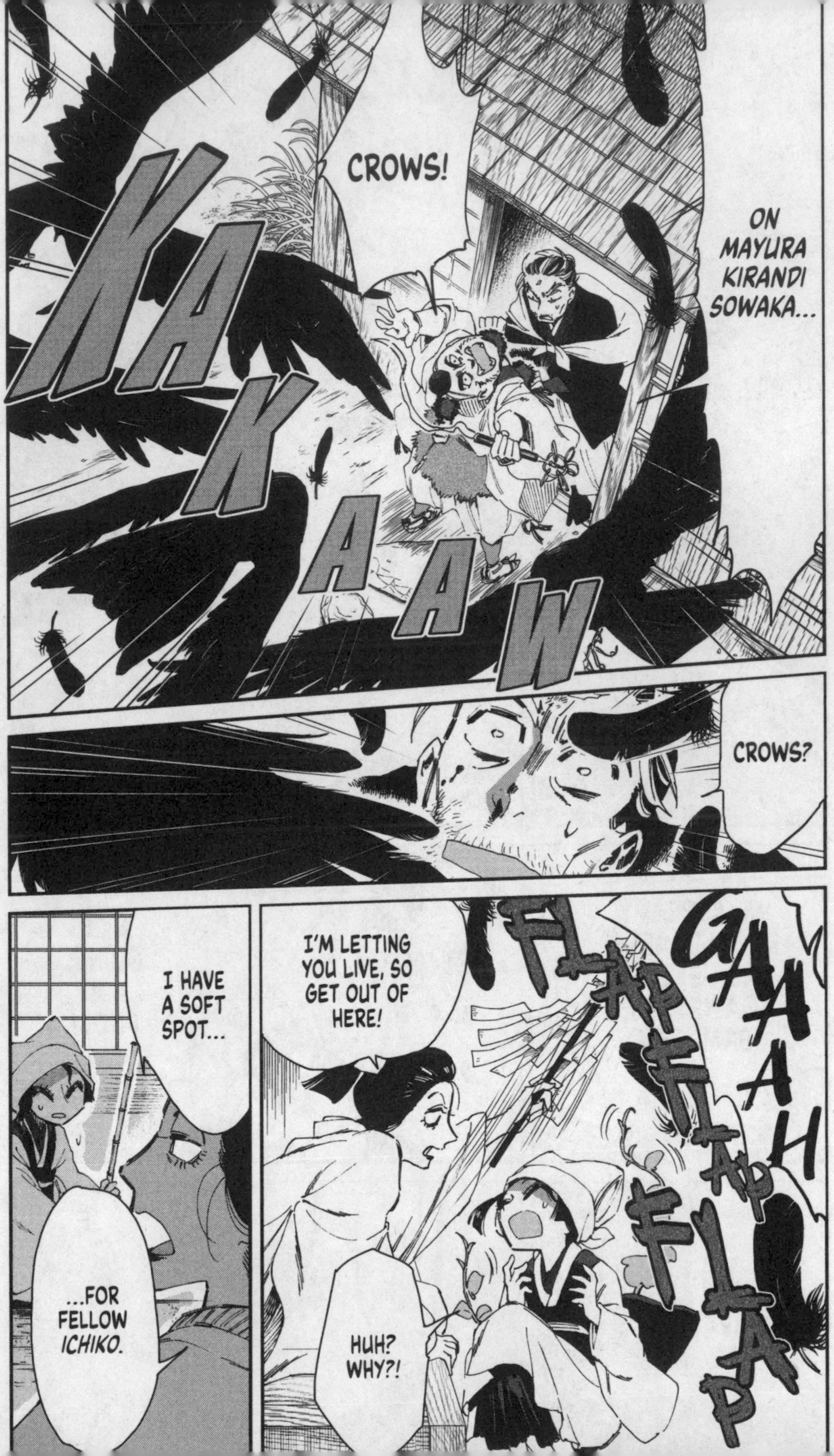
ON MAYURA KIRANDI SOWAKA...
CROWS!
KAKAAAW
CROWS?
GAAAAH
FLAP FLAP FLAP FLAP
I'M LETTING YOU LIVE, SO GET OUT OF HERE!
HUH? WHY?!
I HAVE A SOFT SPOT...
...FOR FELLOW ICHIKO.

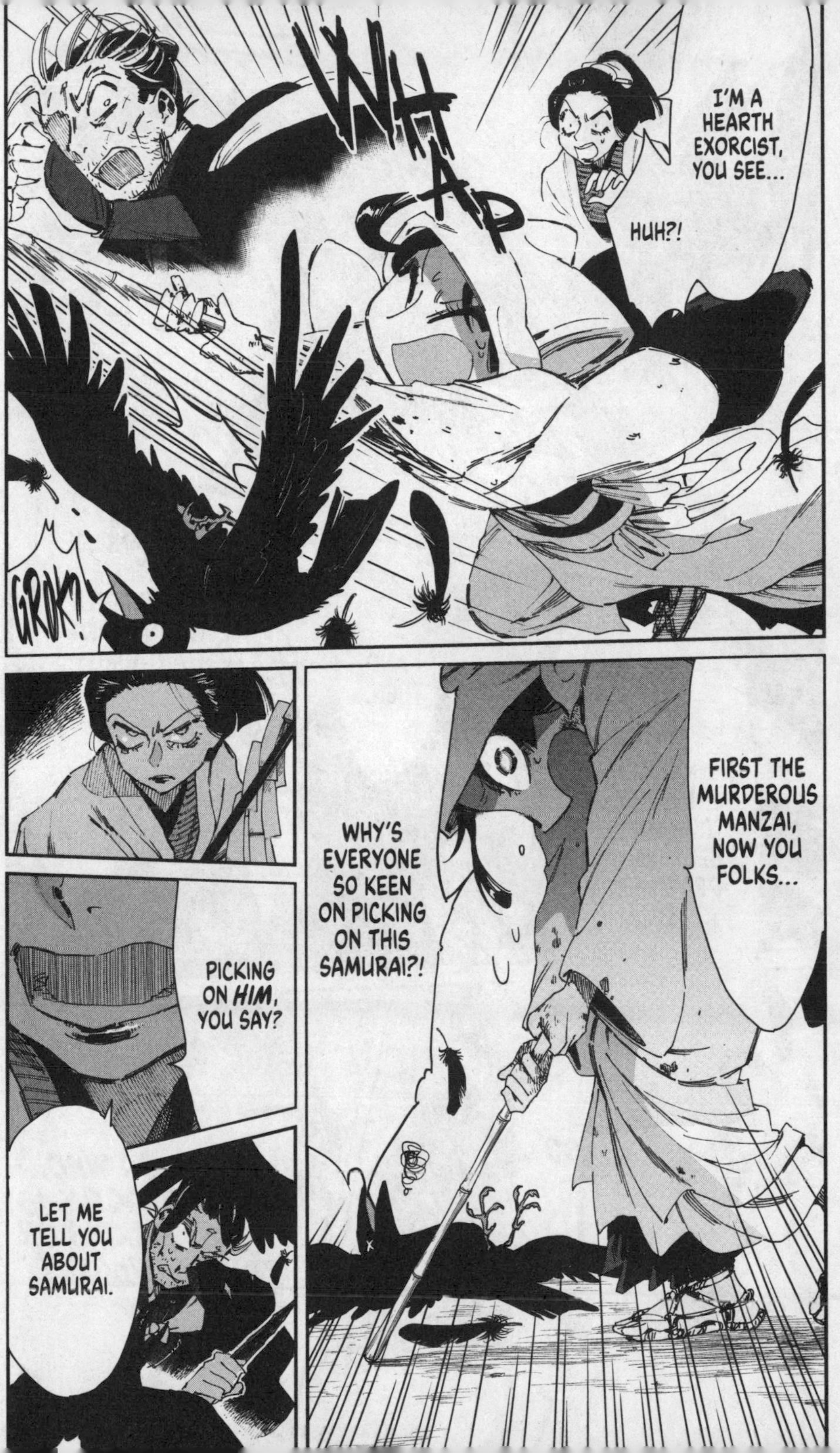
I'M A HEARTH EXORCIST, YOU SEE...
HUH?!
WHAP
GROK?!
FIRST THE MURDEROUS MANZAI, NOW YOU FOLKS...
WHY'S EVERYONE SO KEEN ON PICKING ON THIS SAMURAI?!
PICKING ON *HIM*, YOU SAY?
LET ME TELL YOU ABOUT SAMURAI.

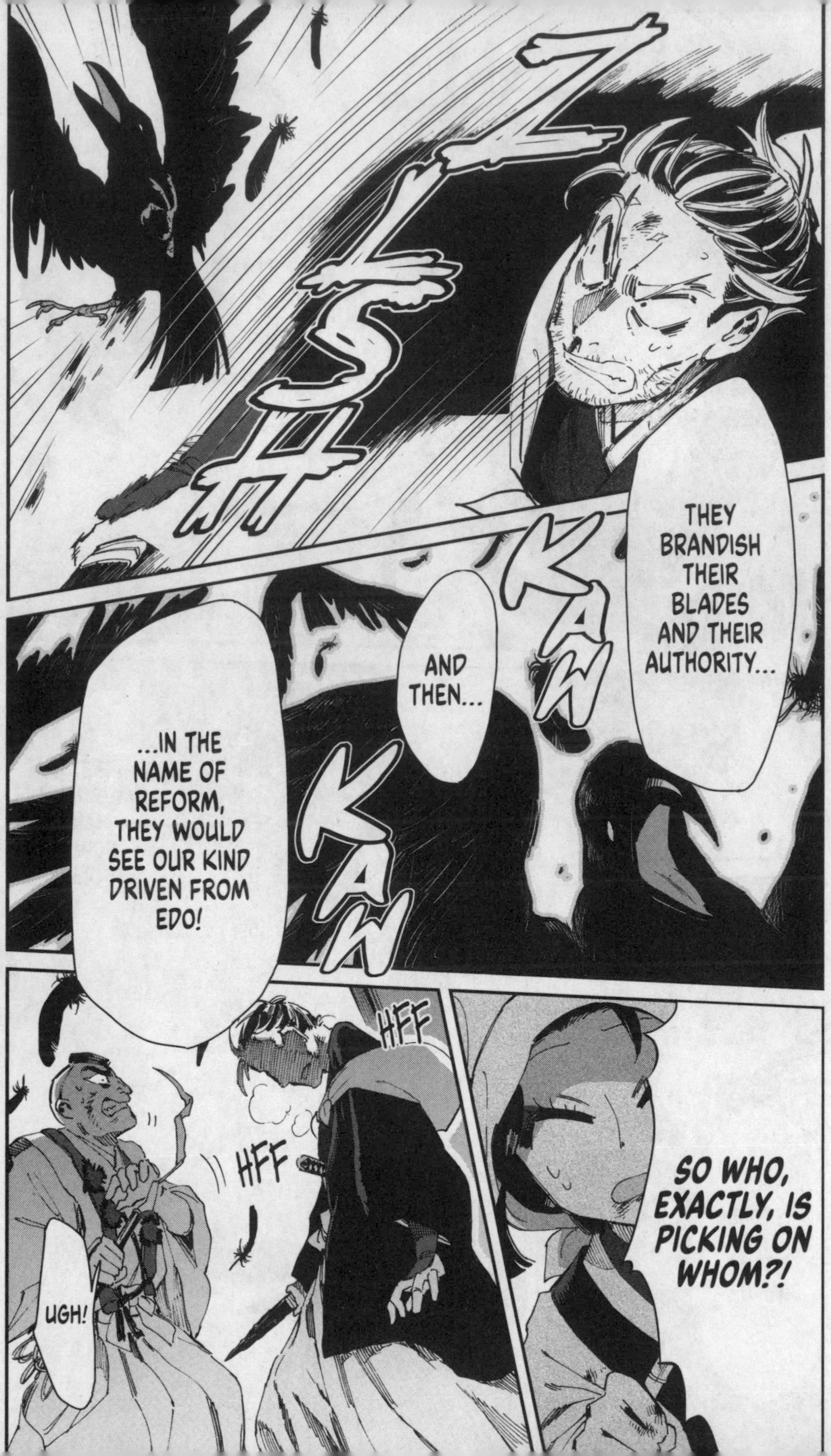

SHH
THEY BRANDISH THEIR BLADES AND THEIR AUTHORITY...
KAW
AND THEN...
KAW
...IN THE NAME OF REFORM, THEY WOULD SEE OUR KIND DRIVEN FROM EDO!
HFF
HFF
UGH!
SO WHO, EXACTLY, IS PICKING ON WHOM?!

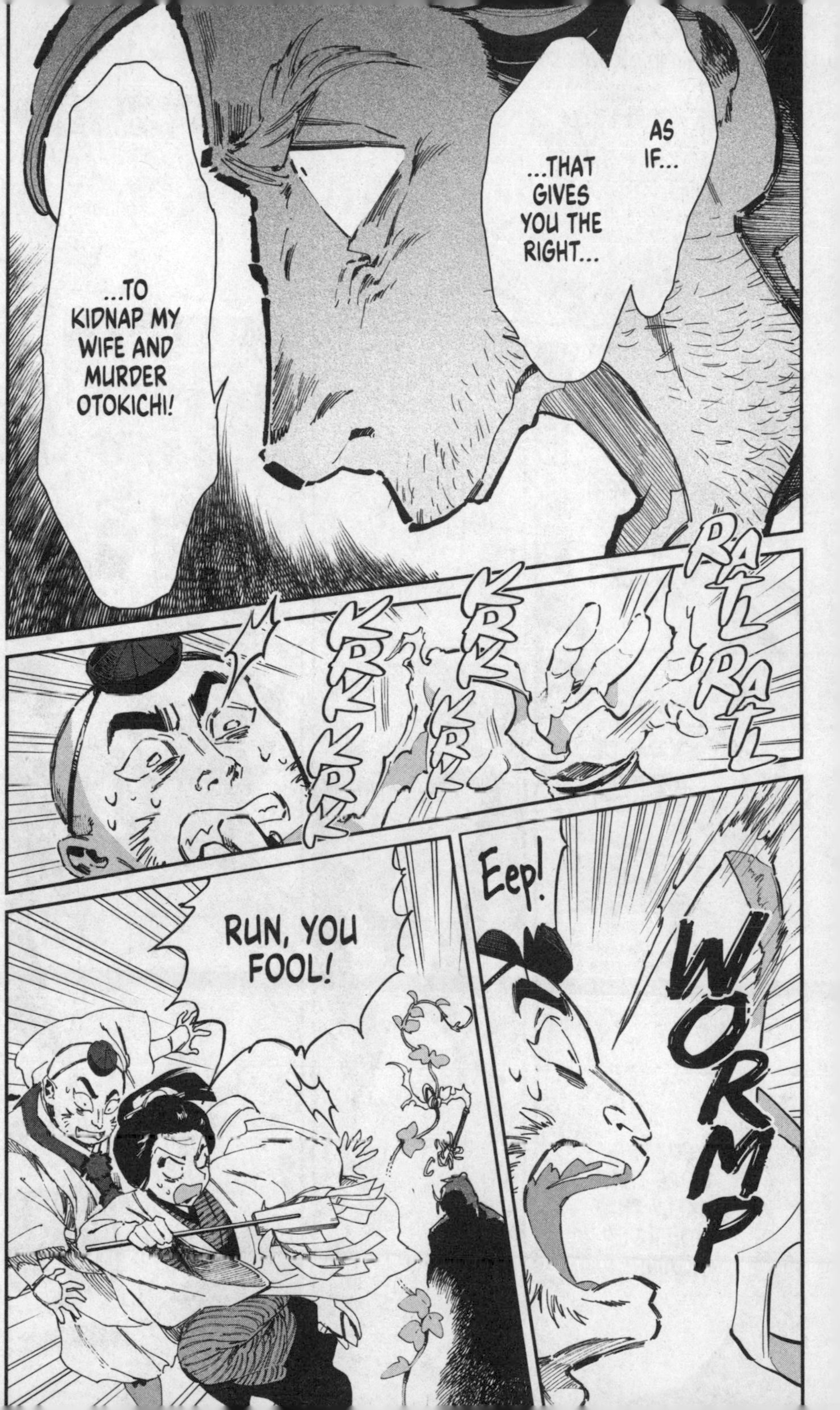
AS IF...
...THAT GIVES YOU THE RIGHT...
...TO KIDNAP MY WIFE AND MURDER OTOKICHI!
RATL RATL
Eep!
WORMP
RUN, YOU FOOL!

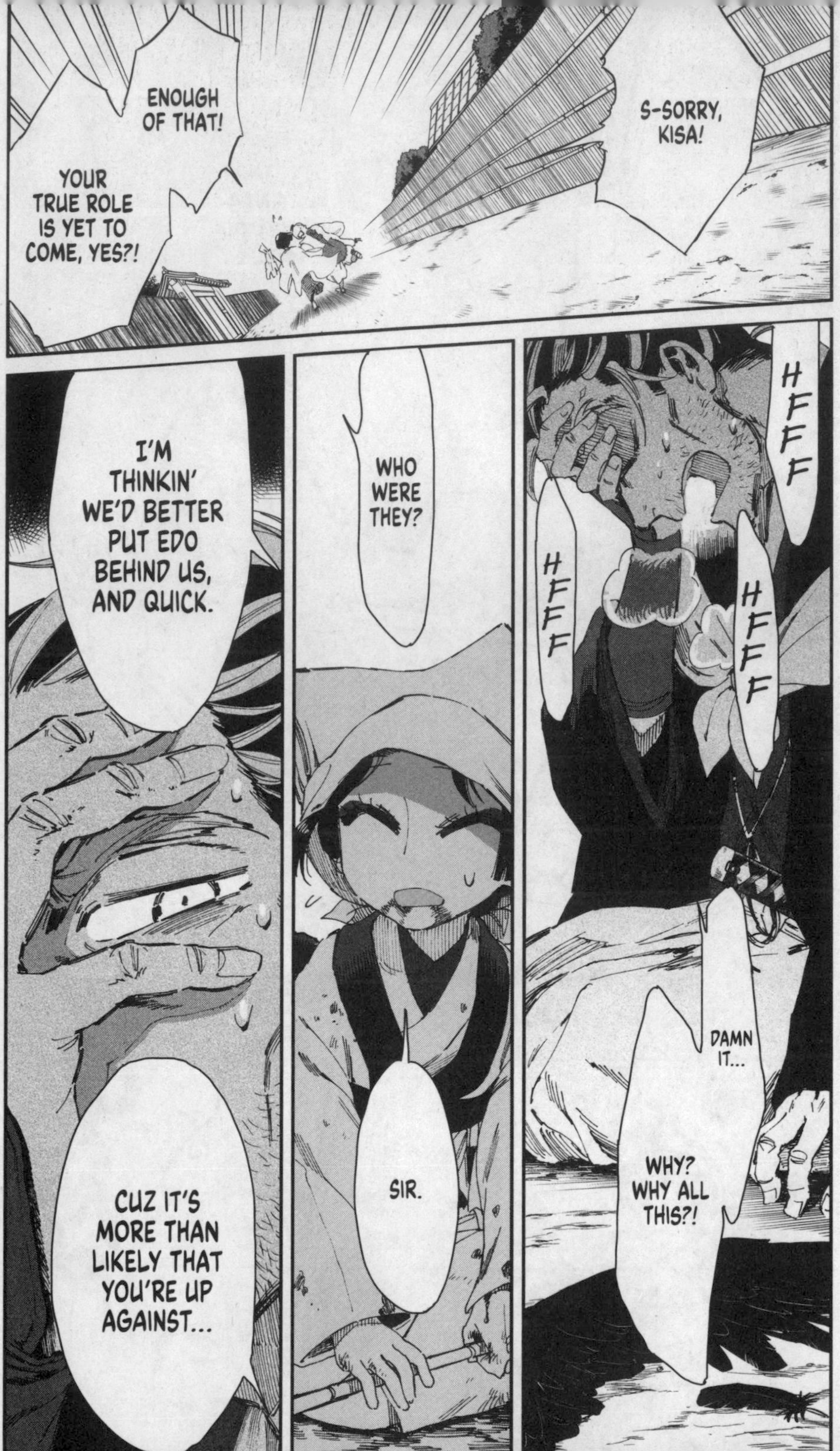
ENOUGH OF THAT!
YOUR TRUE ROLE IS YET TO COME, YES?!
S-SORRY, KISA!
HFFF
HFFF
HFFF
DAMN IT...
WHY? WHY ALL THIS?!
WHO WERE THEY?
SIR.
I'M THINKIN' WE'D BETTER PUT EDO BEHIND US, AND QUICK.
CUZ IT'S MORE THAN LIKELY THAT YOU'RE UP AGAINST...

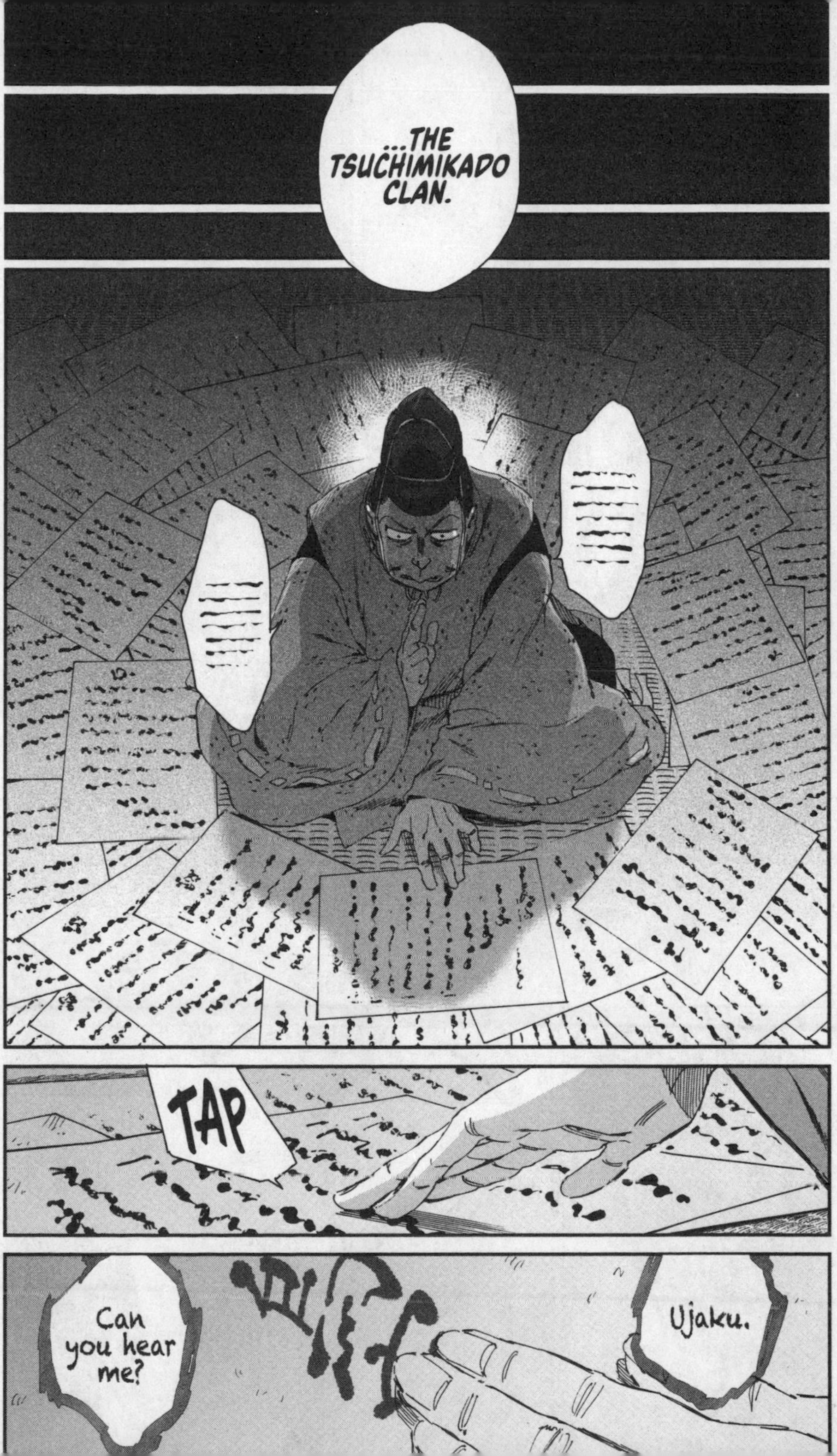
...THE TSUCHIMIKADO CLAN.
TAP
Ujaku.
Can you hear me?

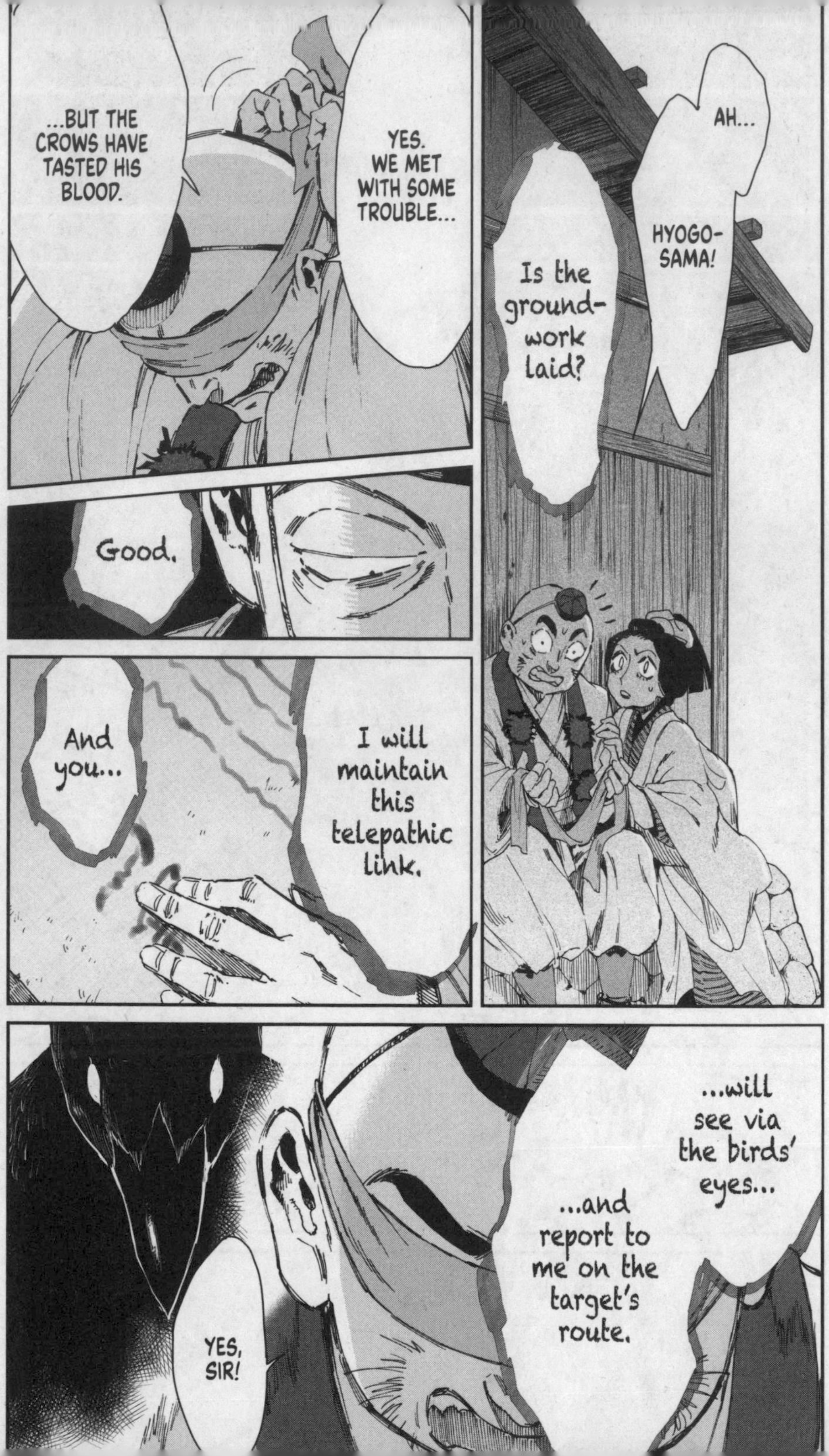

AH...
HYOGO-SAMA!
Is the groundwork laid?
YES. WE MET WITH SOME TROUBLE...
...BUT THE CROWS HAVE TASTED HIS BLOOD.
Good.
I will maintain this telepathic link.
And you...
...will see via the birds' eyes...
...and report to me on the target's route.
YES, SIR!

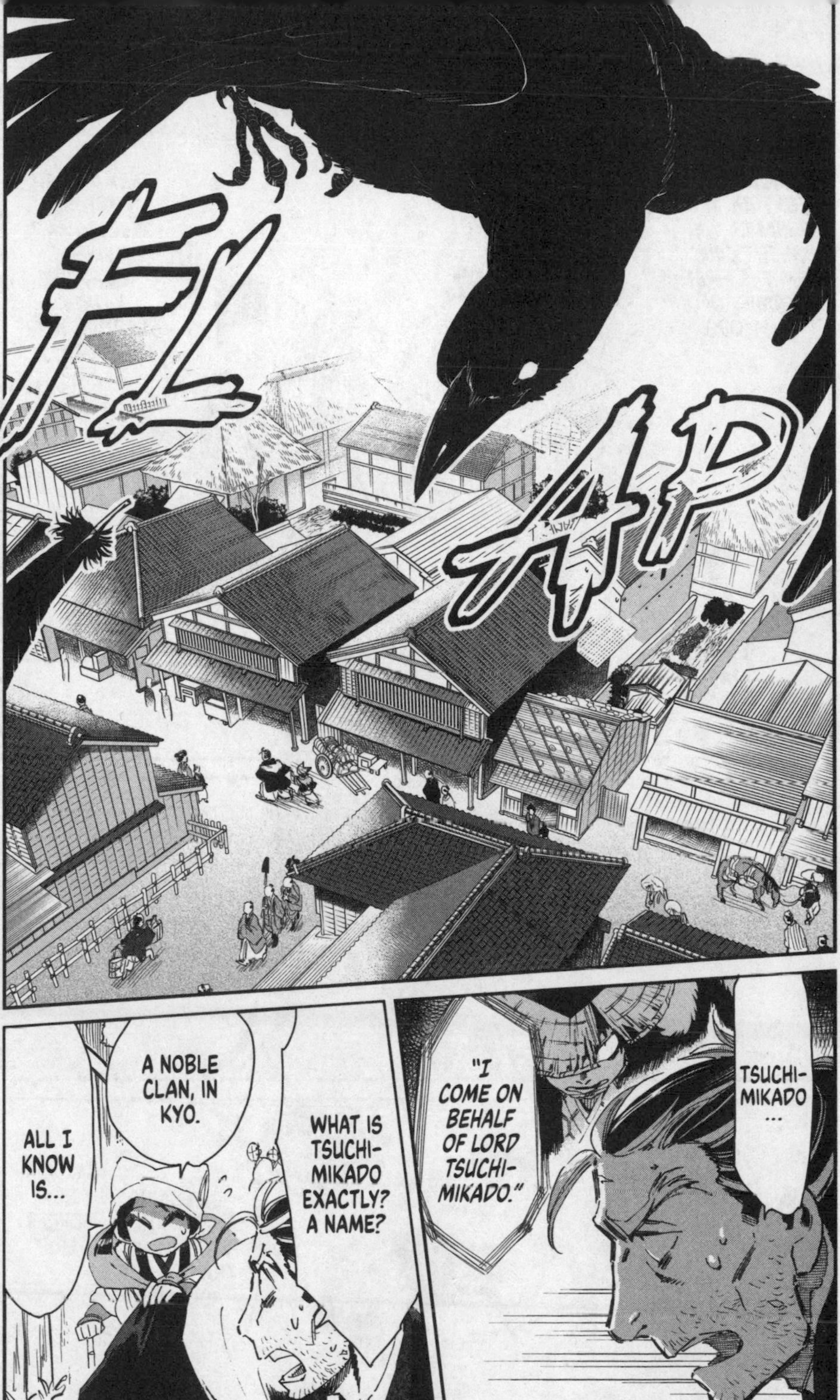
FLAP
TSUCHI-MIKADO...
"I COME ON BEHALF OF LORD TSUCHI-MIKADO."
WHAT IS TSUCHI-MIKADO EXACTLY? A NAME?
ALL I KNOW IS...
A NOBLE CLAN, IN KYO.

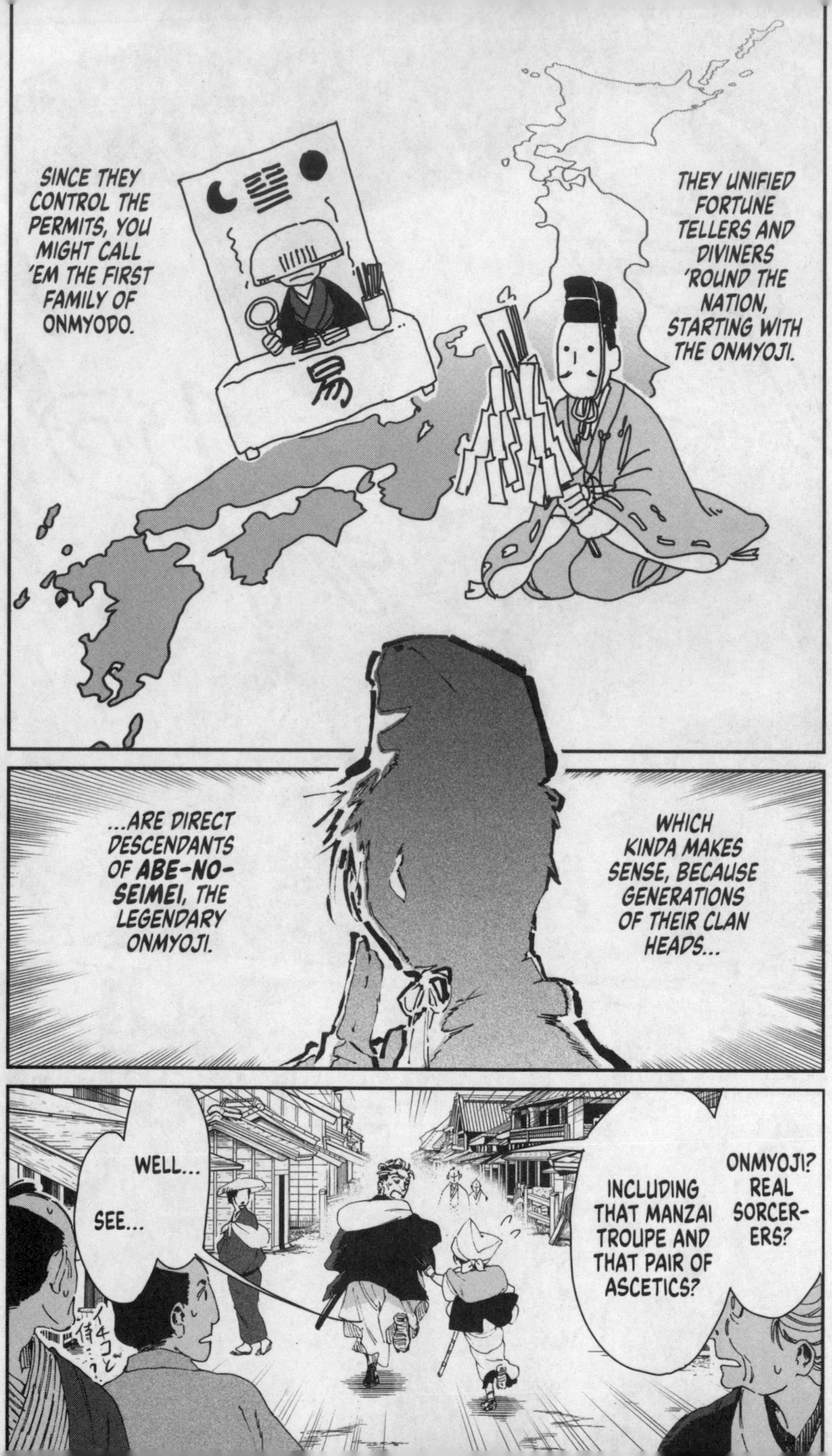
THEY UNIFIED FORTUNE TELLERS AND DIVINERS 'ROUND THE NATION, STARTING WITH THE ONMYOJI.
SINCE THEY CONTROL THE PERMITS, YOU MIGHT CALL 'EM THE FIRST FAMILY OF ONMYODO.
易
WHICH KINDA MAKES SENSE, BECAUSE GENERATIONS OF THEIR CLAN HEADS...
...ARE DIRECT DESCENDANTS OF **ABE-NO-SEIMEI**, THE LEGENDARY ONMYOJI.
ONMYOJI? REAL SORCERER-ERS?
INCLUDING THAT MANZAI TROUPE AND THAT PAIR OF ASCETICS?
WELL...
SEE...

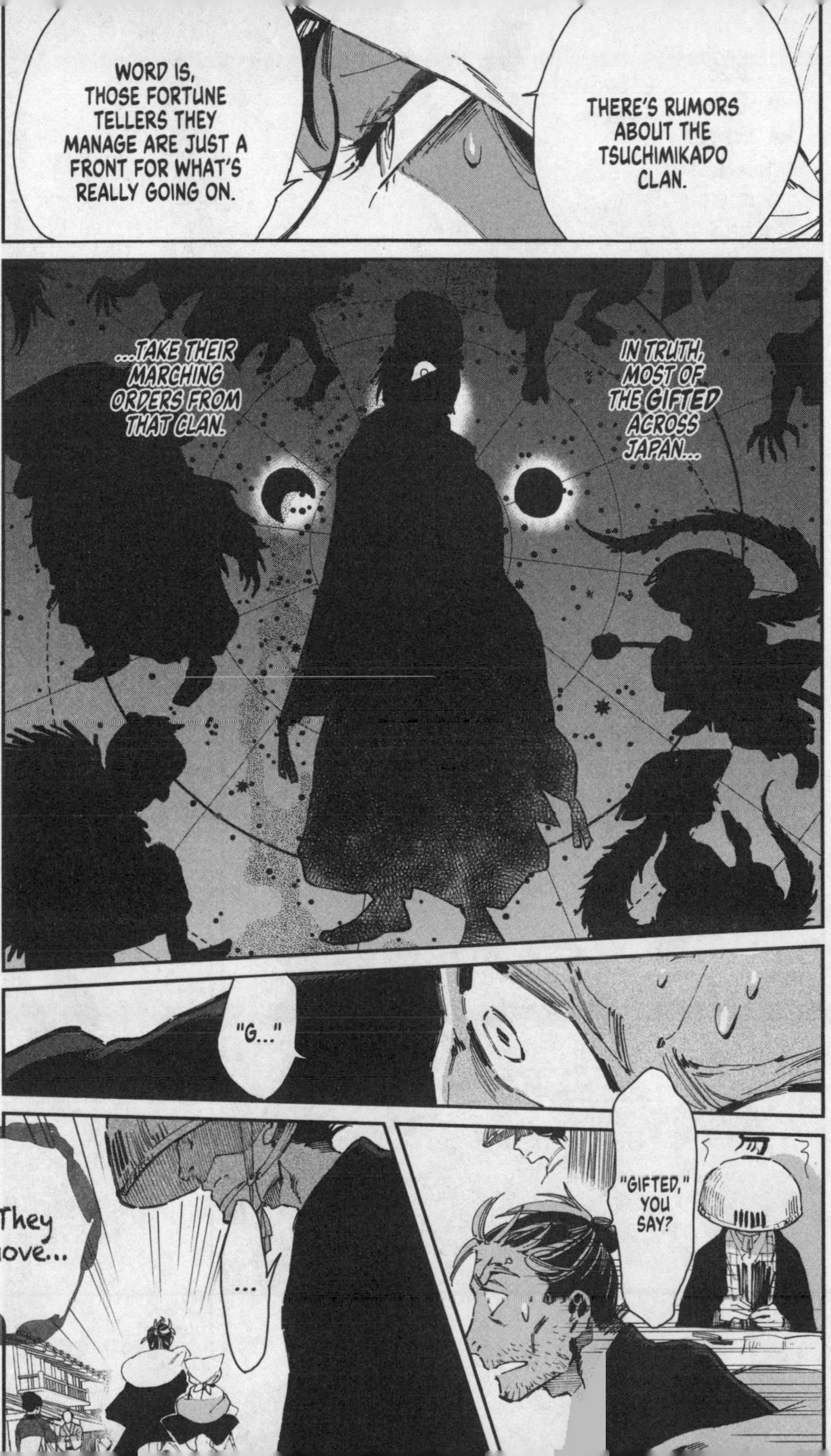
THERE'S RUMORS ABOUT THE TSUCHIMIKADO CLAN.
WORD IS, THOSE FORTUNE TELLERS THEY MANAGE ARE JUST A FRONT FOR WHAT'S REALLY GOING ON.
IN TRUTH, MOST OF THE GIFTED ACROSS JAPAN...
...TAKE THEIR MARCHING ORDERS FROM THAT CLAN.
"G..."
"GIFTED," YOU SAY?
...
They move...

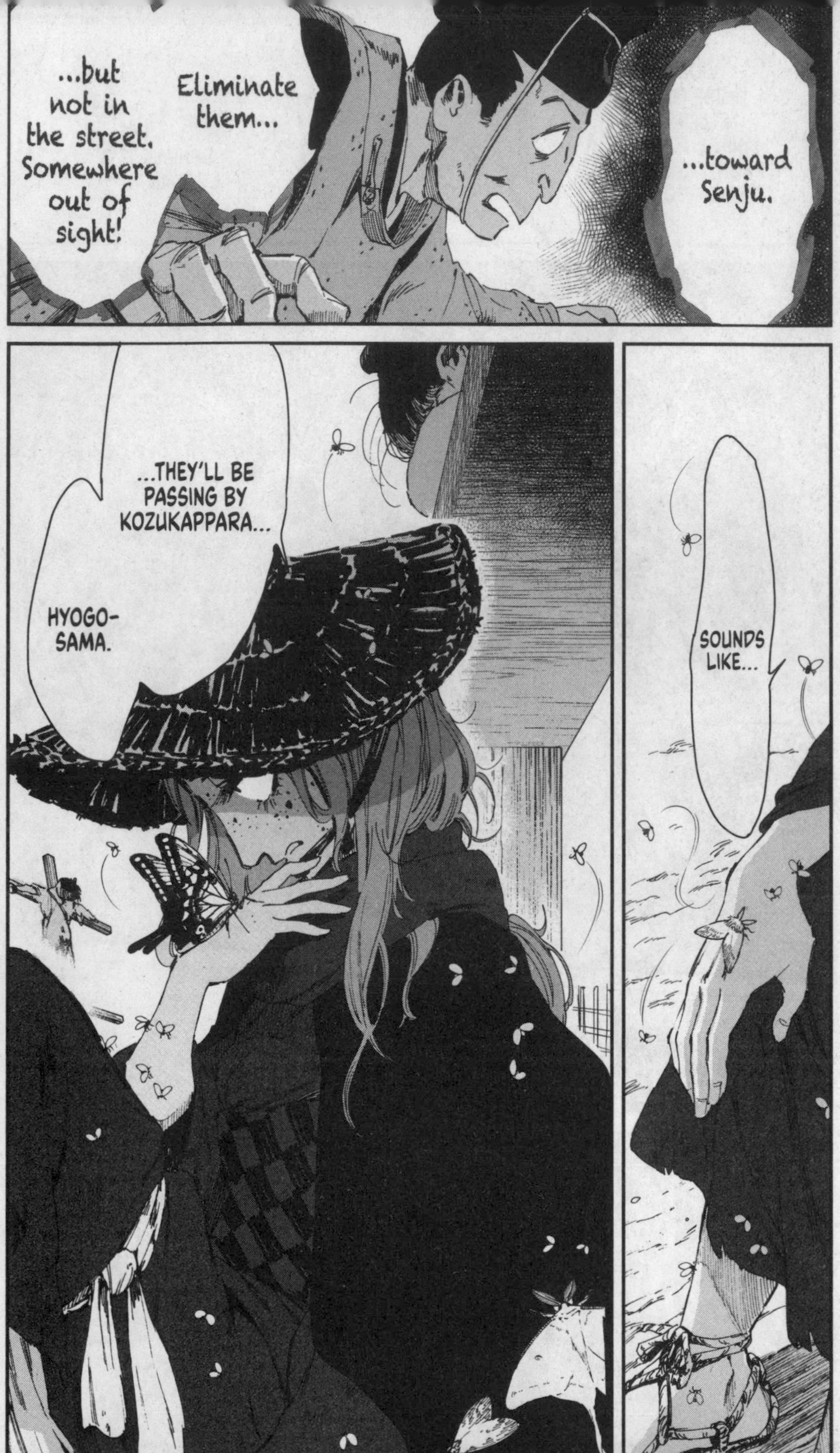
...toward Senju.
Eliminate them...
...but not in the street. Somewhere out of sight!
SOUNDS LIKE...
...THEY'LL BE PASSING BY KOZUKAPPARA...
HYOGO-SAMA.

STEEL of the CELESTIAL SHADOWS

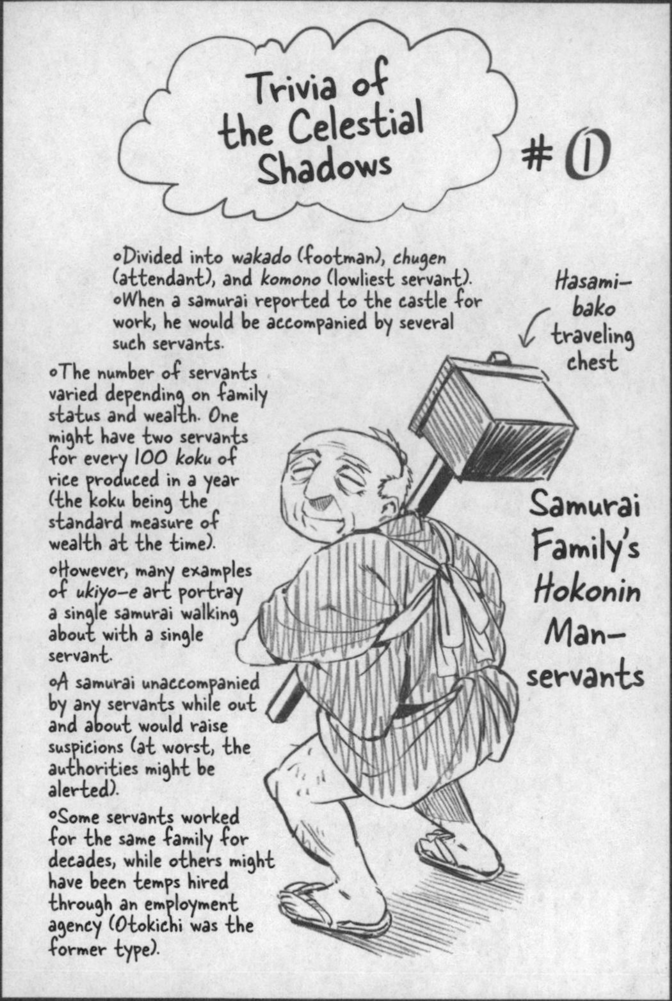

Trivia of the Celestial Shadows #①

∘Divided into *wakado* (footman), *chugen* (attendant), and *komono* (lowliest servant).
∘When a samurai reported to the castle for work, he would be accompanied by several such servants.

∘The number of servants varied depending on family status and wealth. One might have two servants for every 100 *koku* of rice produced in a year (the *koku* being the standard measure of wealth at the time).

∘However, many examples of *ukiyo-e* art portray a single samurai walking about with a single servant.

∘A samurai unaccompanied by any servants while out and about would raise suspicions (at worst, the authorities might be alerted).

∘Some servants worked for the same family for decades, while others might have been temps hired through an employment agency (Otokichi was the former type).

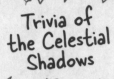

Hasami-bako traveling chest

Samurai Family's Hokonin Man-servants

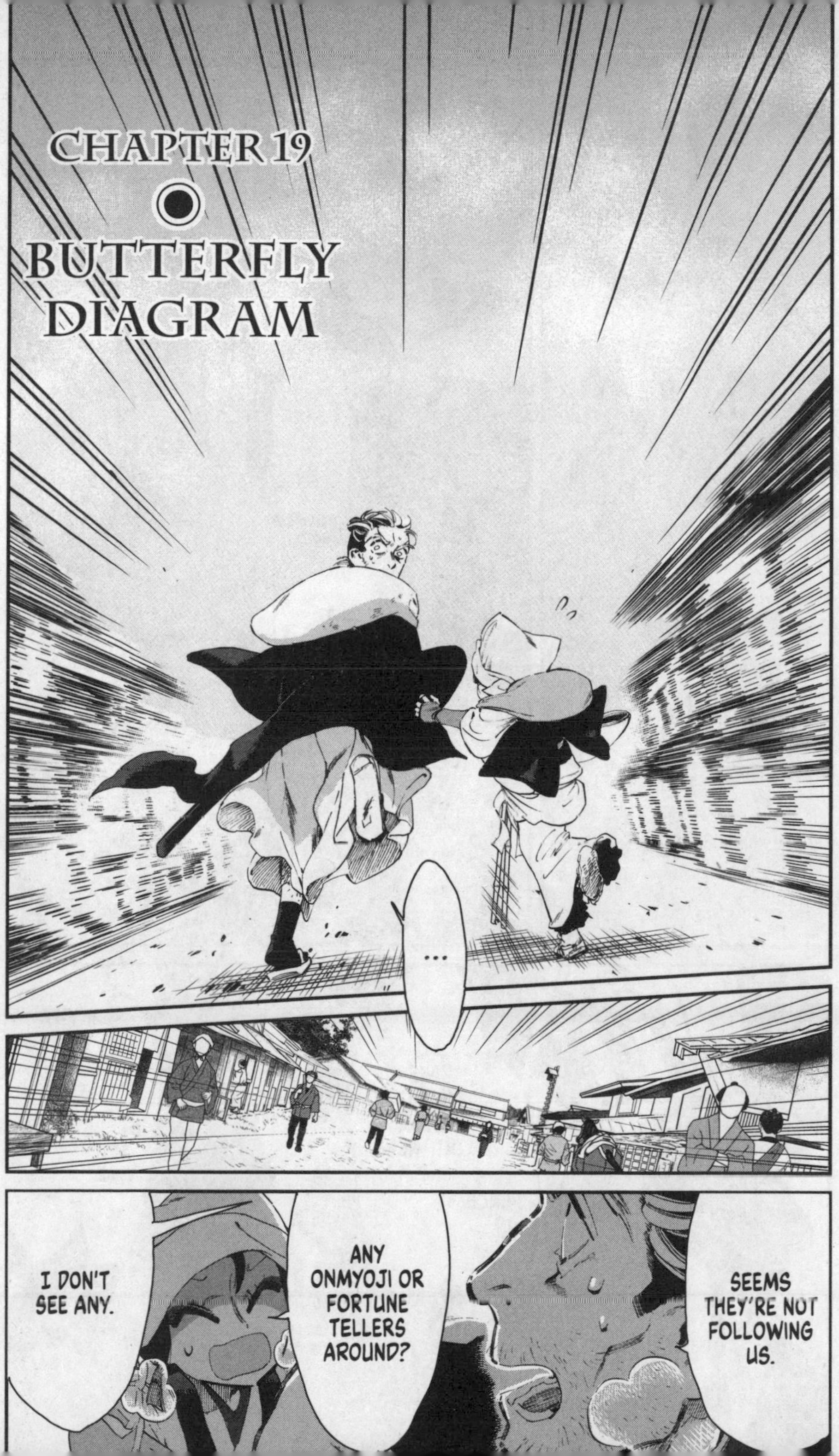

CHAPTER 19
BUTTERFLY DIAGRAM
...
SEEMS THEY'RE NOT FOLLOWING US.
ANY ONMYOJI OR FORTUNE TELLERS AROUND?
I DON'T SEE ANY.

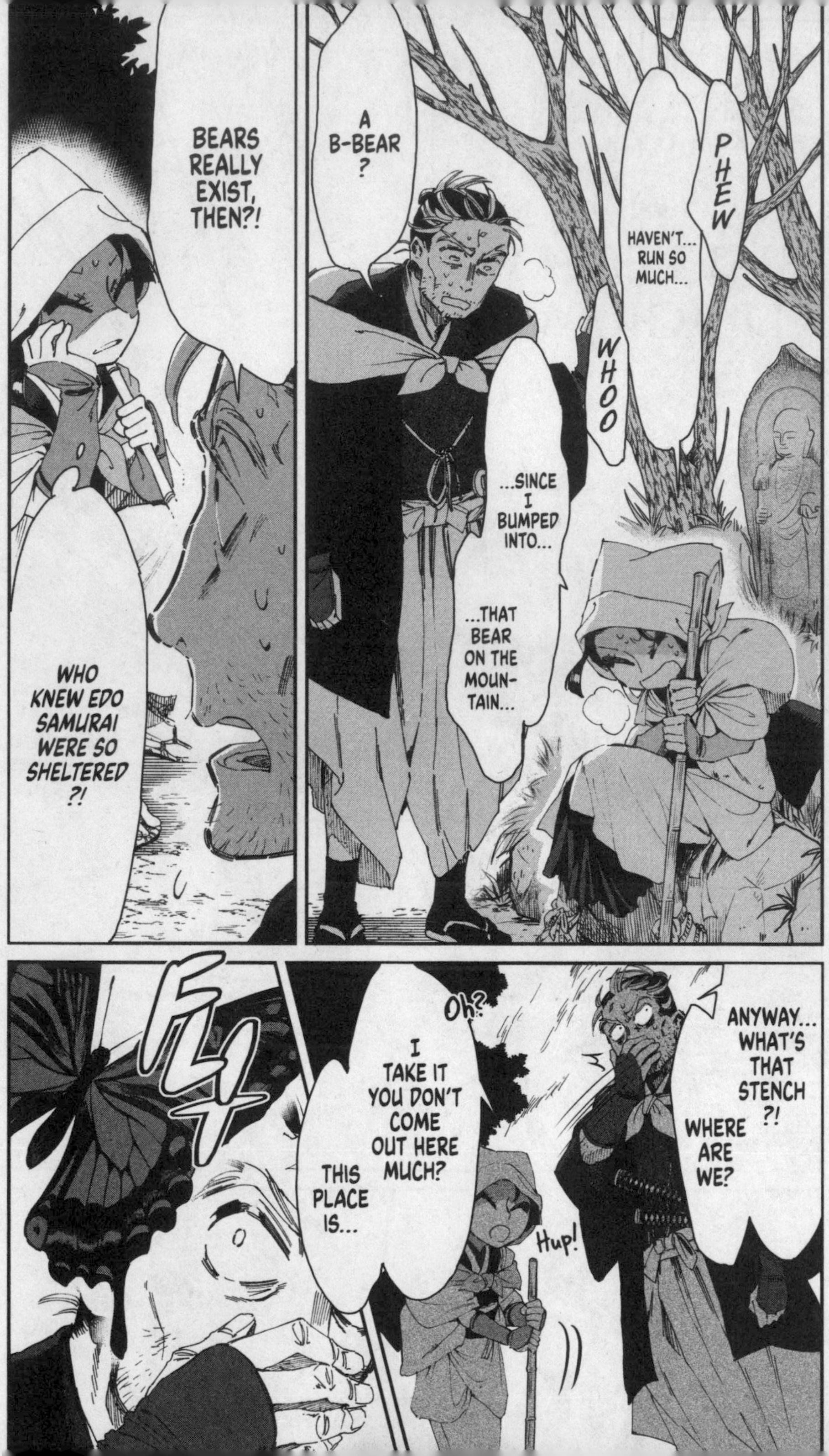
PHEW
HAVEN'T... RUN SO MUCH...
WHOO
...SINCE I BUMPED INTO...
...THAT BEAR ON THE MOUN-TAIN...
A B-BEAR?
BEARS REALLY EXIST, THEN?!
WHO KNEW EDO SAMURAI WERE SO SHELTERED?!
ANYWAY... WHAT'S THAT STENCH?!
WHERE ARE WE?
Hup!
Oh?
I TAKE IT YOU DON'T COME OUT HERE MUCH?
THIS PLACE IS...

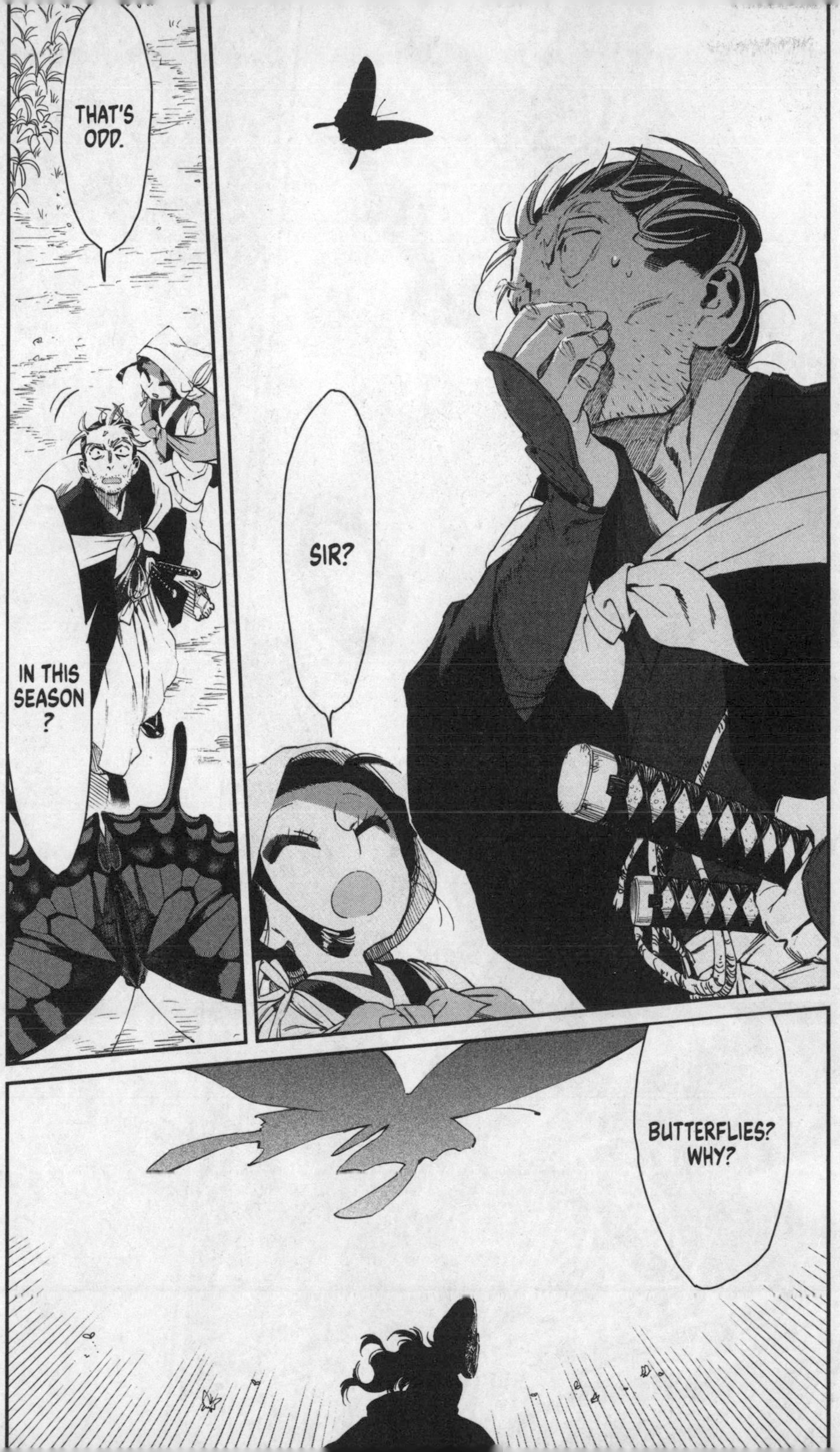
SIR?
THAT'S ODD.
IN THIS SEASON?
BUTTERFLIES? WHY?

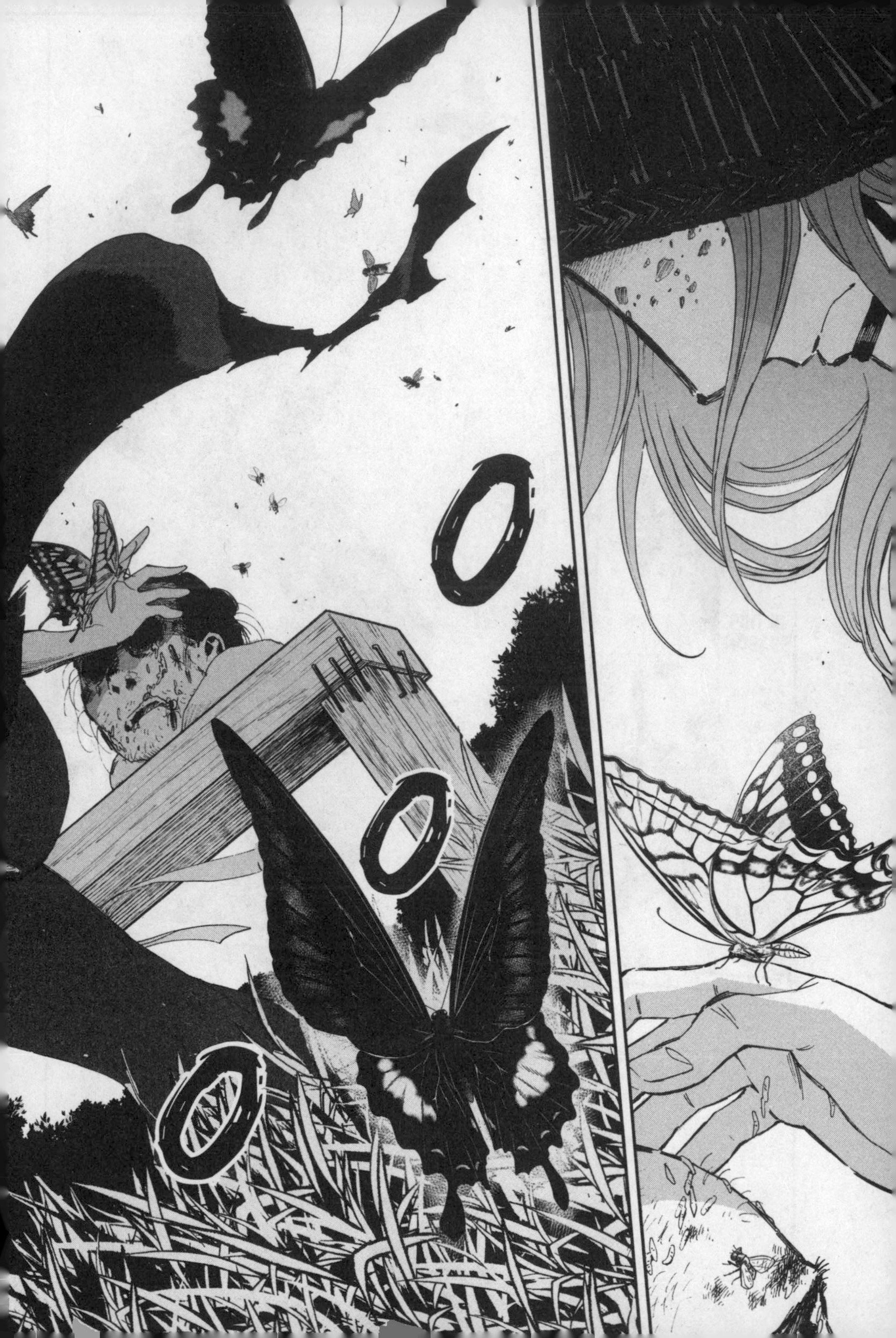

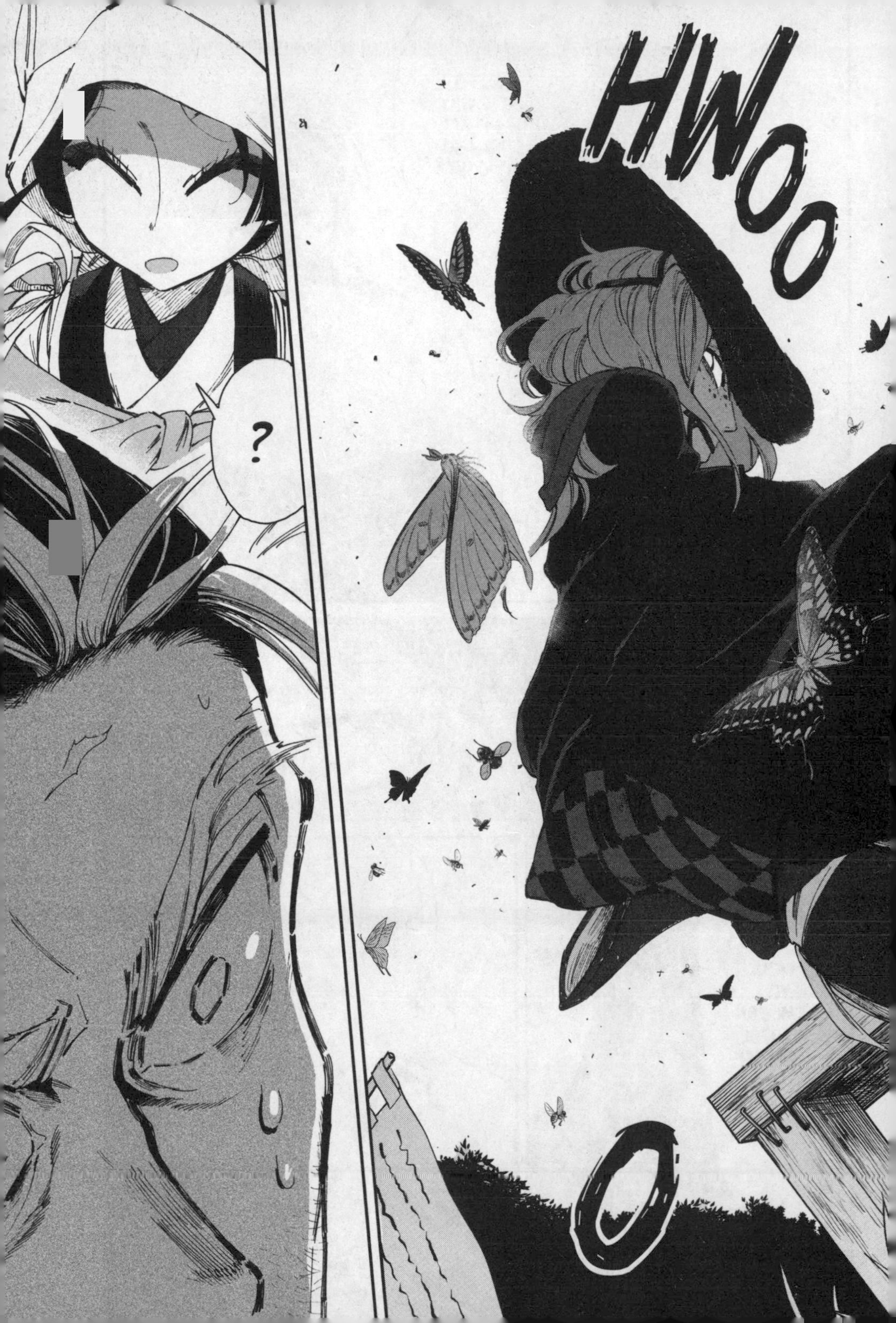
HWOOO
?

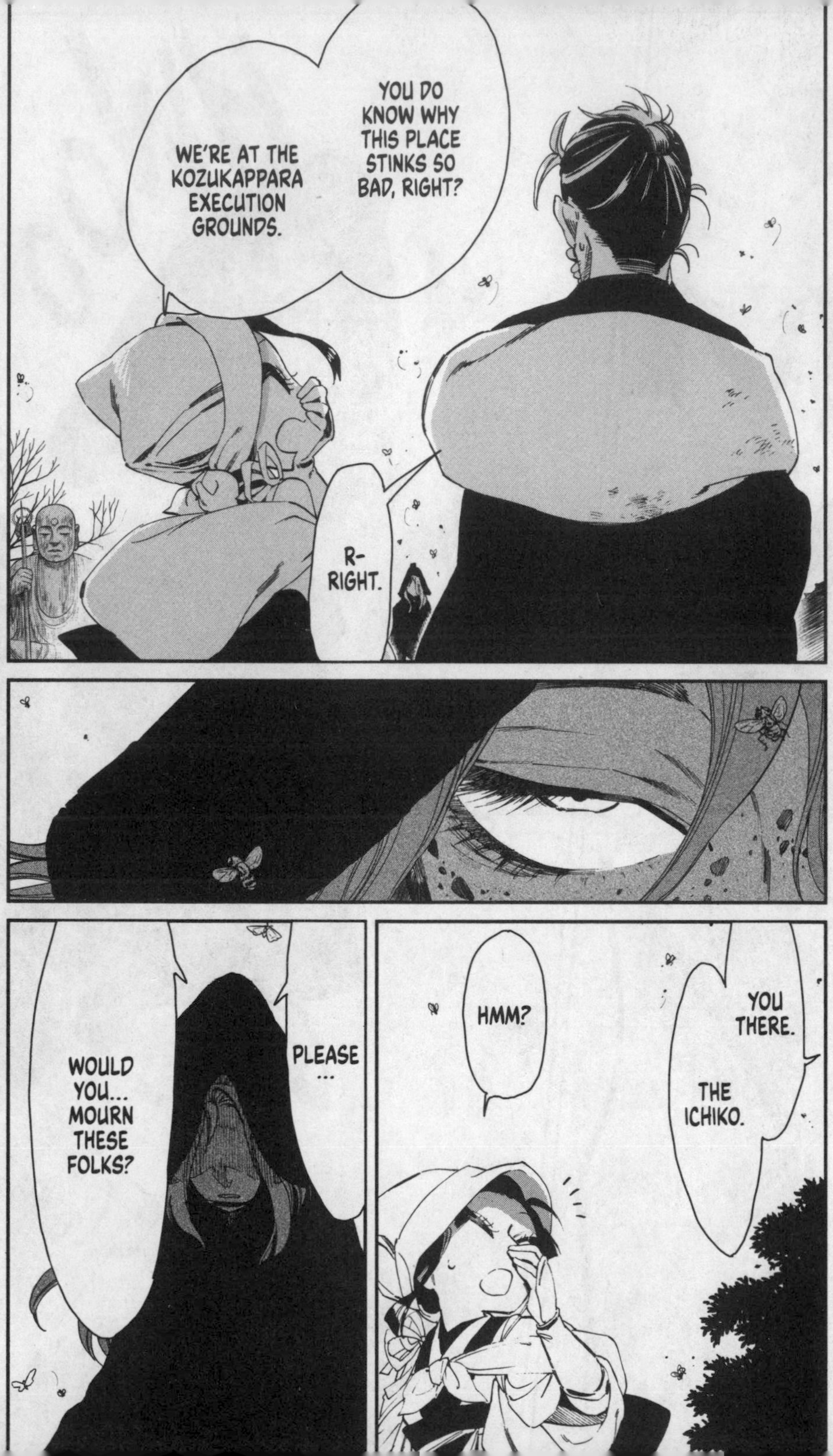
YOU DO KNOW WHY THIS PLACE STINKS SO BAD, RIGHT?
WE'RE AT THE KOZUKAPPARA EXECUTION GROUNDS.
R-RIGHT.
YOU THERE.
THE ICHIKO.
HMM?
PLEASE...
WOULD YOU... MOURN THESE FOLKS?

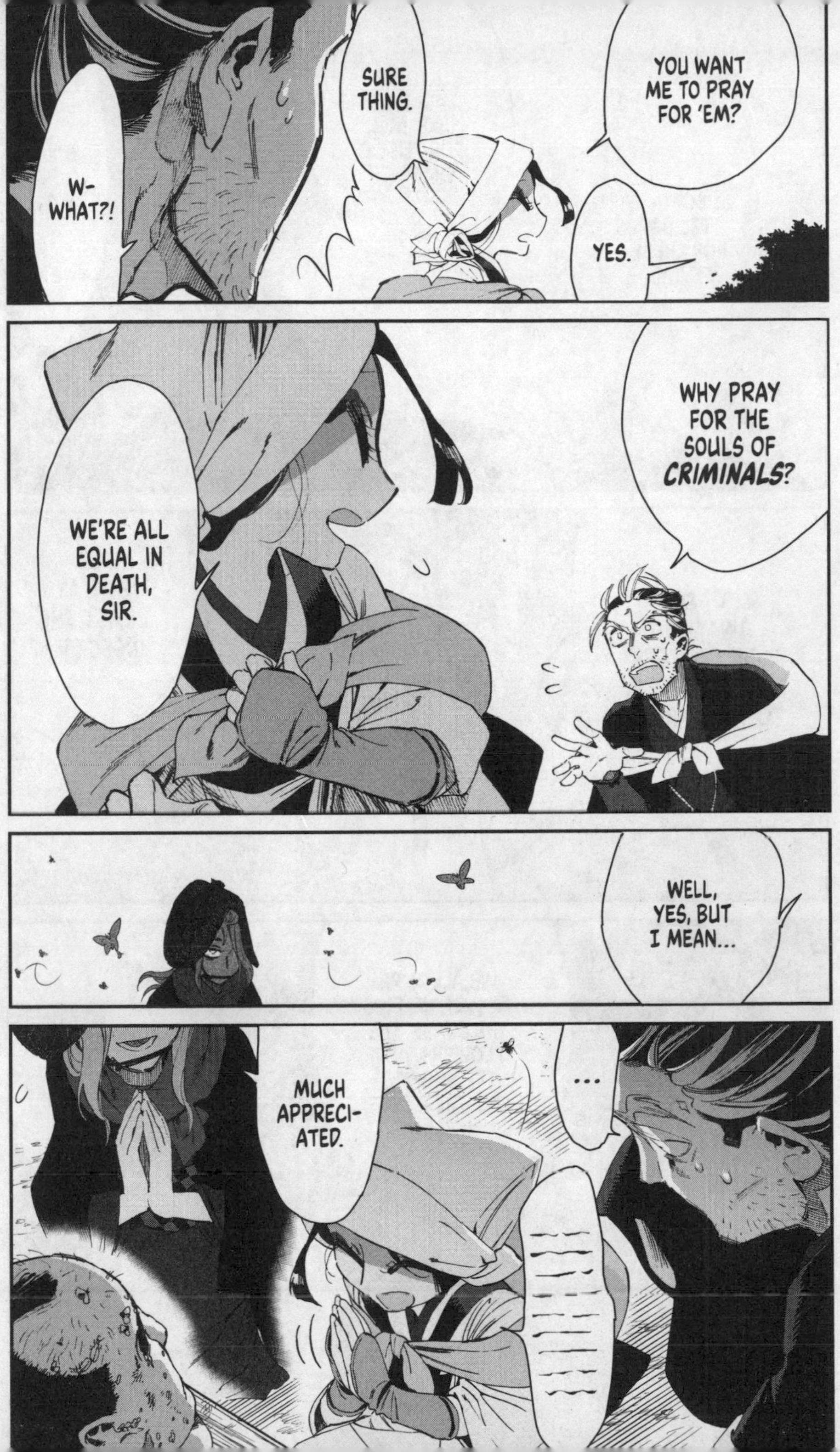
YOU WANT ME TO PRAY FOR 'EM?
YES.
SURE THING.
W-WHAT?!
WHY PRAY FOR THE SOULS OF *CRIMINALS*?
WE'RE ALL EQUAL IN DEATH, SIR.
WELL, YES, BUT I MEAN...
...
MUCH APPRECIATED.

GOTTA FEEL BAD FOR THESE FELLAS.

...TO BE LAID BARE LIKE THIS, FOR PUBLIC SHAMING?

GUILTY OR NOT...

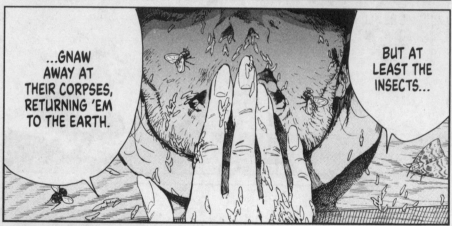

...GNAW AWAY AT THEIR CORPSES, RETURNING 'EM TO THE EARTH.

BUT AT LEAST THE INSECTS...

DON'T YOU THINK...

WE ALL TURN TO DIRT, HELPING THE GRASS, THE FLOWERS, AND THE BUGS TO LIVE THEIR BEST LIVES...

WHETHER GOOD OR EVIL...

MAN OR WOMAN...

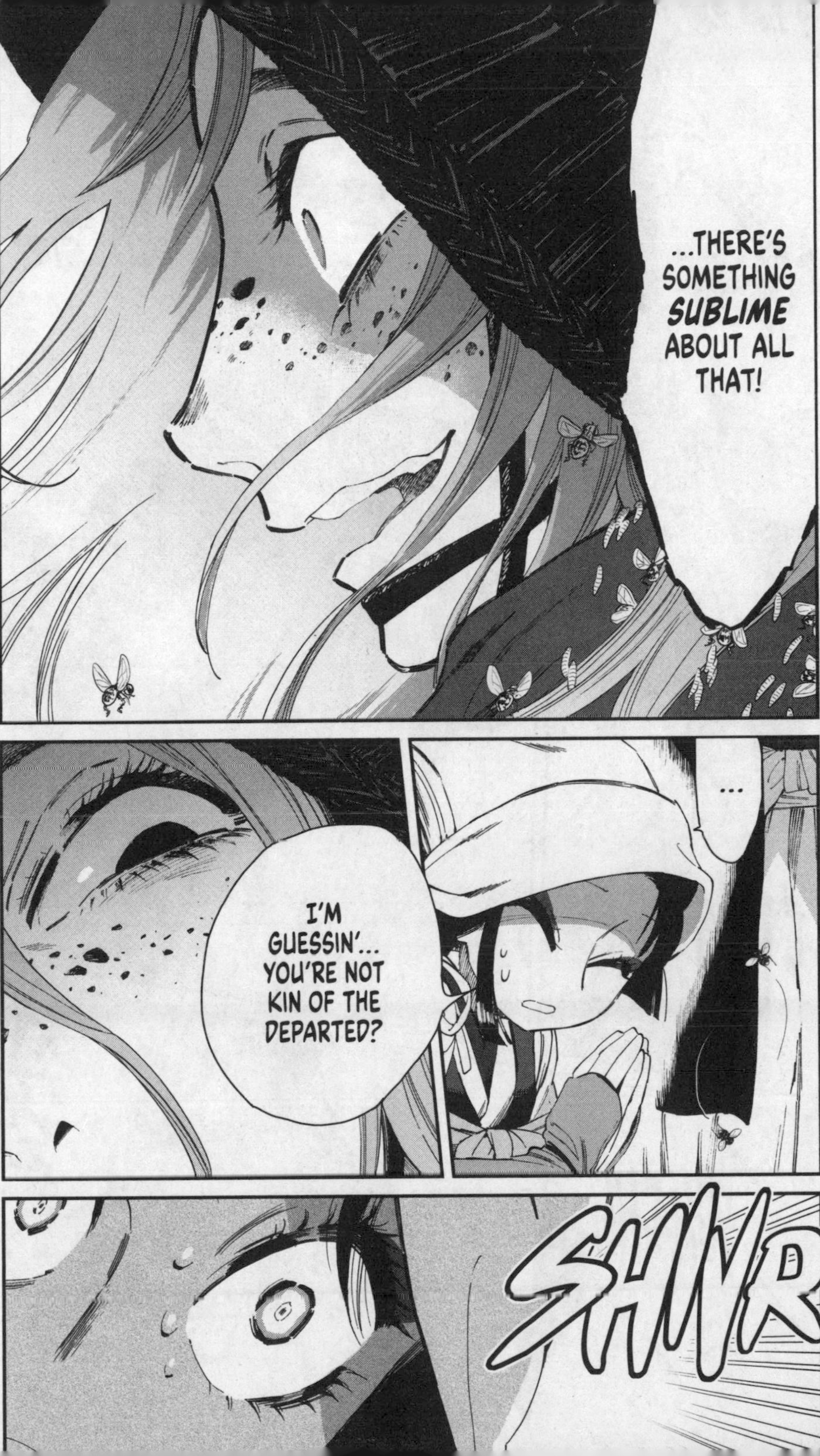
...THERE'S SOMETHING SUBLIME ABOUT ALL THAT!
...
I'M GUESSIN'... YOU'RE NOT KIN OF THE DEPARTED?
SHNR

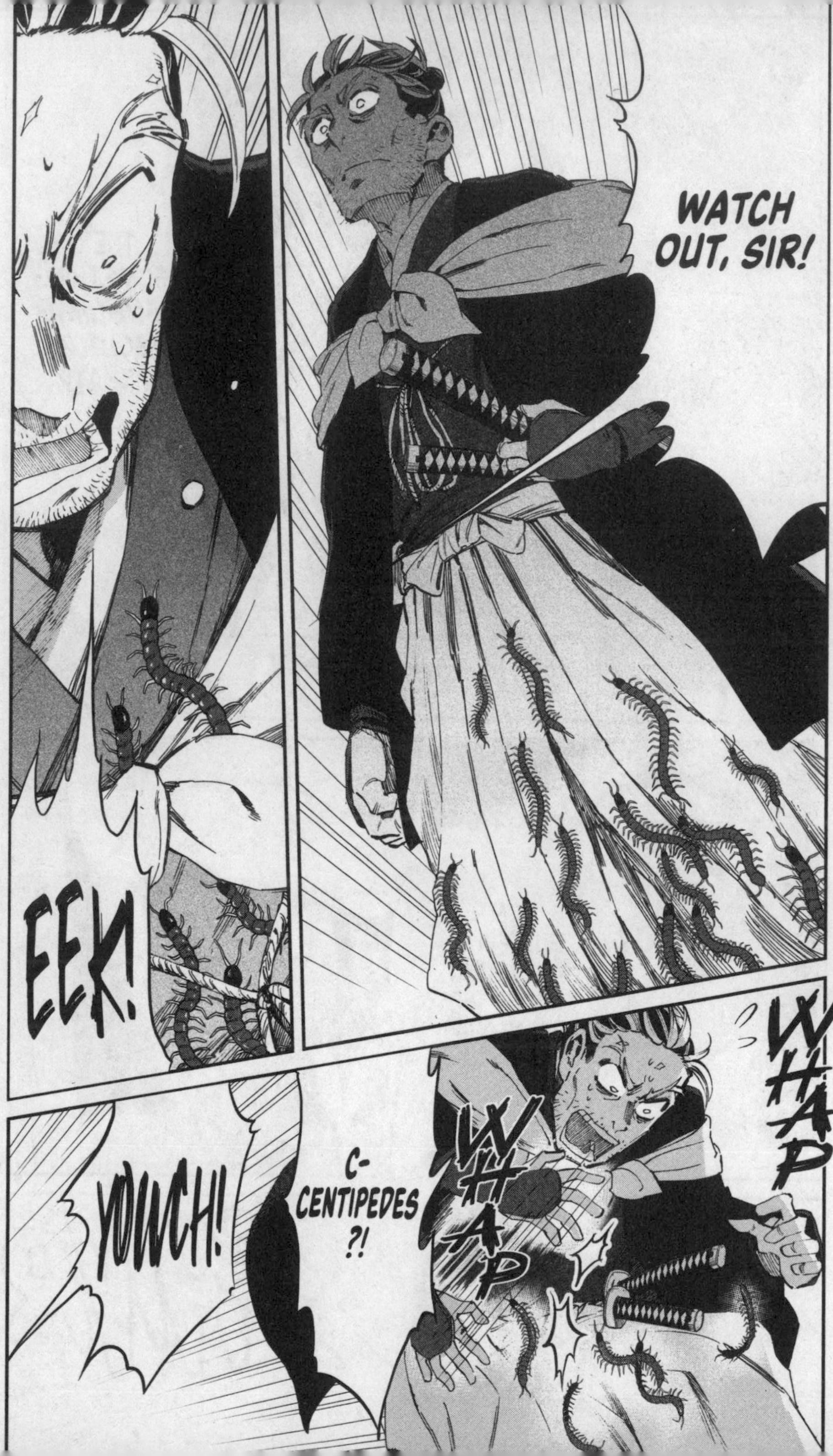
WATCH OUT, SIR!
EEK!
WHAP
WHAP
C-CENTIPEDES?!
YOUCH!

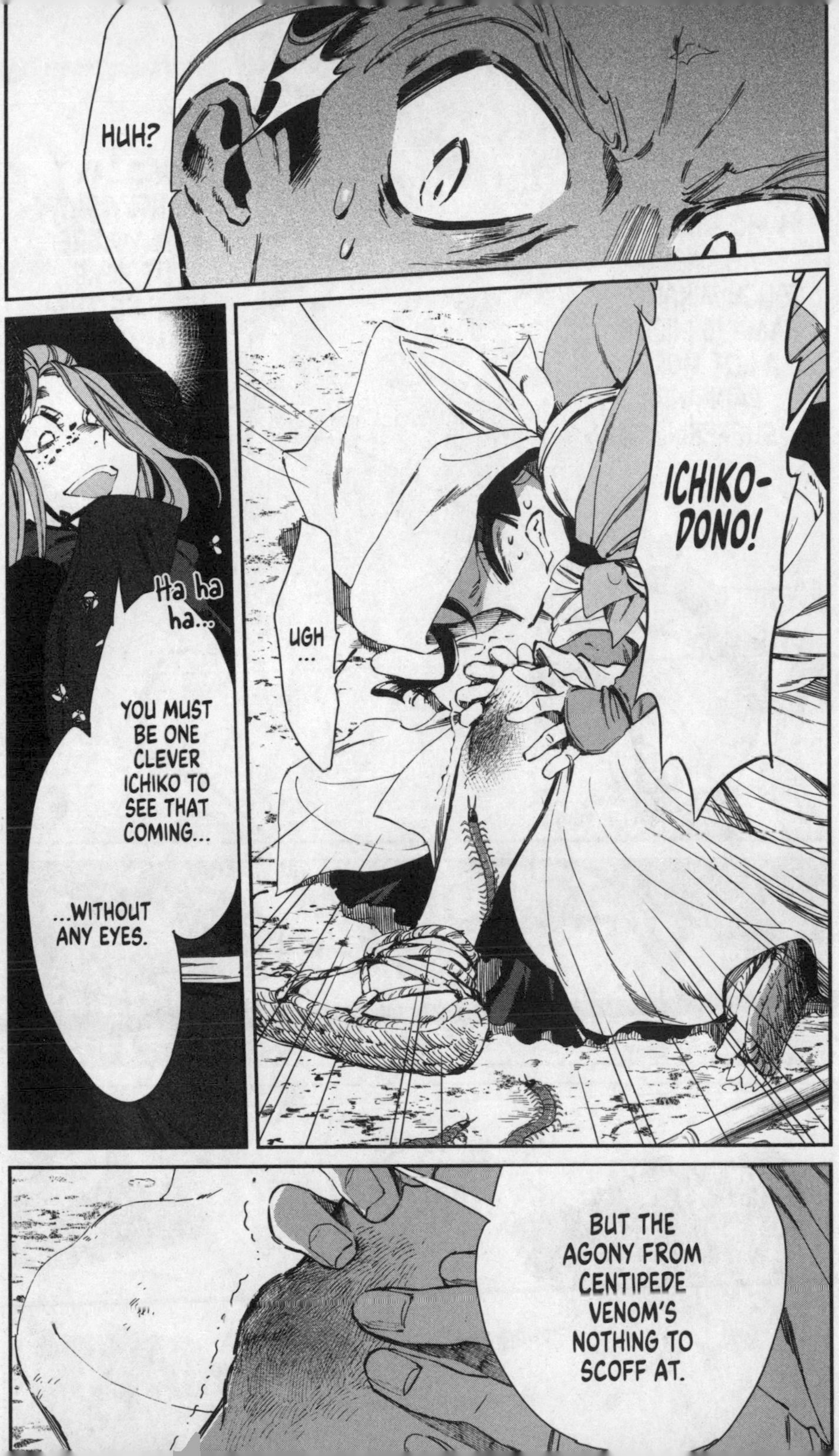
HUH?
ICHIKO-DONO!
UGH...
Ha ha ha...
YOU MUST BE ONE CLEVER ICHIKO TO SEE THAT COMING...
...WITHOUT ANY EYES.
BUT THE AGONY FROM CENTIPEDE VENOM'S NOTHING TO SCOFF AT.

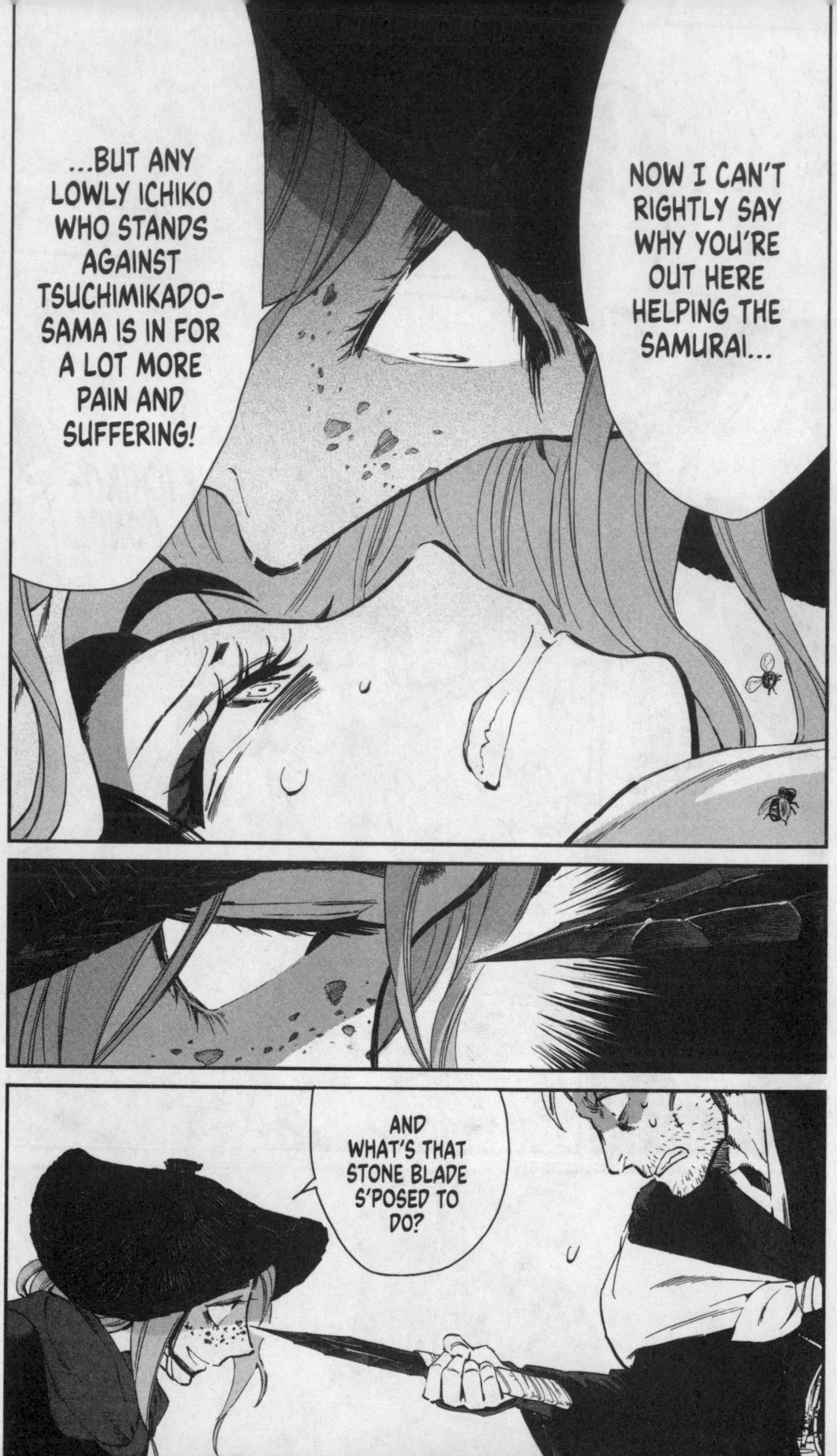
NOW I CAN'T RIGHTLY SAY WHY YOU'RE OUT HERE HELPING THE SAMURAI...
...BUT ANY LOWLY ICHIKO WHO STANDS AGAINST TSUCHIMIKADO-SAMA IS IN FOR A LOT MORE PAIN AND SUFFERING!
AND WHAT'S THAT STONE BLADE S'POSED TO DO?

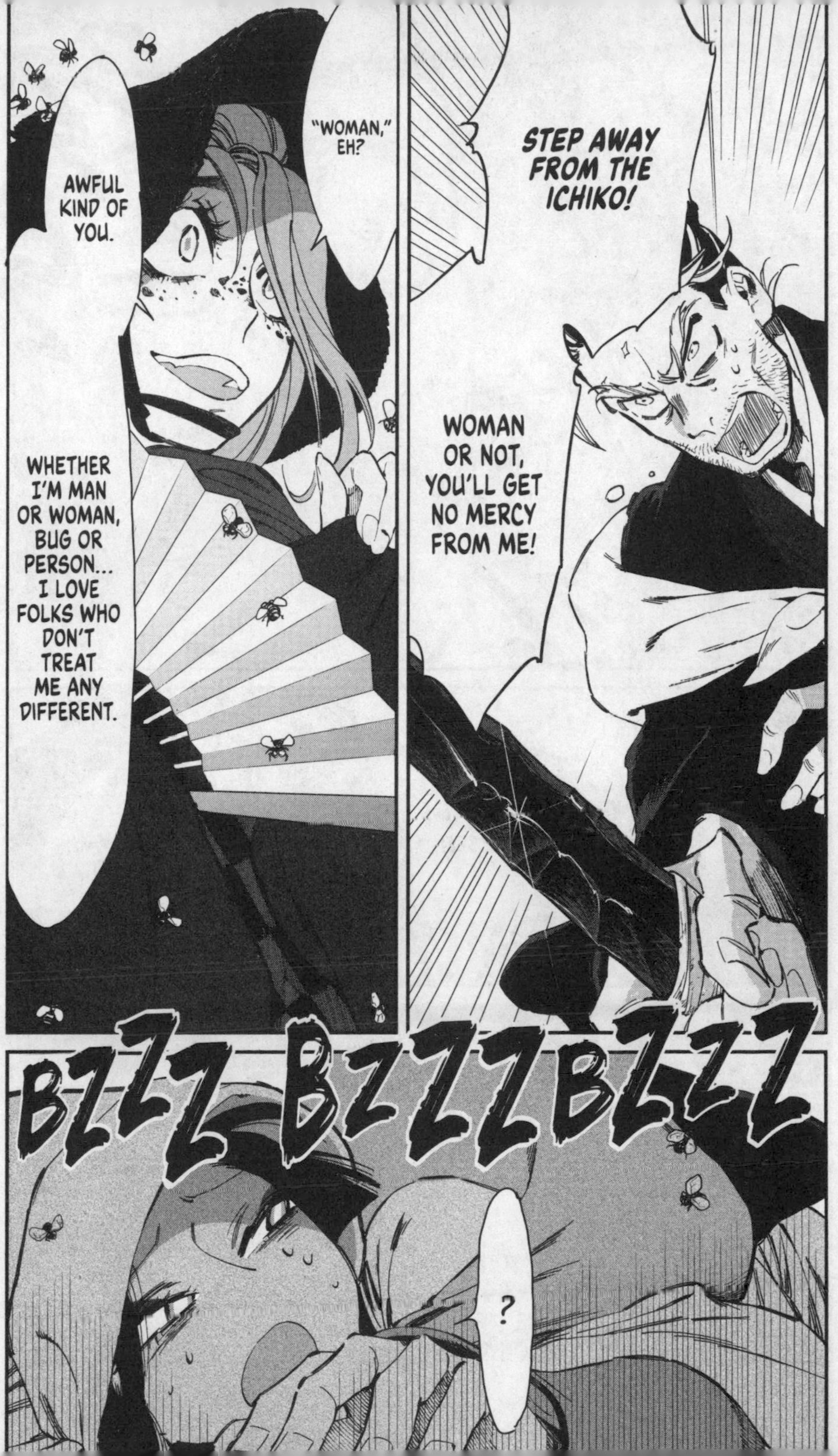
STEP AWAY FROM THE ICHIKO!
WOMAN OR NOT, YOU'LL GET NO MERCY FROM ME!
"WOMAN," EH?
AWFUL KIND OF YOU.
WHETHER I'M MAN OR WOMAN, BUG OR PERSON... I LOVE FOLKS WHO DON'T TREAT ME ANY DIFFERENT.
BZZZ BZZZZBZZZ
?

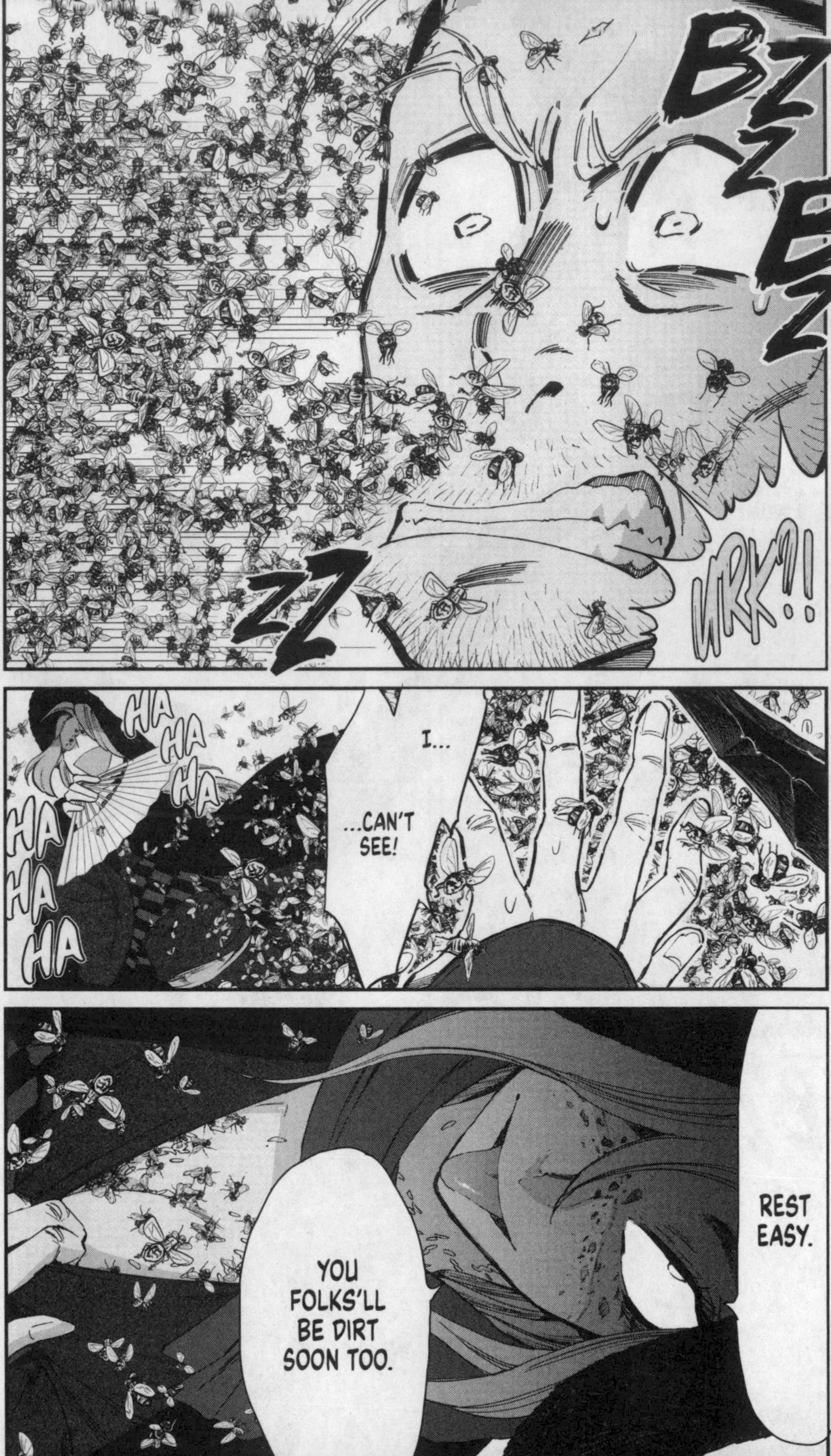
BZZ BZZ
URK?!
ZZ
I...
...CAN'T SEE!
HA HA HA HA
HA HA HA HA
REST EASY.
YOU FOLKS'LL BE DIRT SOON TOO.

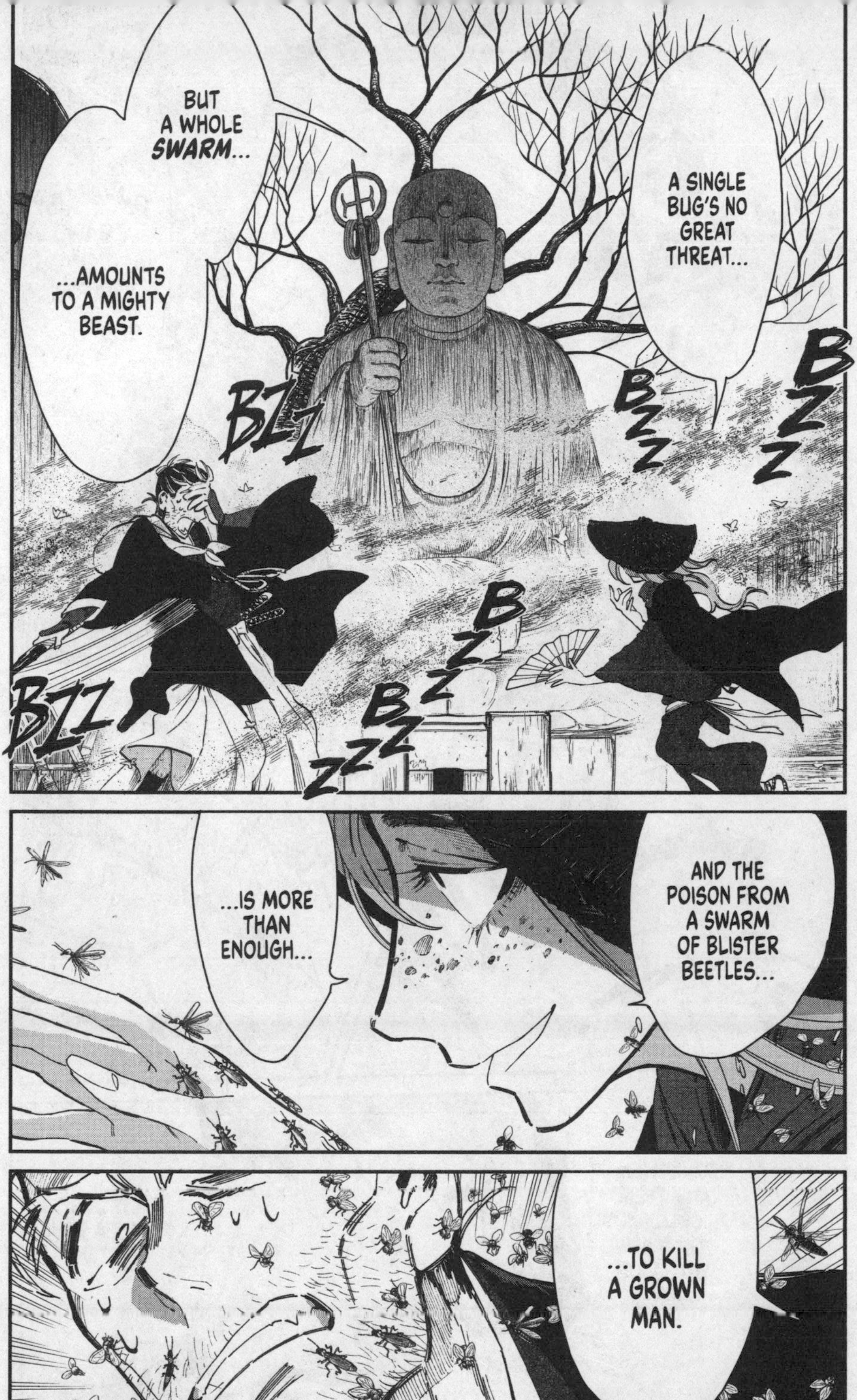
A SINGLE BUG'S NO GREAT THREAT...
BUT A WHOLE *SWARM*...
...AMOUNTS TO A MIGHTY BEAST.
BZZ
BZZ
BZZ
BZZ
BZZZ
BZZZ
AND THE POISON FROM A SWARM OF BLISTER BEETLES...
...IS MORE THAN ENOUGH...
...TO KILL A GROWN MAN.

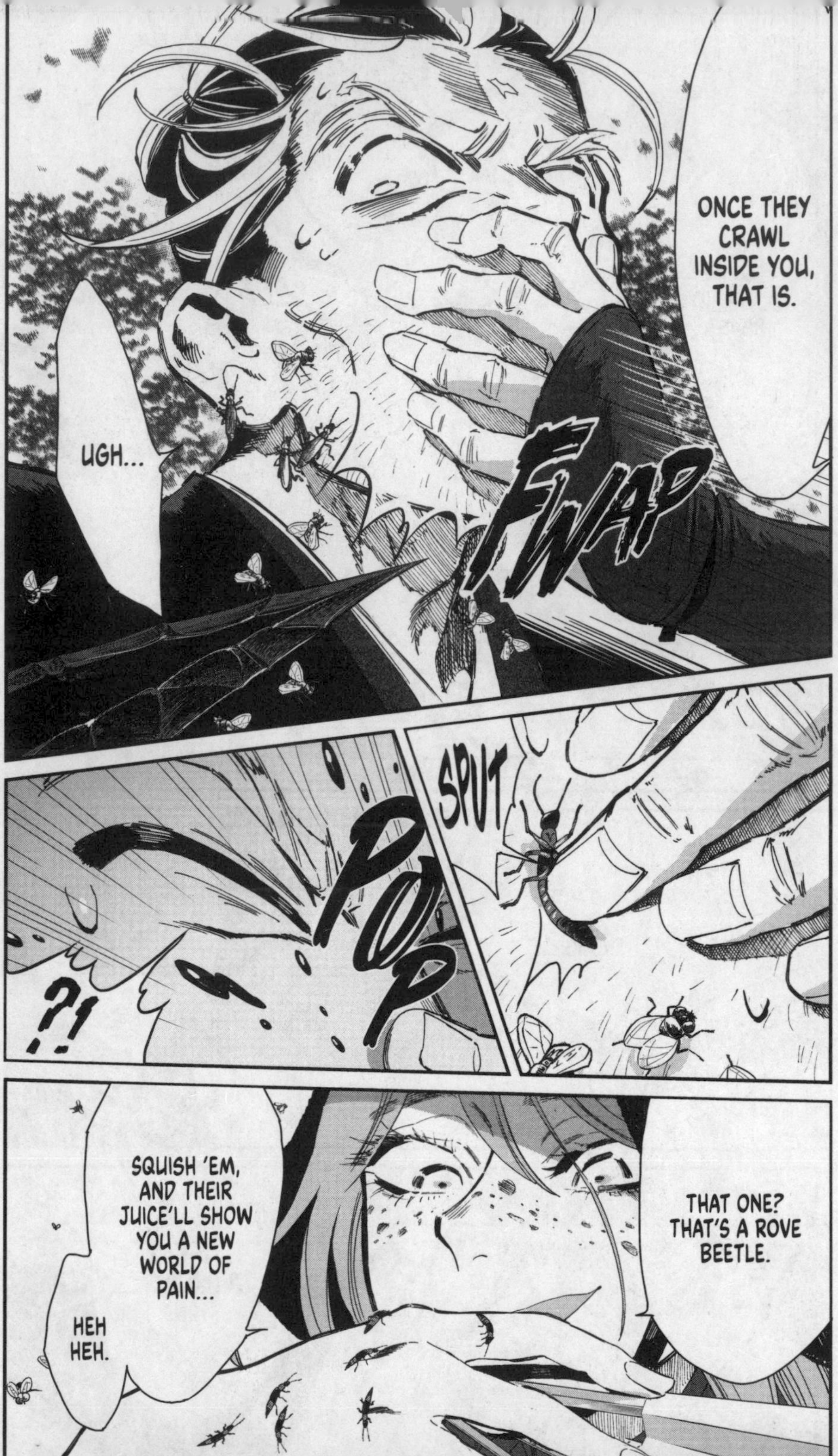
ONCE THEY CRAWL INSIDE YOU, THAT IS.
UGH...
FWAP
SPUT
POP
?!
THAT ONE? THAT'S A ROVE BEETLE.
SQUISH 'EM, AND THEIR JUICE'LL SHOW YOU A NEW WORLD OF PAIN...
HEH HEH.

LOTTA DIFFERENT KINDS GOT INTO THAT SWARM.

YOU'LL NEVER MANAGE TO SWAT AWAY JUST THE BLISTER BEETLES.

HECK, THEY'LL CRAWL INTO YOUR EYE SOCKETS.

OR EVEN YOUR EARS!

COVER YOUR MOUTH, AND THEY'LL FIND YOUR NOSE.

WHP

WHP

FWMP

!

BZZ

BZZ

BZZ

OWW...

DAMN!

HFF

HFF

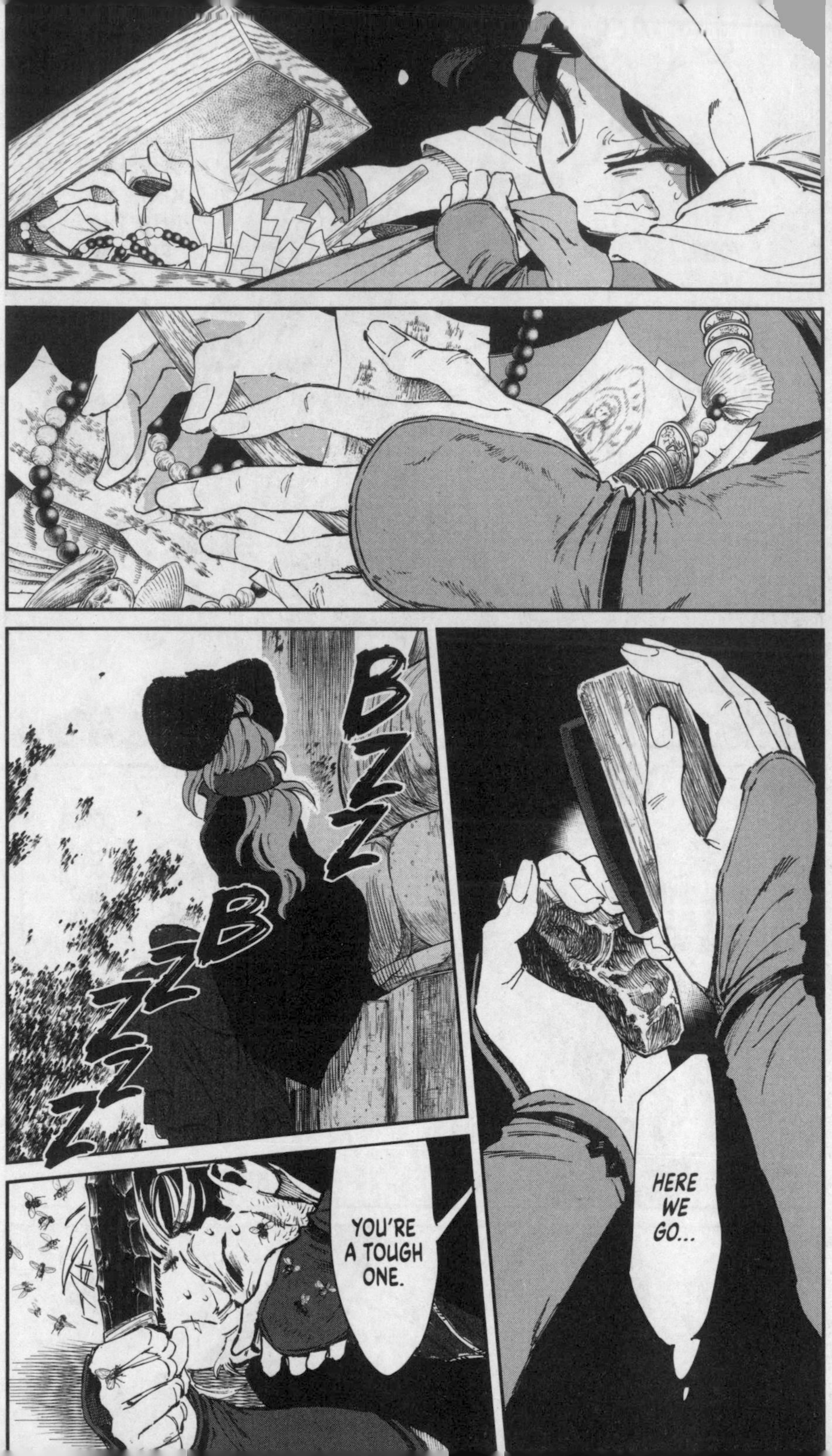
HERE WE GO...
BZZ
BZZZZ
YOU'RE A TOUGH ONE.

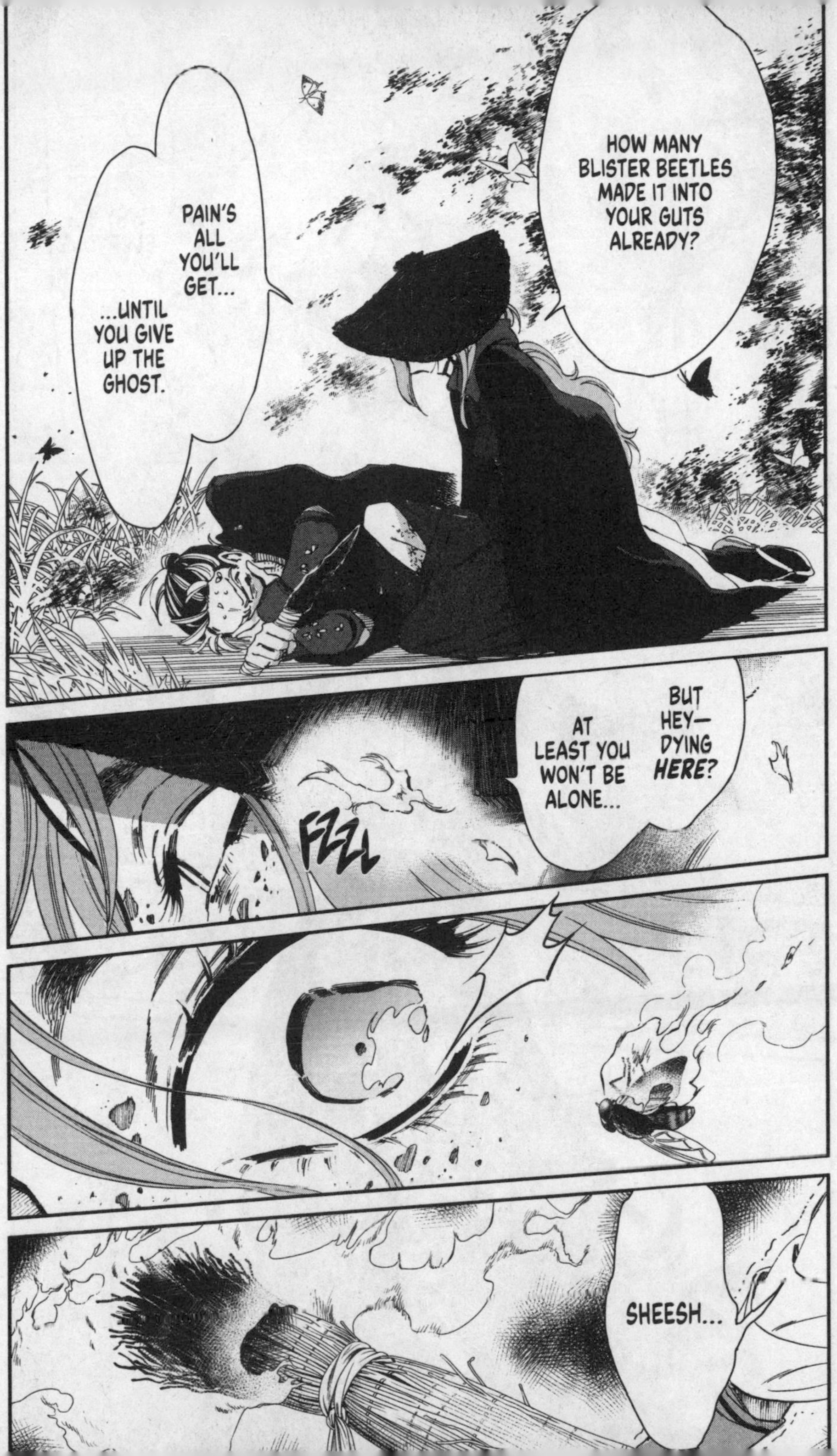
HOW MANY BLISTER BEETLES MADE IT INTO YOUR GUTS ALREADY?
PAIN'S ALL YOU'LL GET...
...UNTIL YOU GIVE UP THE GHOST.
BUT HEY—DYING *HERE*?
AT LEAST YOU WON'T BE ALONE...
FZZZ
SHEESH...

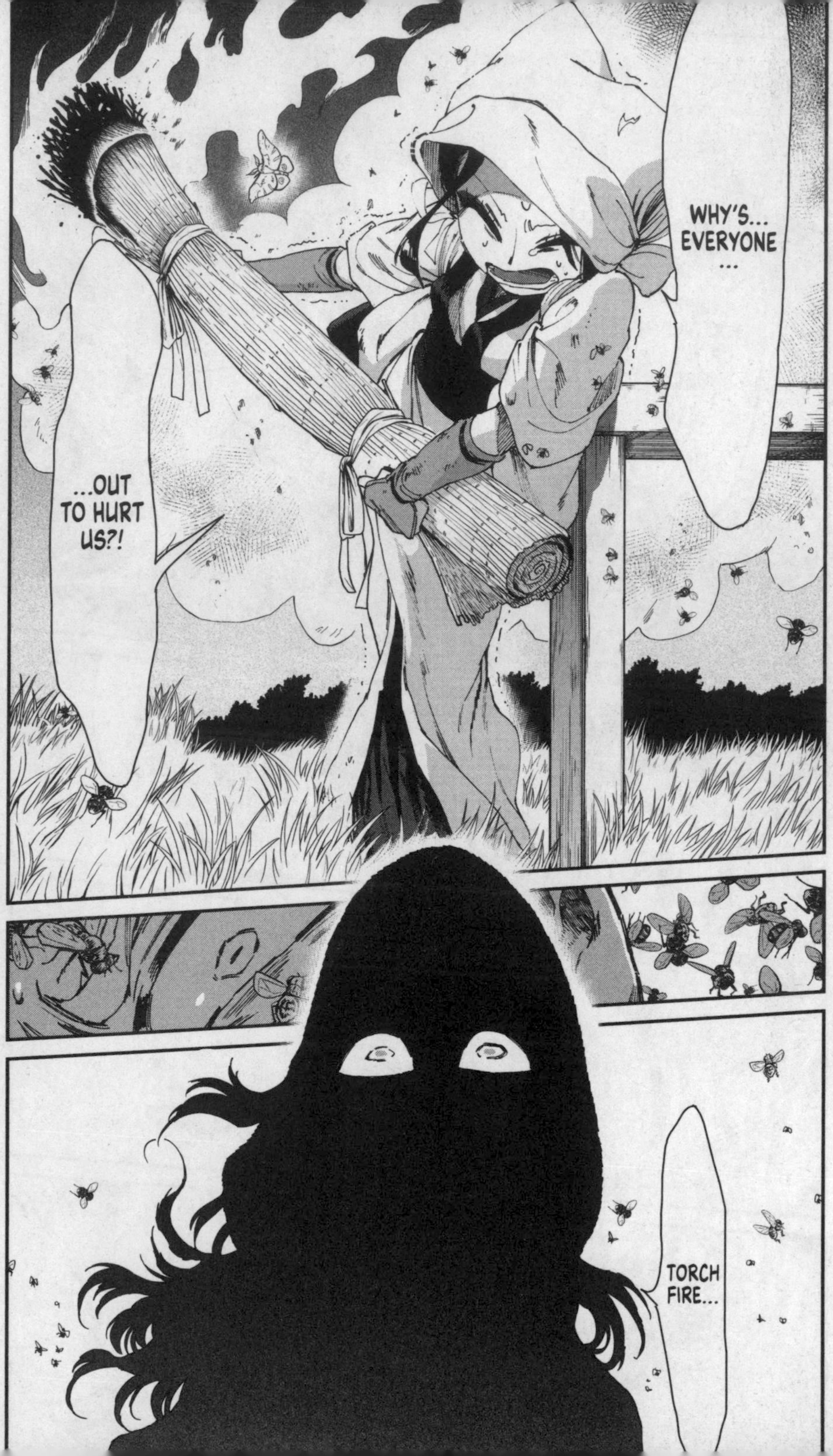
WHY'S... EVERYONE ...
...OUT TO HURT US?!
TORCH FIRE...

STEEL of the
CELESTIAL
SHADOWS

Trivia of
the Celestial
Shadows #②

Goze
Buskers

°Blind female performers
who roam the land, singing
gozeuta songs.

oThey usually traveled in
groups, with a sighted goze
leading the way.

oThey returned home
annually, at the end of
the year. Those who
came from snowy
regions had a hard
time getting
home if their
return trip
was delayed.

oTo hone their
craft, they
endured strict
training from
a young age.

I can't elaborate
too much on this,
but there was more
I wanted to do with
these characters.
I'd like to have
them appear
again.

You can find
Showa-era
goze songs
on YouTube,
if you're
interested.

Those strong
voices really hit
you deep down.

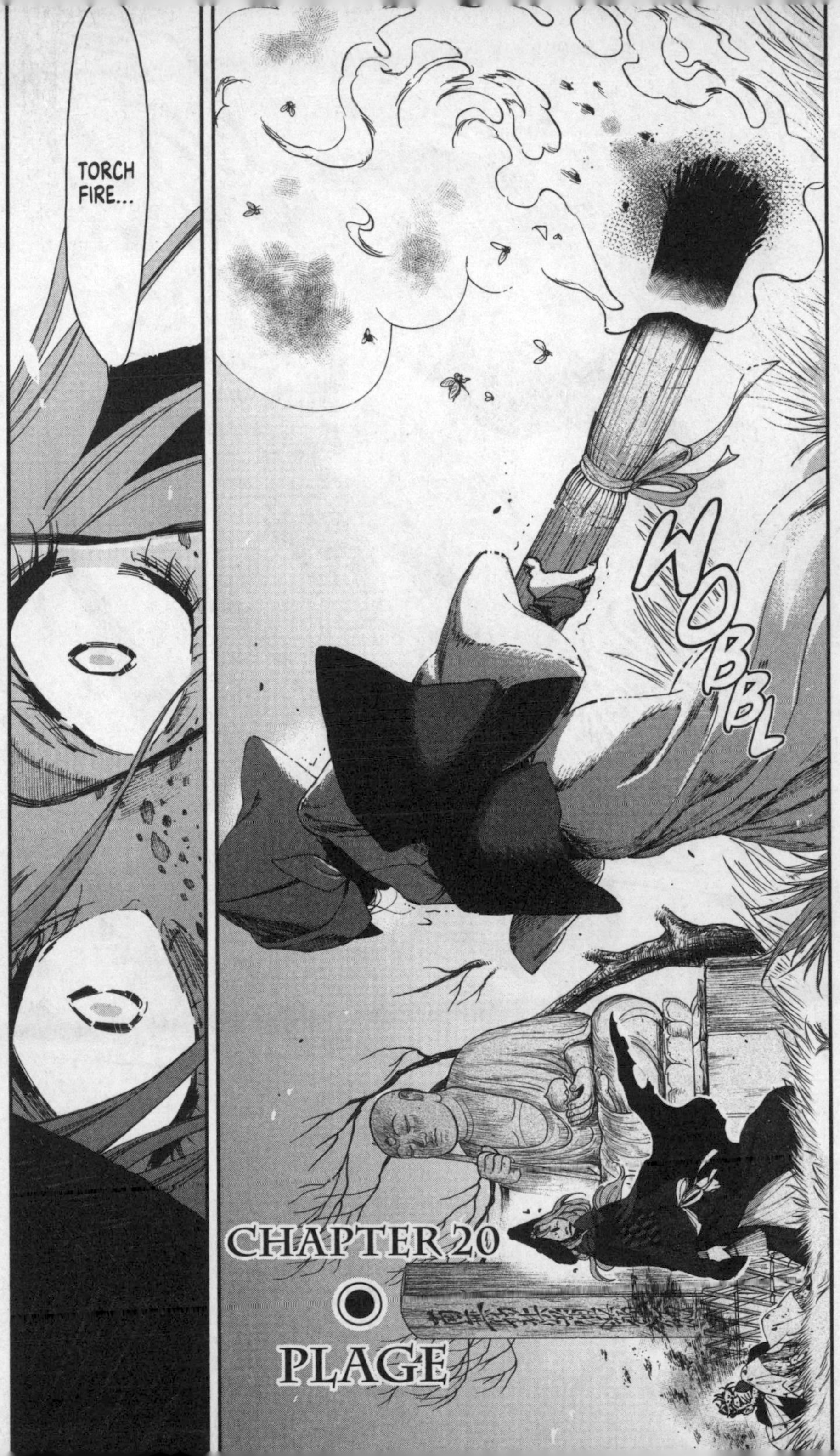
WOBBL
CHAPTER 20
PLAGE
TORCH FIRE...

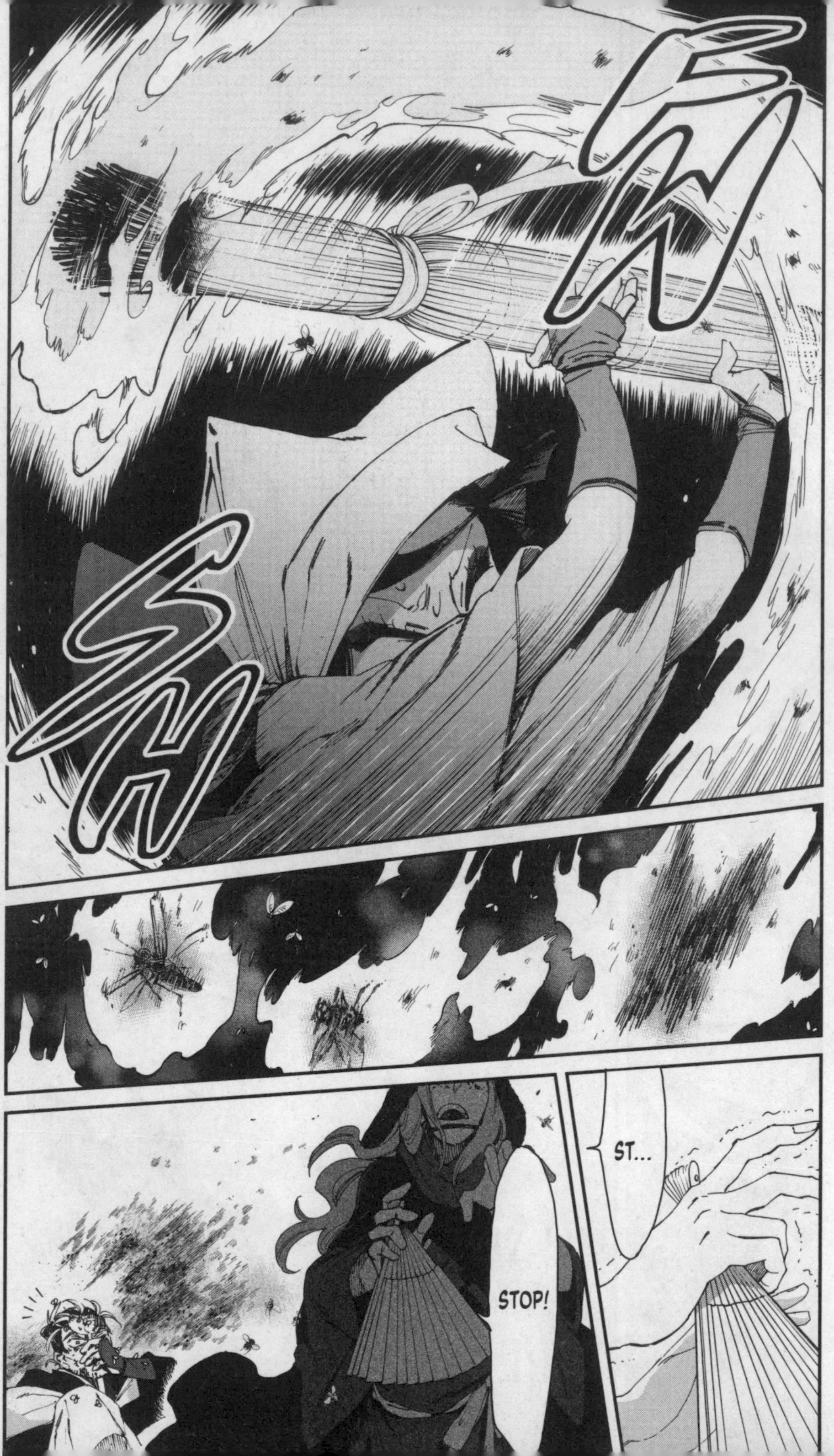
ST...
STOP!

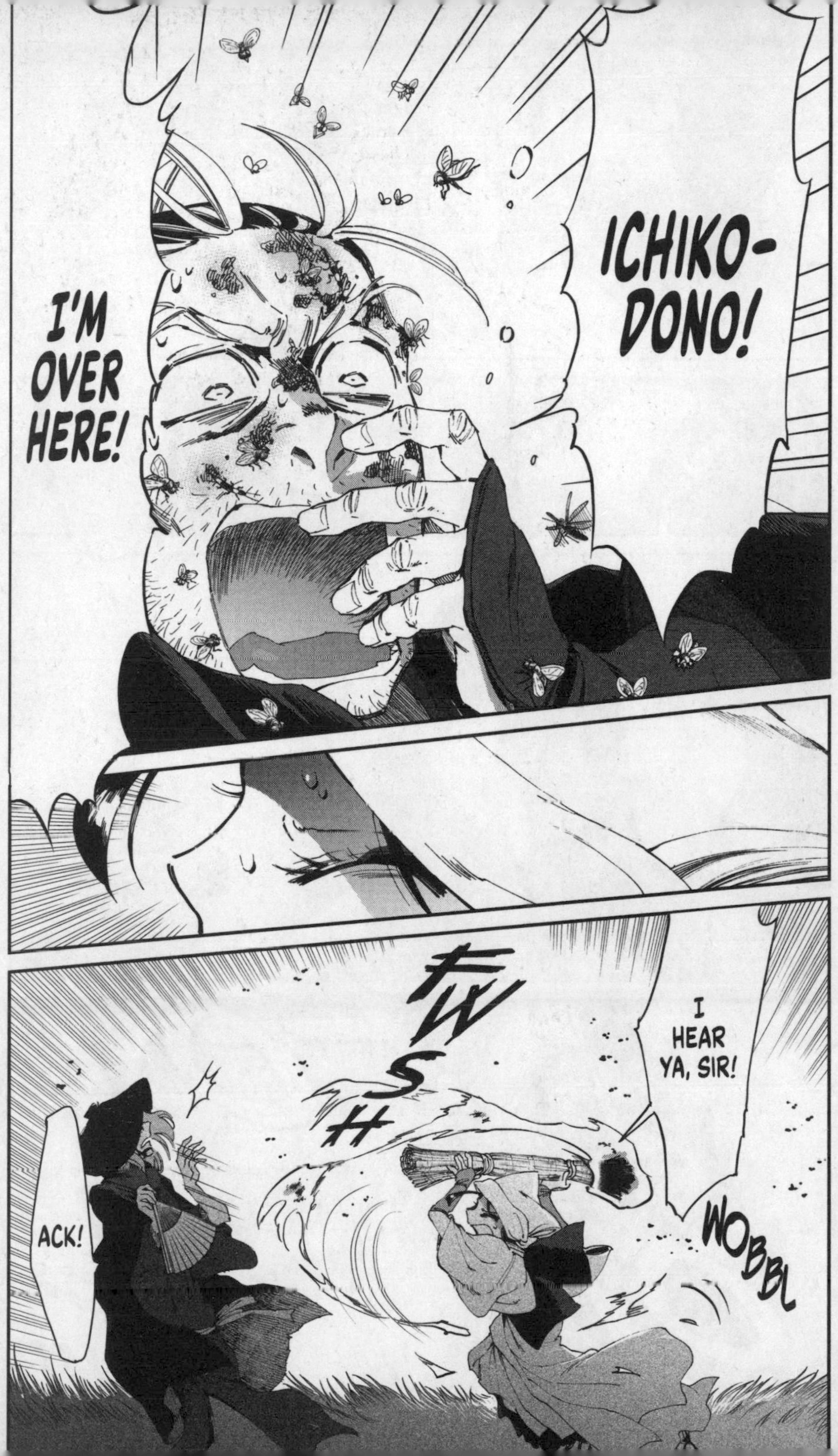
ICHIKO-DONO!
I'M OVER HERE!
FWSH
I HEAR YA, SIR!
WOBBL
ACK!

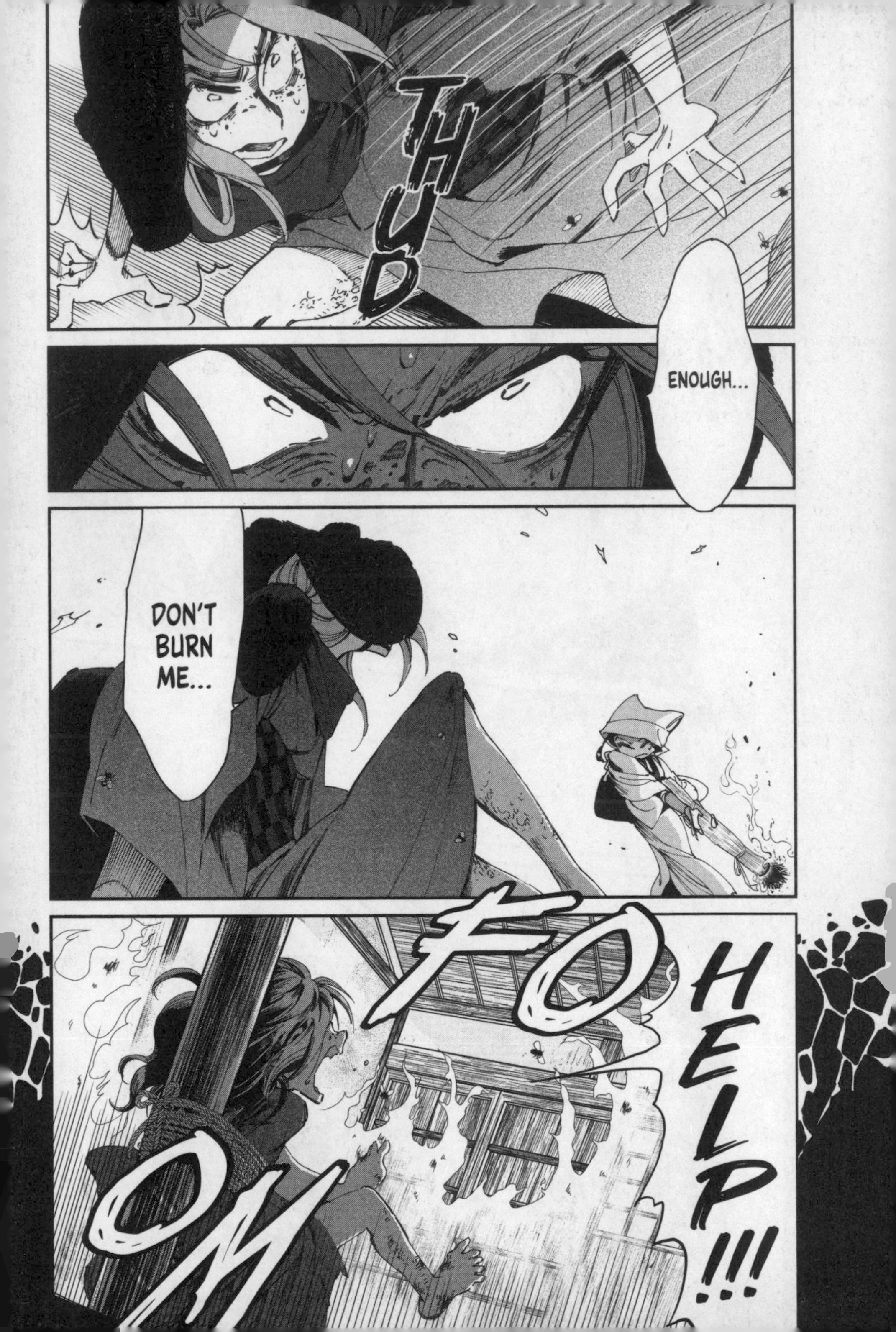
THUD
ENOUGH...
DON'T BURN ME...
HELP!!!
FOOM

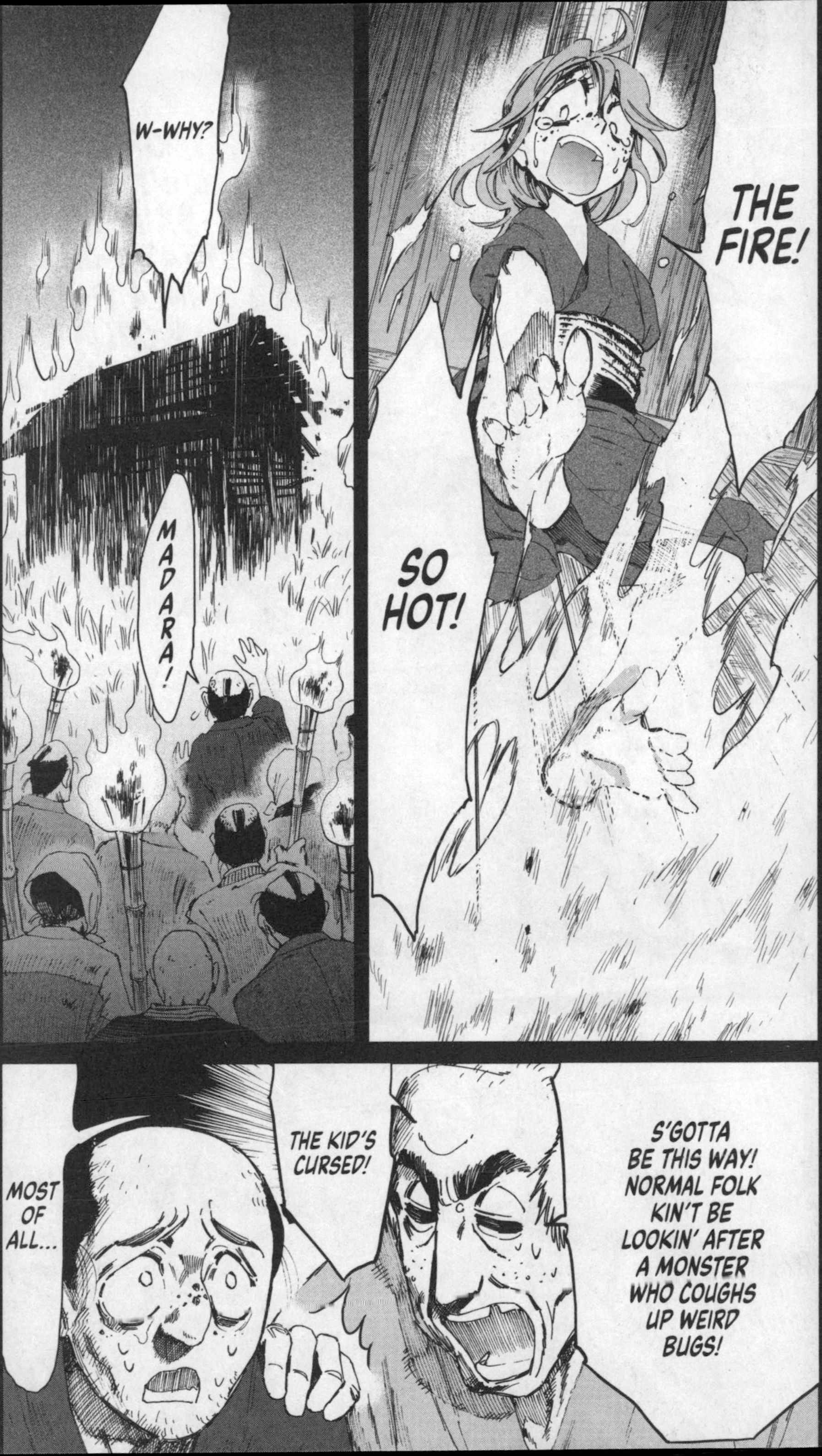
THE FIRE!
SO HOT!
W-WHY?
MADARA!
S'GOTTA BE THIS WAY! NORMAL FOLK KIN'T BE LOOKIN' AFTER A MONSTER WHO COUGHS UP WEIRD BUGS!
THE KID'S CURSED!
MOST OF ALL...

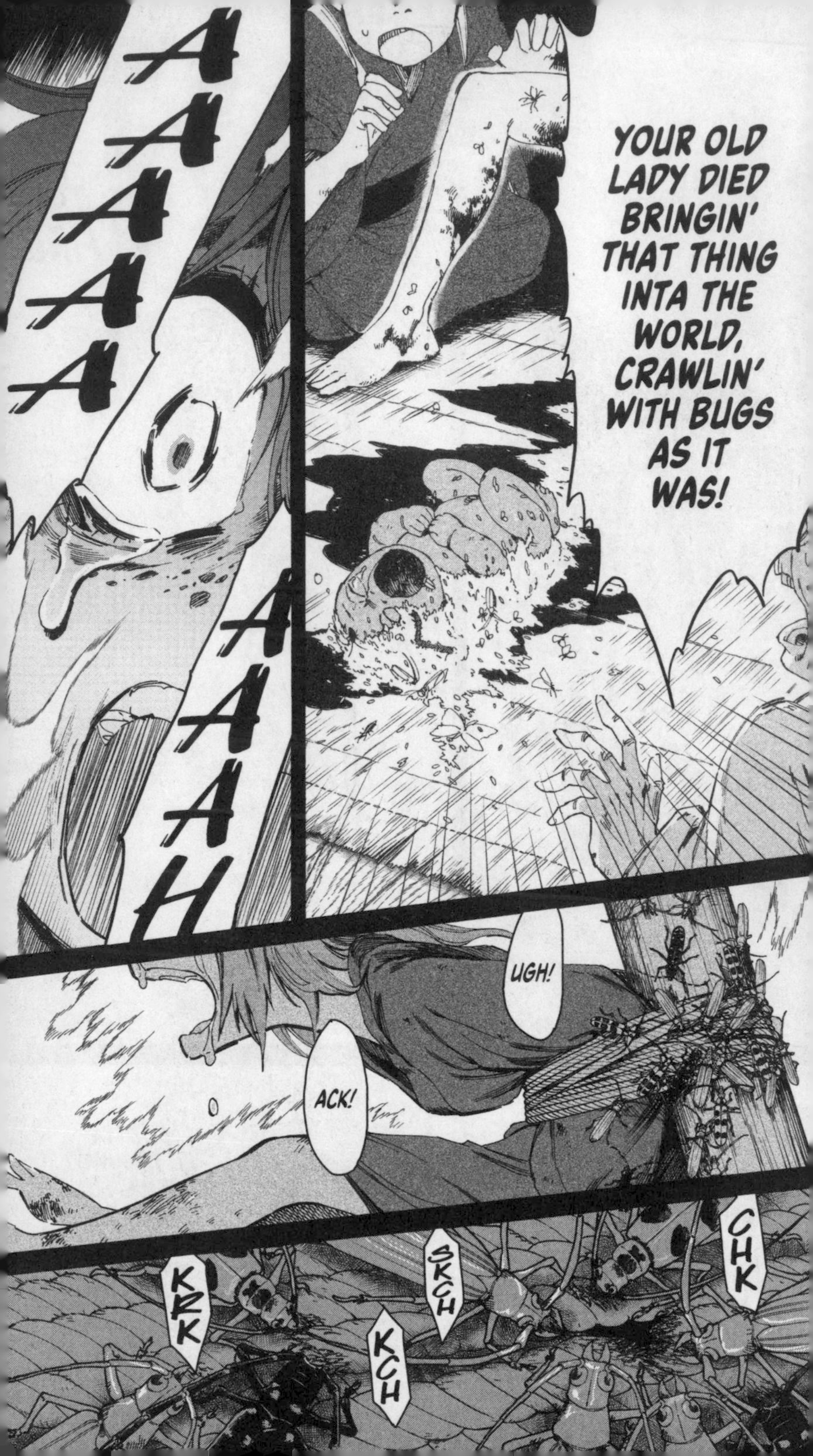
YOUR OLD LADY DIED BRINGIN' THAT THING INTA THE WORLD, CRAWLIN' WITH BUGS AS IT WAS!
AAAAAAAAAH
UGH!
ACK!
CHK
SKCH
KCH
KRK

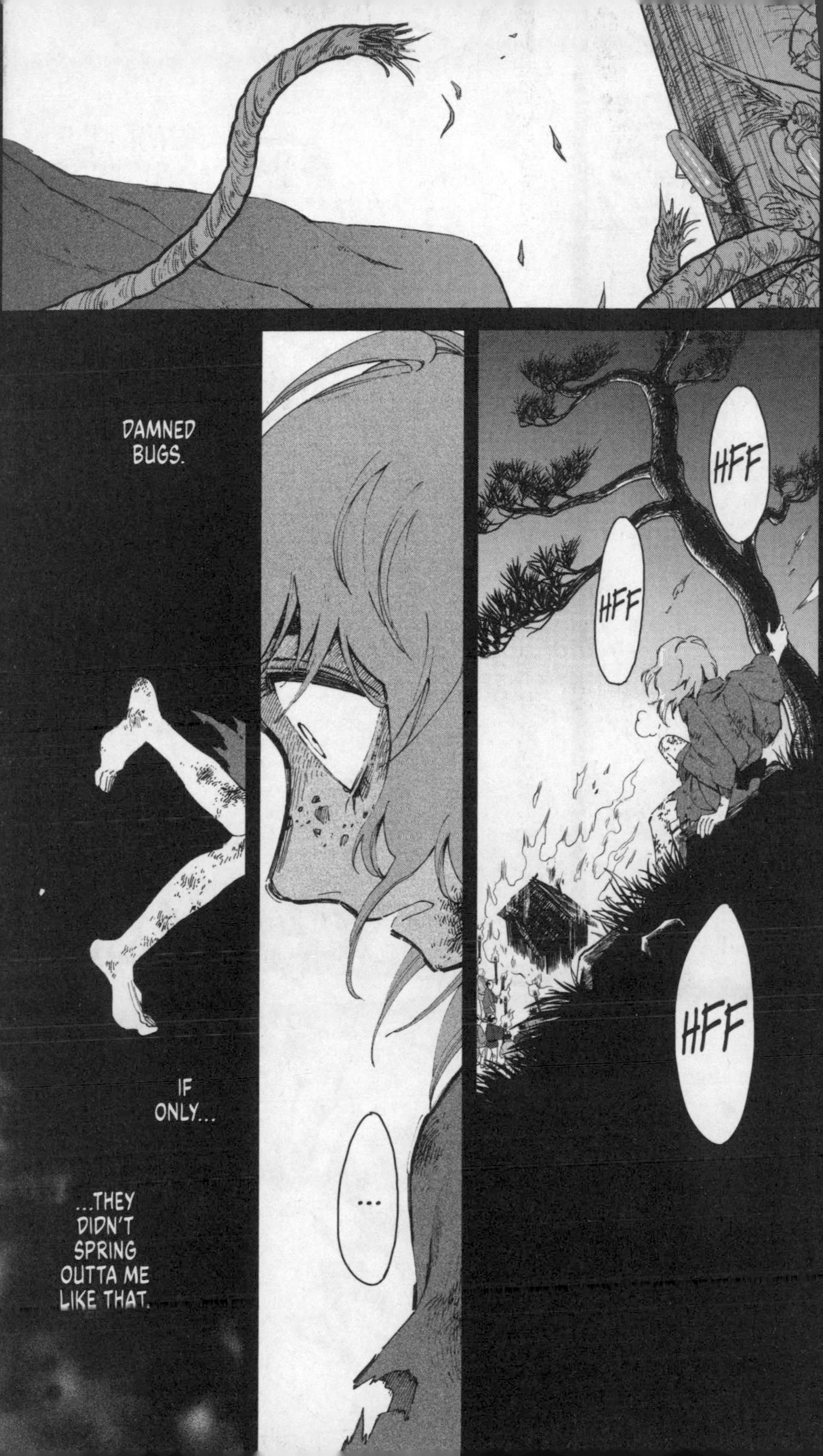
HFF
HFF
HFF
...
DAMNED BUGS.
IF ONLY...
...THEY DIDN'T SPRING OUTTA ME LIKE THAT.

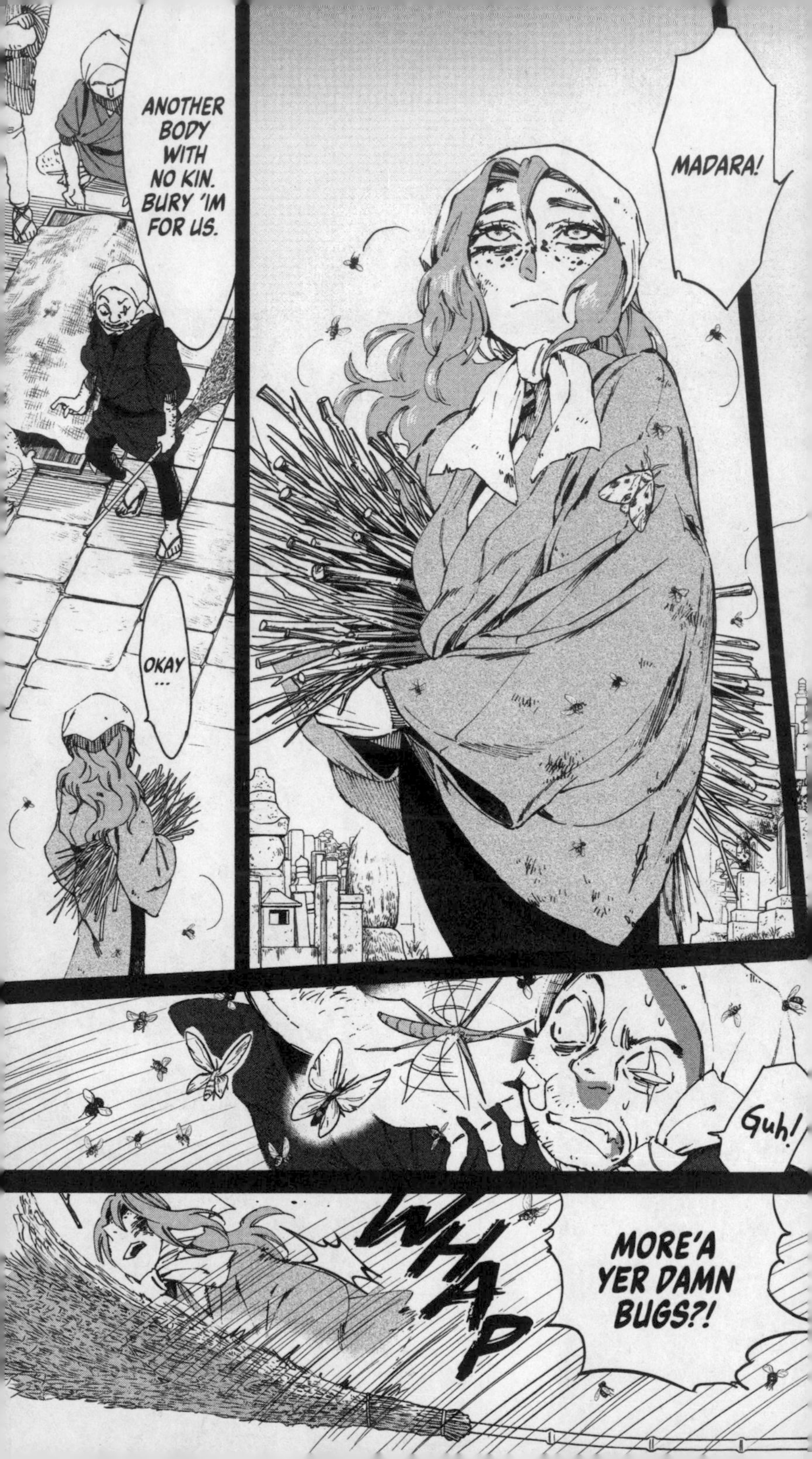
MADARA!
ANOTHER BODY WITH NO KIN. BURY 'IM FOR US.
OKAY ...
Guh!
MORE'A YER DAMN BUGS?!
WHAP

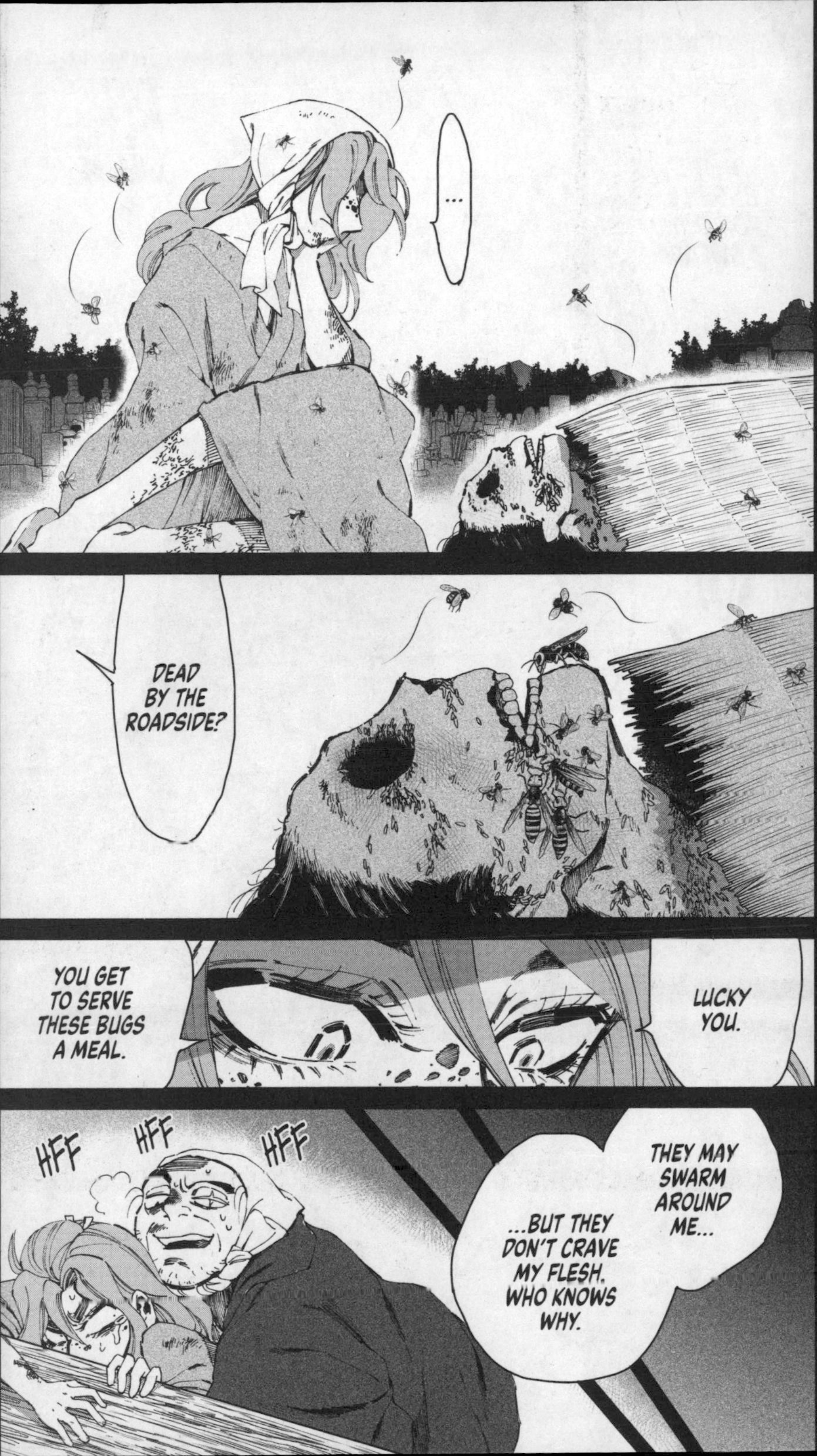
...
DEAD BY THE ROADSIDE?
YOU GET TO SERVE THESE BUGS A MEAL.
LUCKY YOU.
HFF HFF HFF
THEY MAY SWARM AROUND ME...
...BUT THEY DON'T CRAVE MY FLESH. WHO KNOWS WHY.

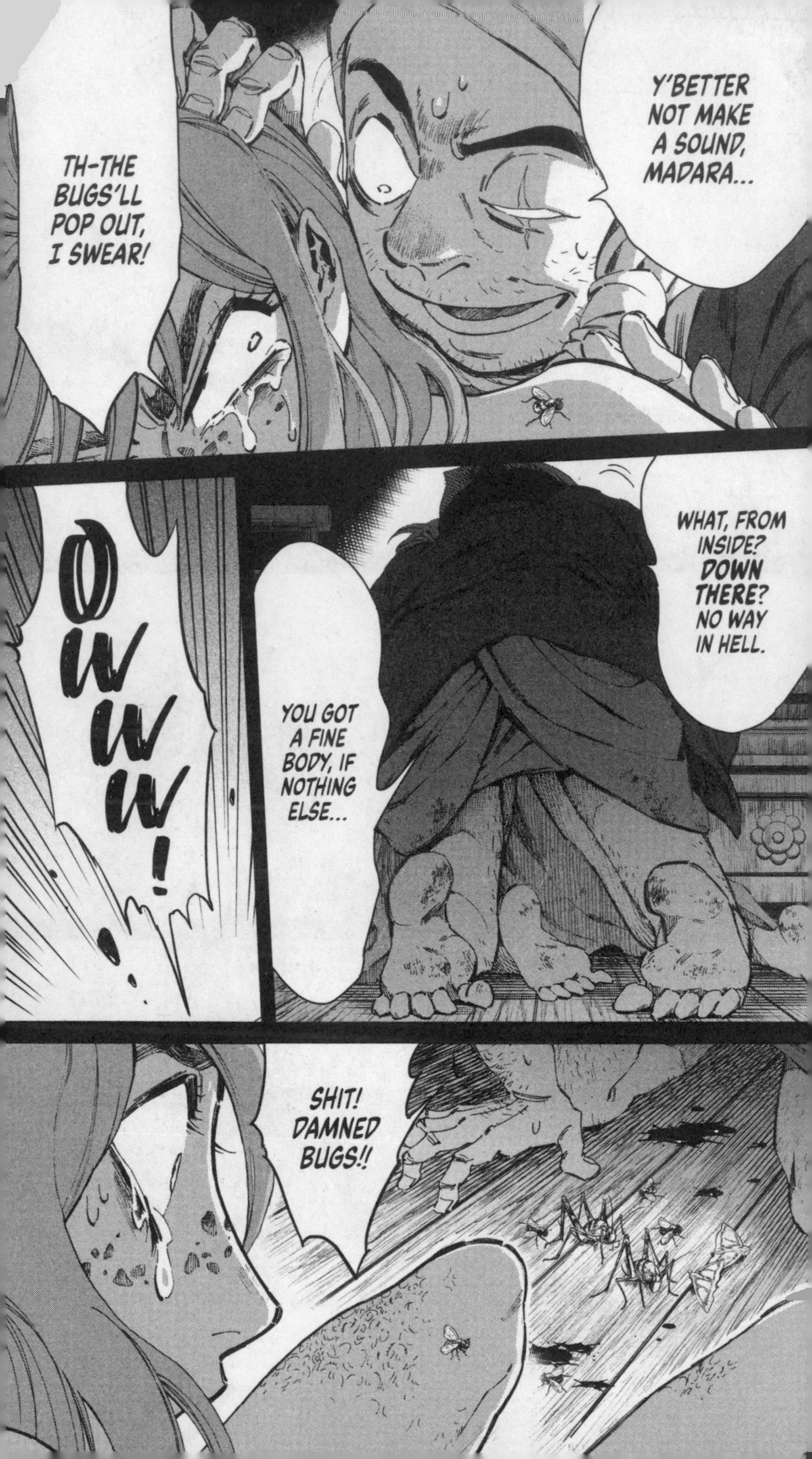
Y'BETTER NOT MAKE A SOUND, MADARA...
TH-THE BUGS'LL POP OUT, I SWEAR!
WHAT, FROM INSIDE? DOWN THERE? NO WAY IN HELL.
YOU GOT A FINE BODY, IF NOTHING ELSE...
OWWW!
SHIT! DAMNED BUGS!!

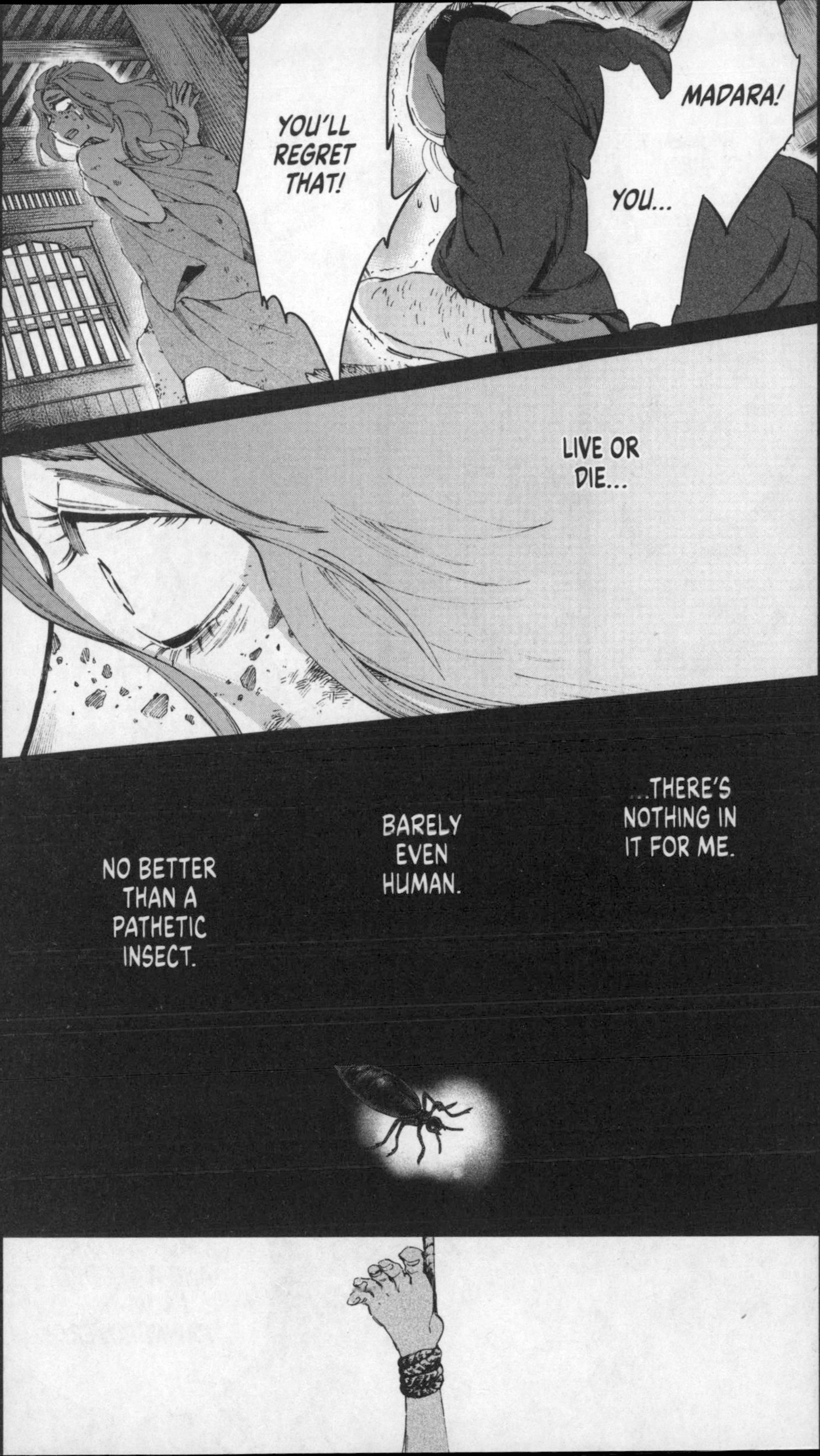
MADARA!
YOU...
YOU'LL REGRET THAT!
LIVE OR DIE...
...THERE'S NOTHING IN IT FOR ME.
BARELY EVEN HUMAN.
NO BETTER THAN A PATHETIC INSECT.

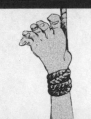

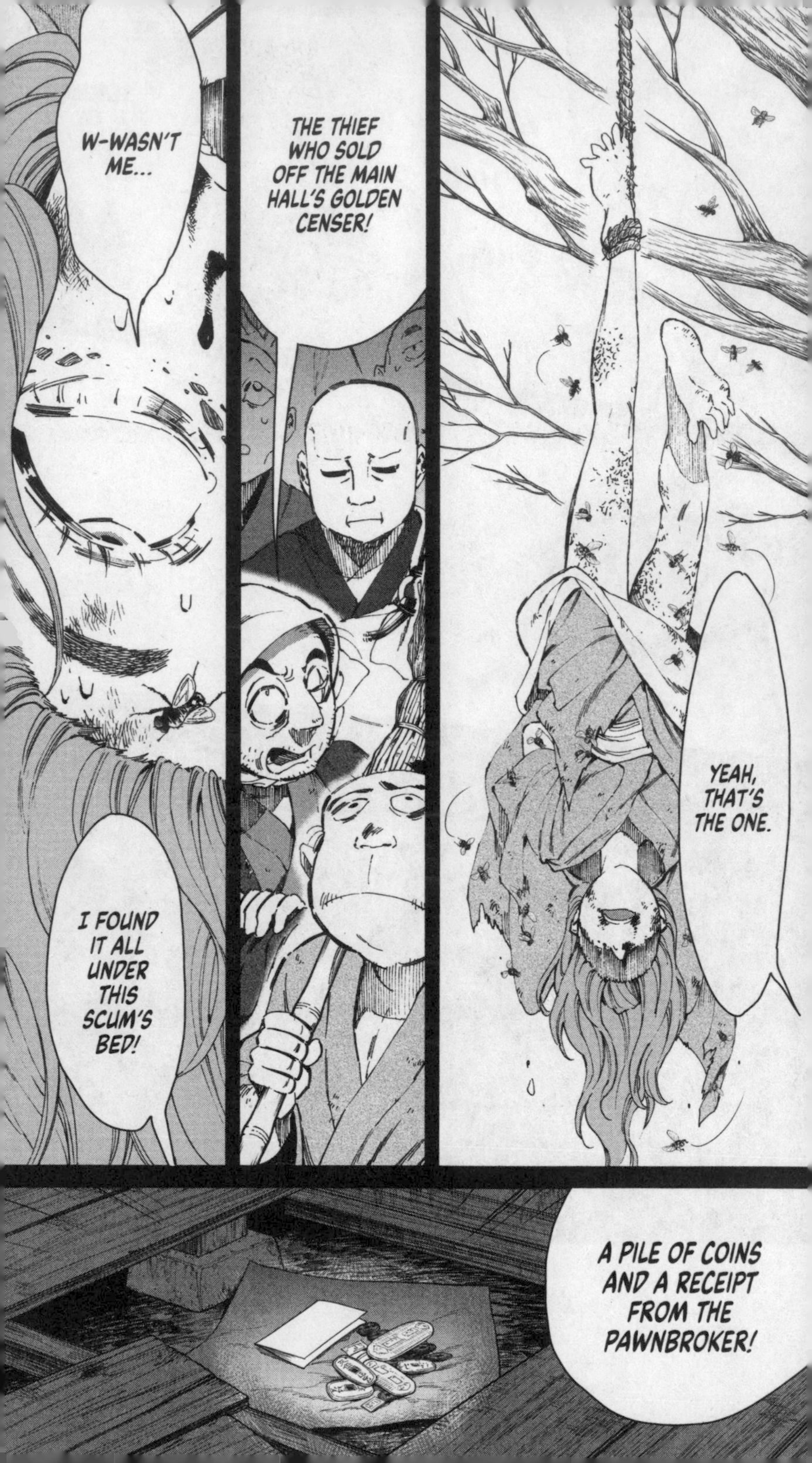
YEAH, THAT'S THE ONE.
THE THIEF WHO SOLD OFF THE MAIN HALL'S GOLDEN CENSER!
W-WASN'T ME...
I FOUND IT ALL UNDER THIS SCUM'S BED!
A PILE OF COINS AND A RECEIPT FROM THE PAWNBROKER!

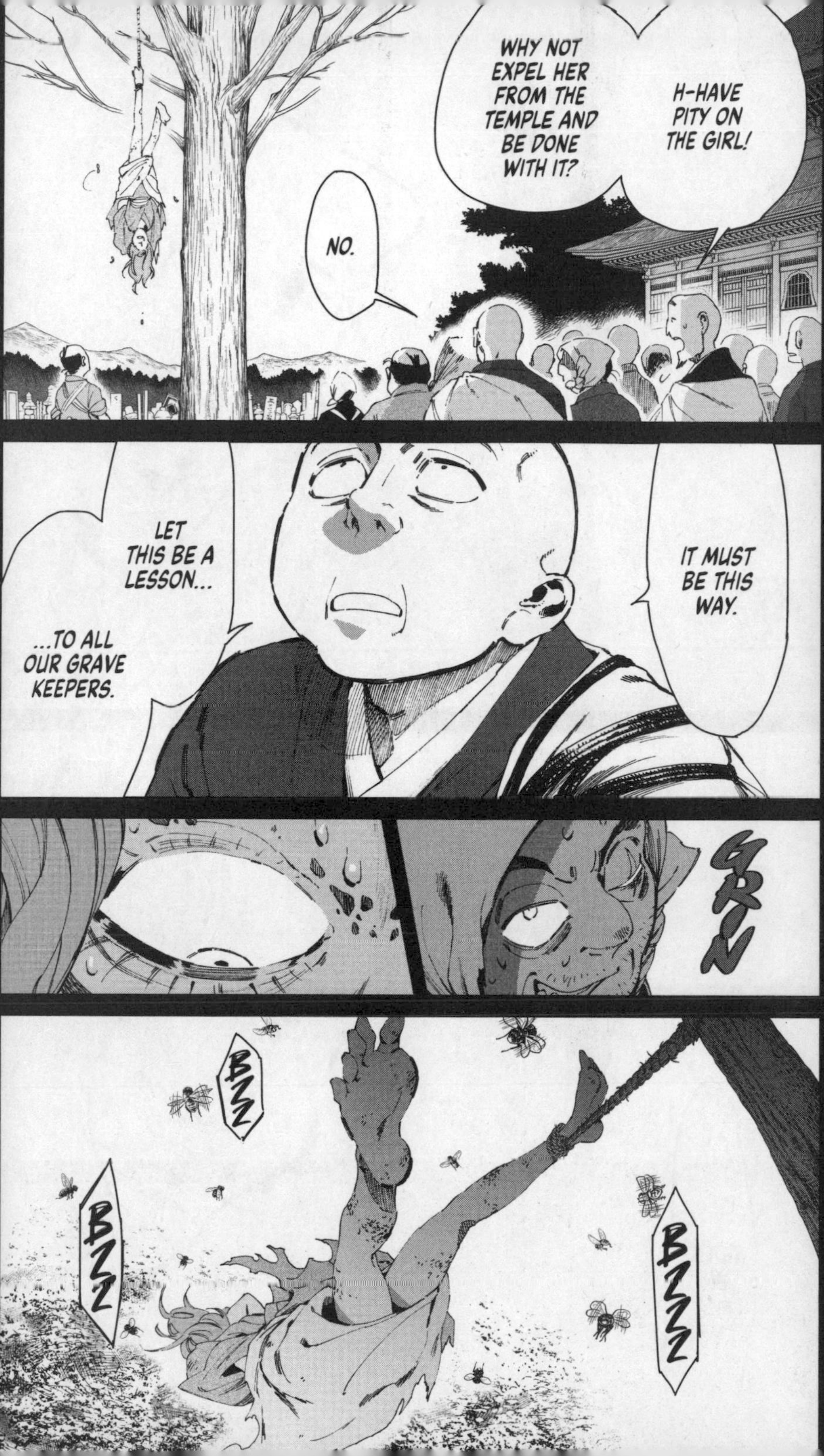
H-HAVE PITY ON THE GIRL!
WHY NOT EXPEL HER FROM THE TEMPLE AND BE DONE WITH IT?
NO.
IT MUST BE THIS WAY.
LET THIS BE A LESSON...
...TO ALL OUR GRAVE KEEPERS.
GRIN
BZZZ
BZZ
BZZ

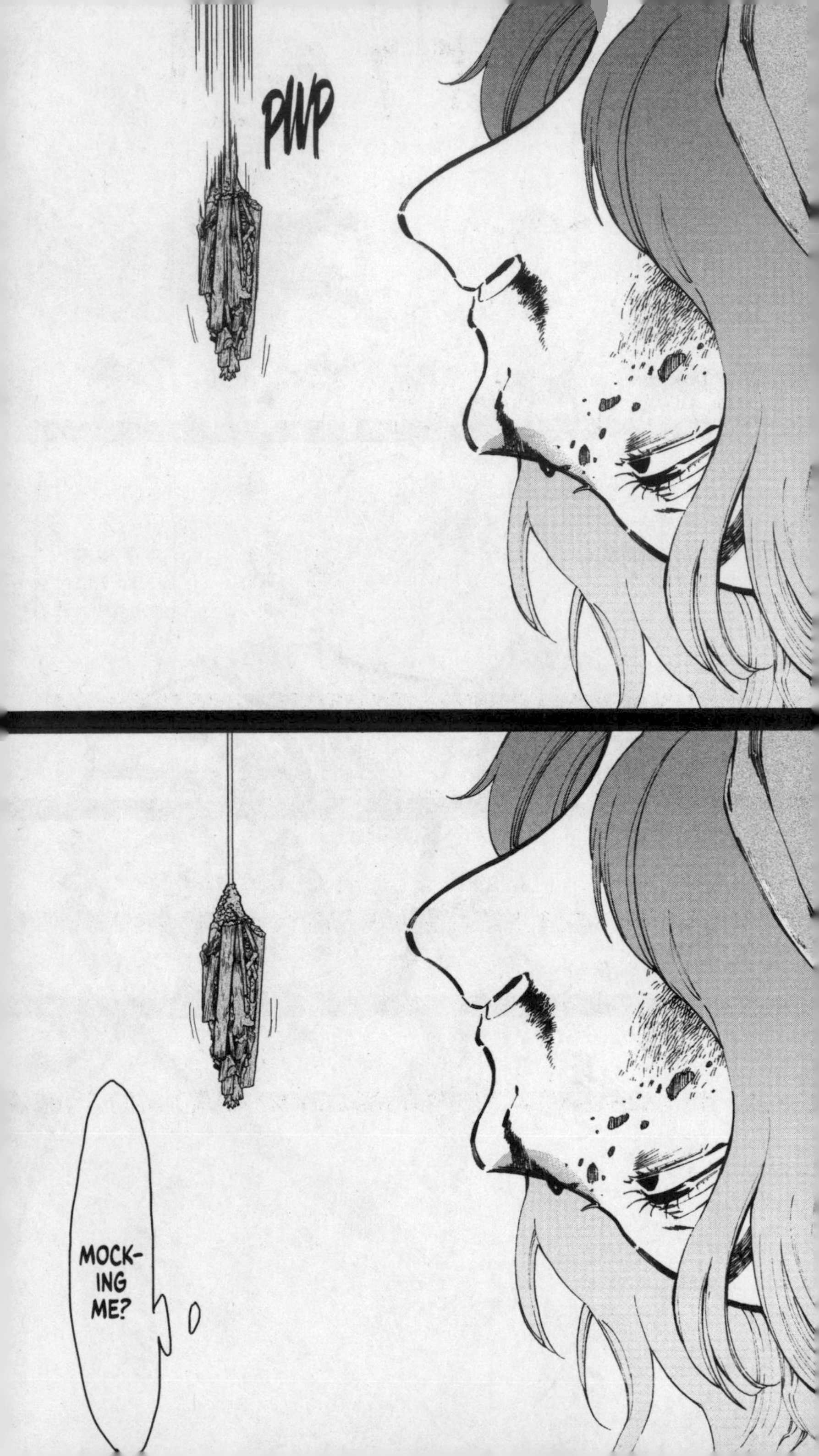
PLIP
MOCK-ING ME?

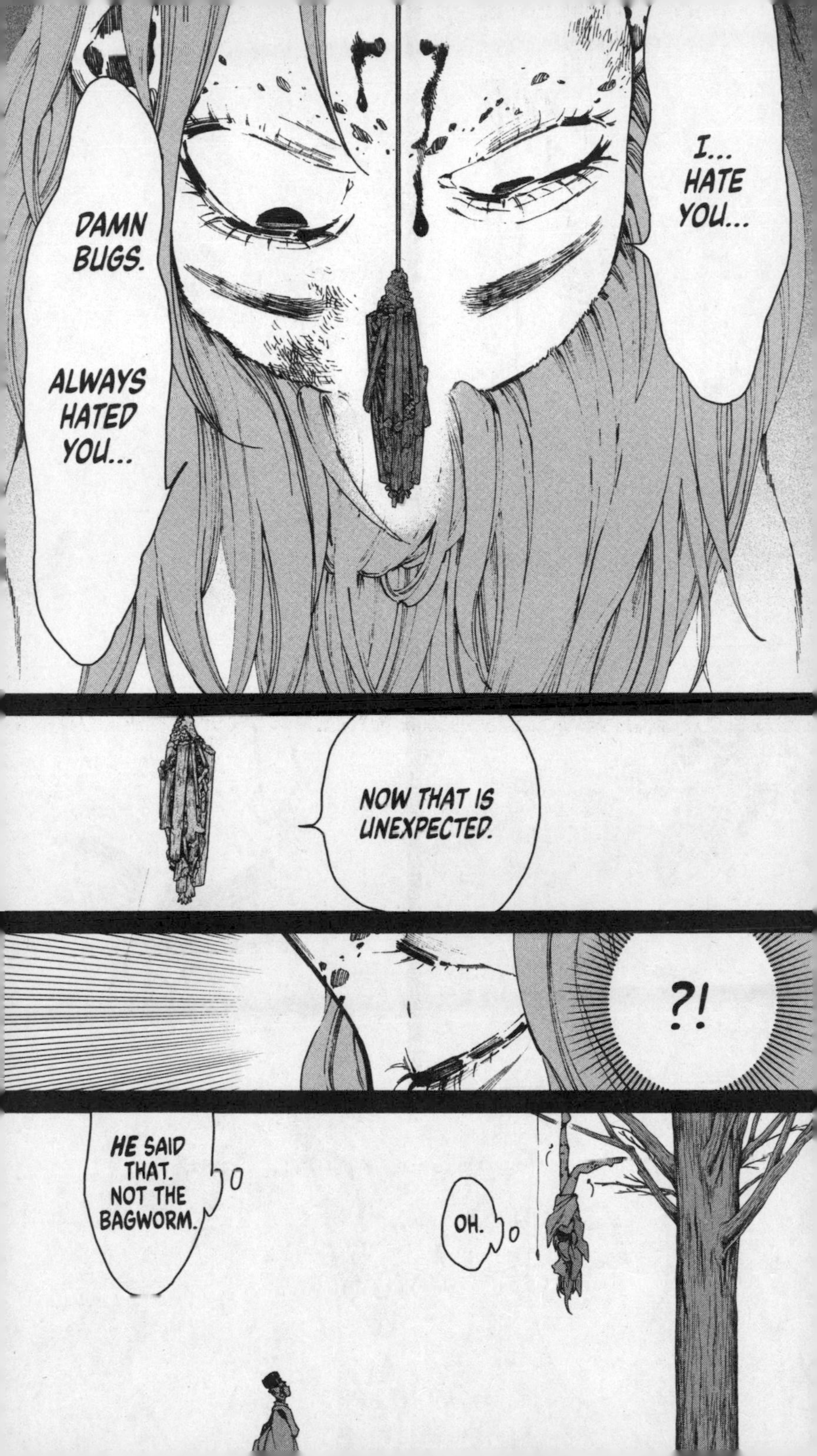
I... HATE YOU...
DAMN BUGS.
ALWAYS HATED YOU...
NOW THAT IS UNEXPECTED.
?!
OH.
HE SAID THAT. NOT THE BAGWORM.

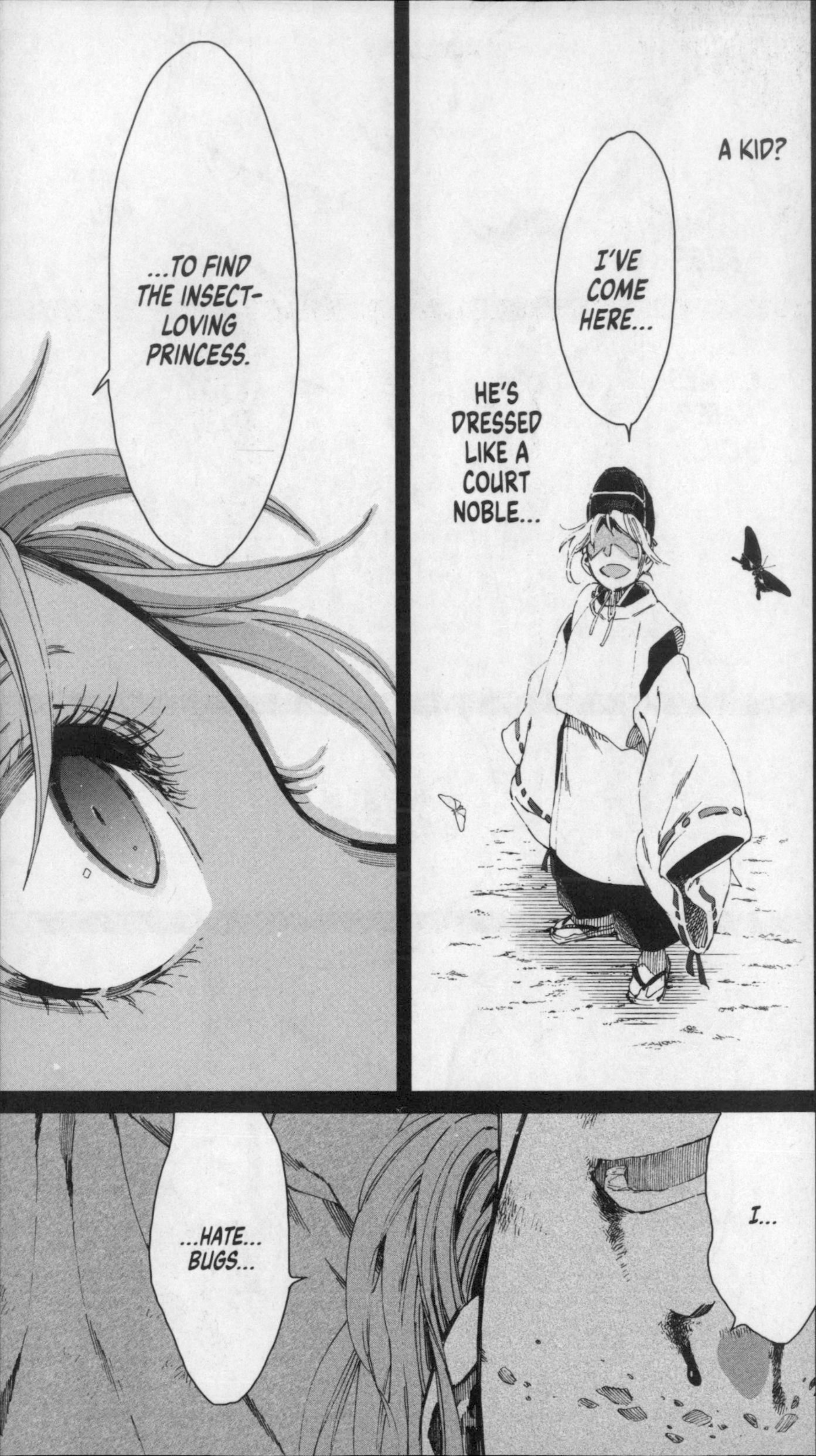
A KID?
HE'S DRESSED LIKE A COURT NOBLE...
I'VE COME HERE...
...TO FIND THE INSECT-LOVING PRINCESS.
I...
...HATE... BUGS...

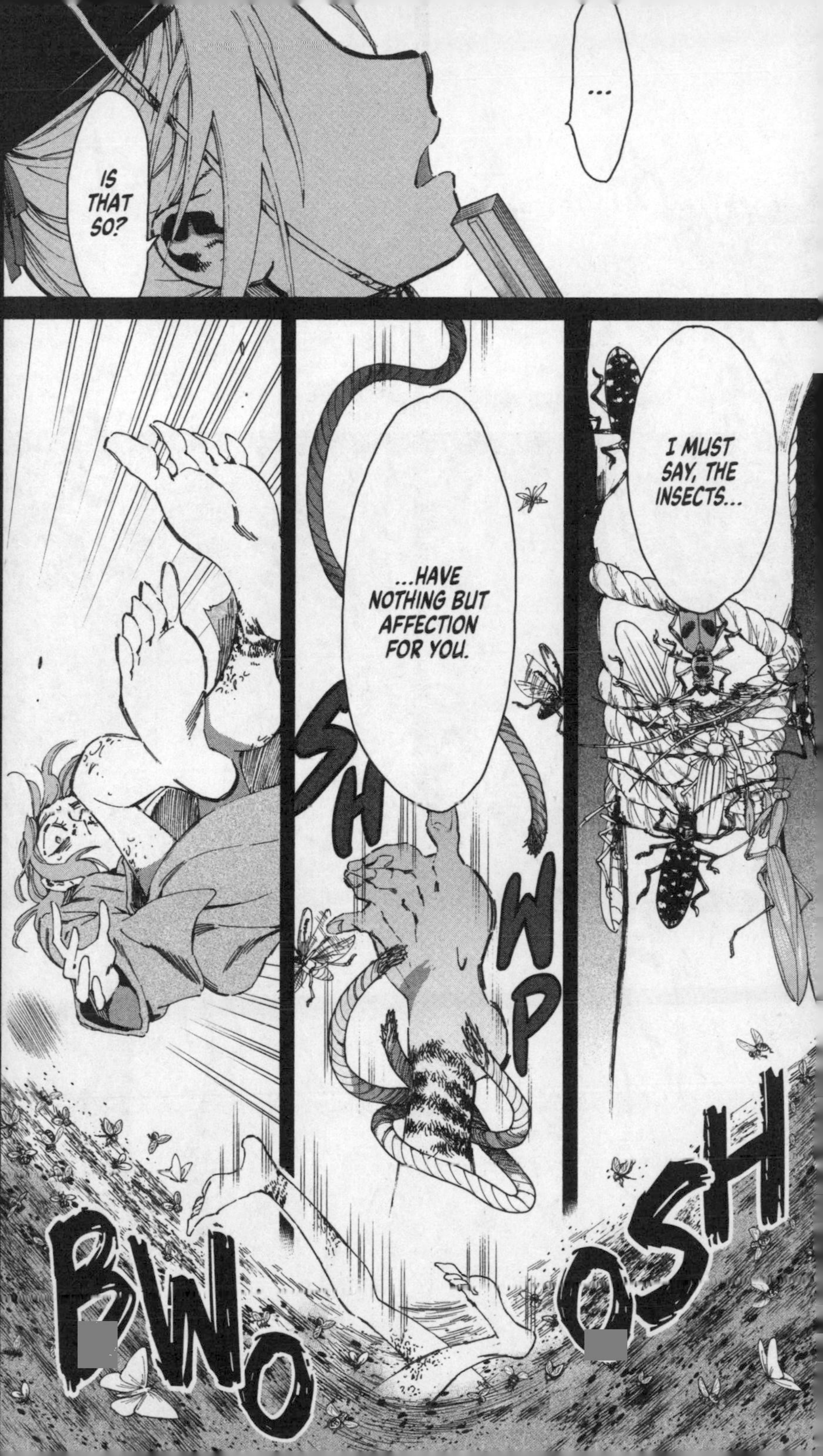
...
IS THAT SO?
I MUST SAY, THE INSECTS...
...HAVE NOTHING BUT AFFECTION FOR YOU.
SHWP
BWOOSH

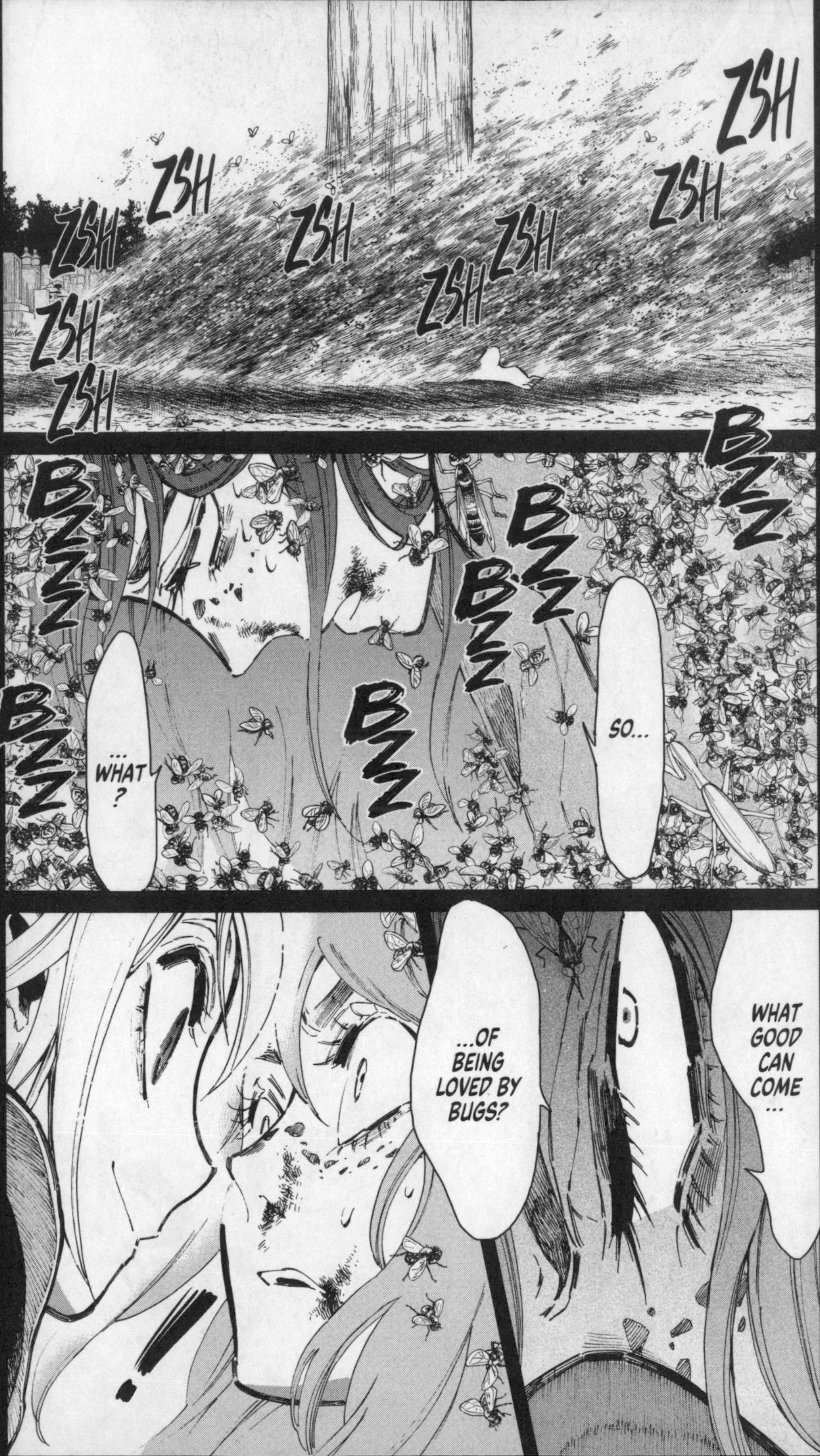
ZSH
ZSH
ZSH
ZSH
ZSH
ZSH
ZSH
ZSH
ZSH
BZZZ
BZZZ
BZZZ
SO...
BZZZ
BZZZ
...WHAT?
WHAT GOOD CAN COME...
...OF BEING LOVED BY BUGS?

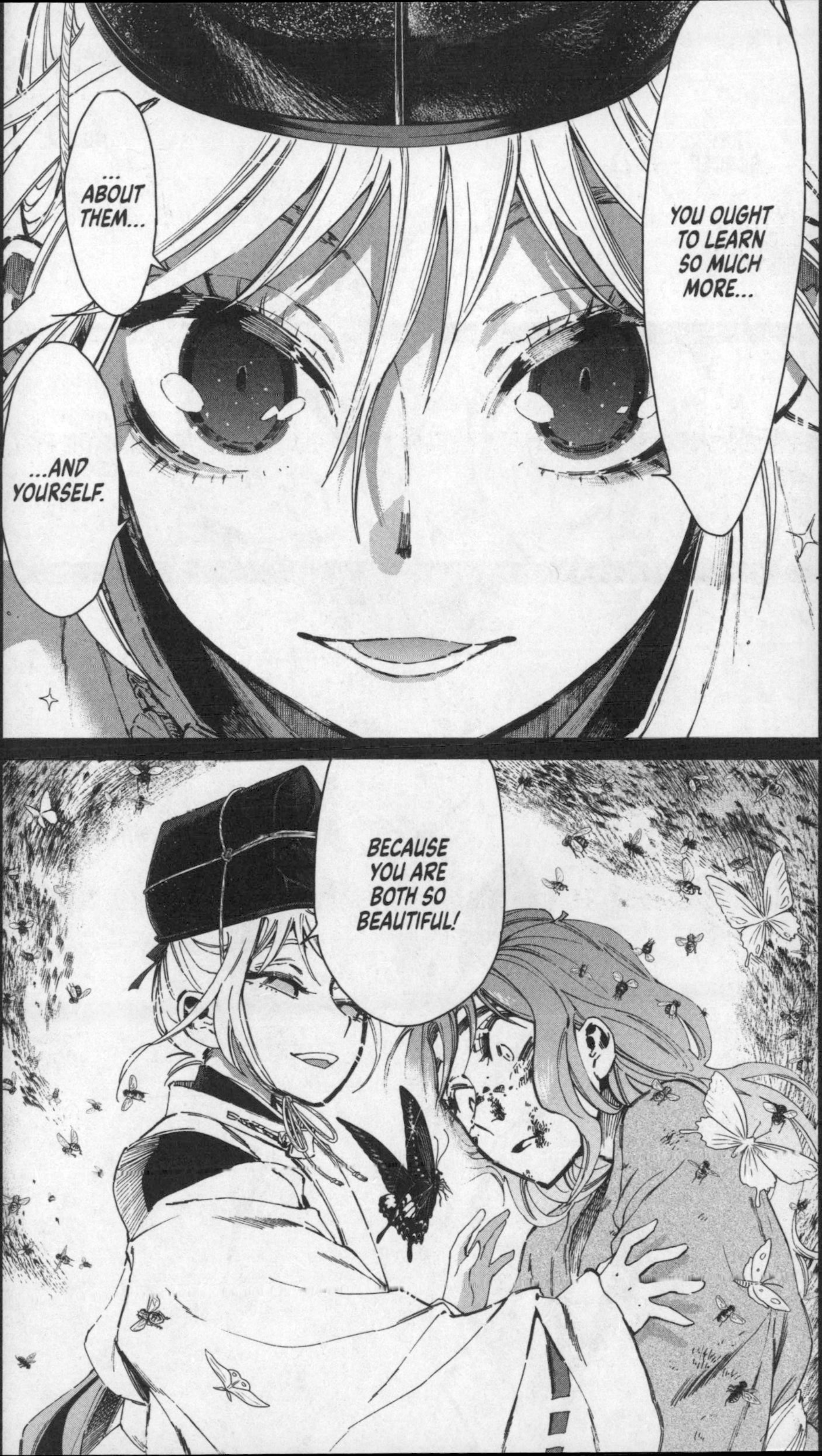
YOU OUGHT TO LEARN SO MUCH MORE...
...ABOUT THEM...
...AND YOURSELF.
BECAUSE YOU ARE BOTH SO BEAUTIFUL!

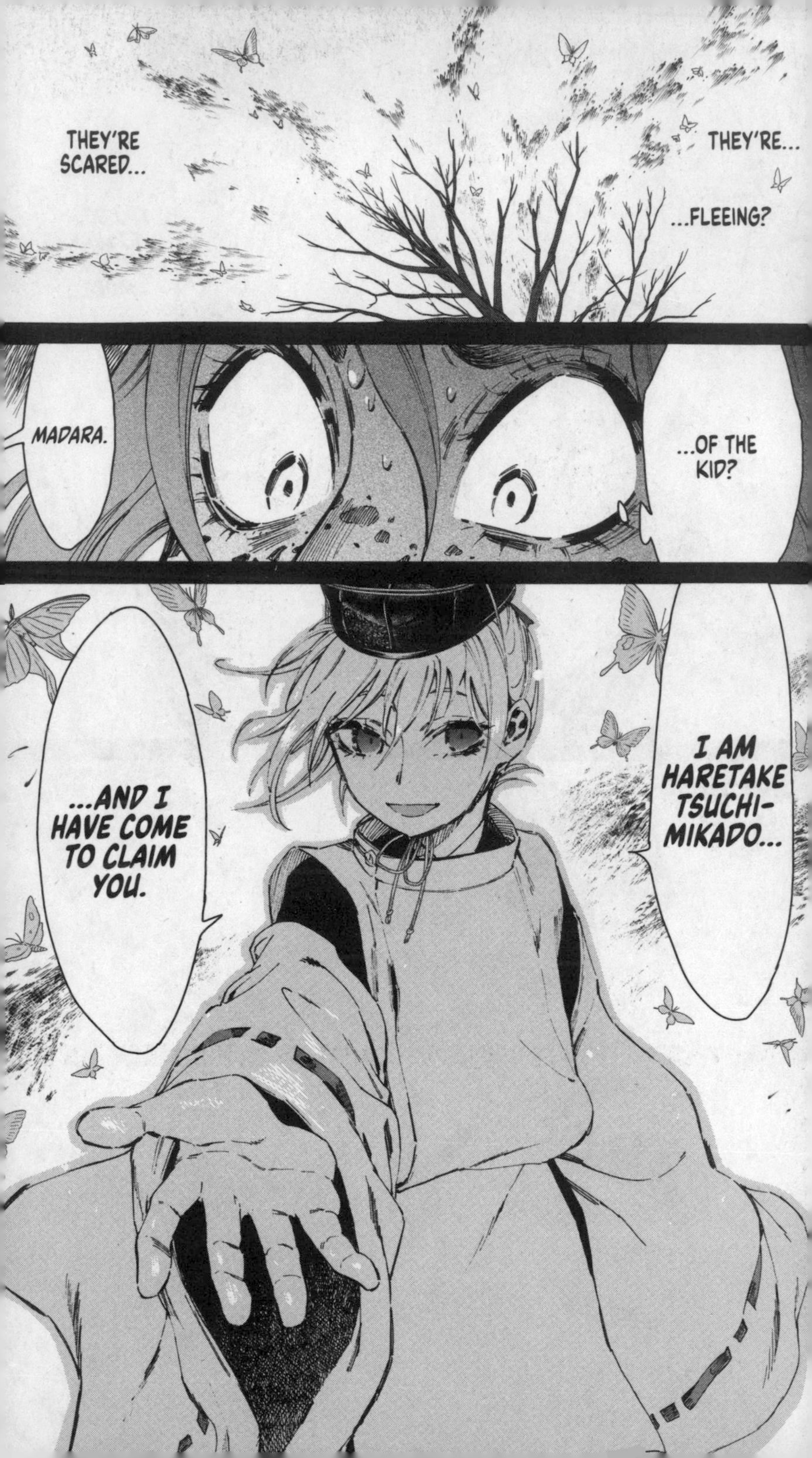
THEY'RE...
...FLEEING?
THEY'RE SCARED...
...OF THE KID?
MADARA.
I AM HARETAKE TSUCHI-MIKADO...
...AND I HAVE COME TO CLAIM YOU.

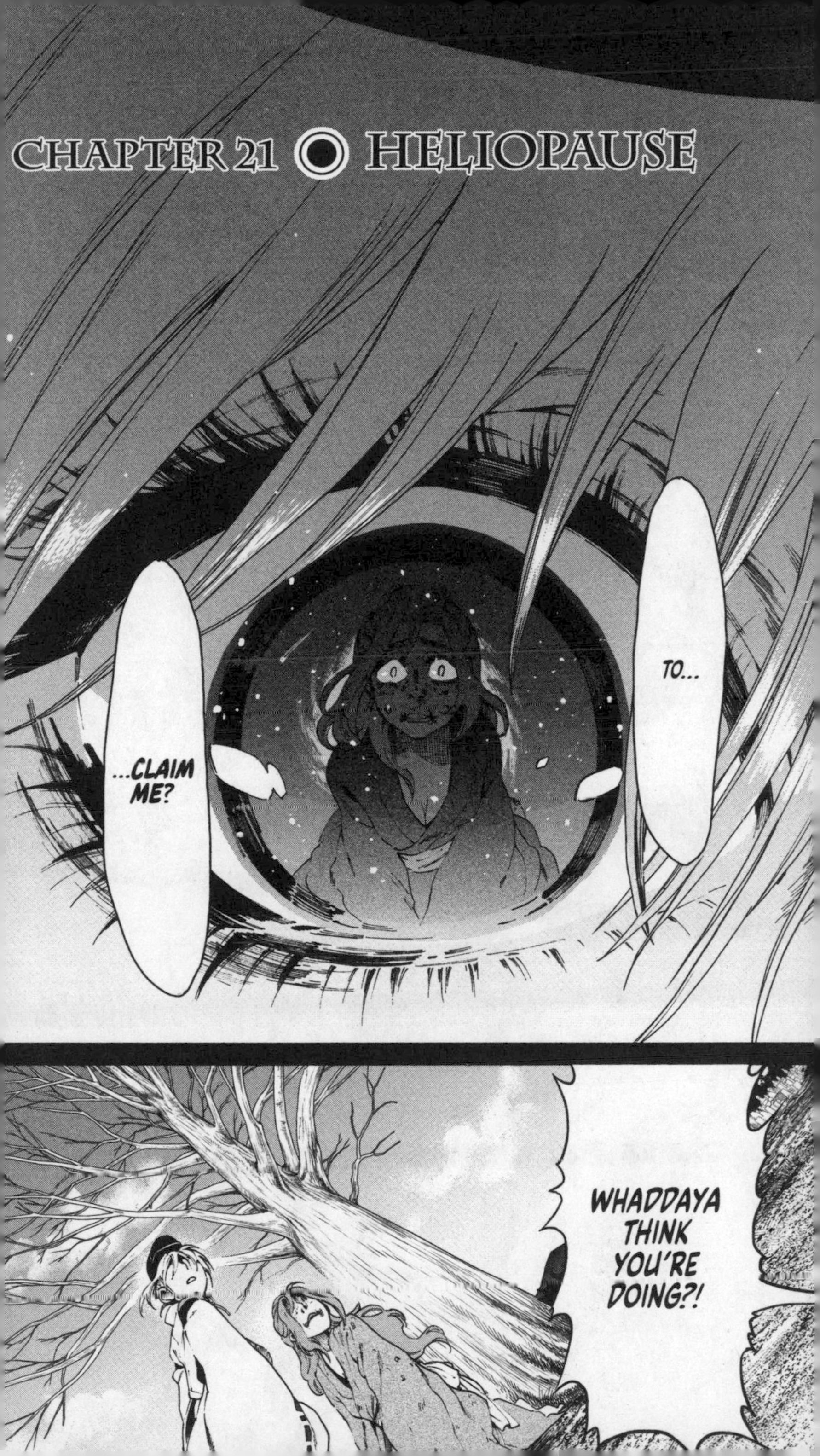
CHAPTER 21 HELIOPAUSE
TO...
...CLAIM ME?
WHADDAYA THINK YOU'RE DOING?!

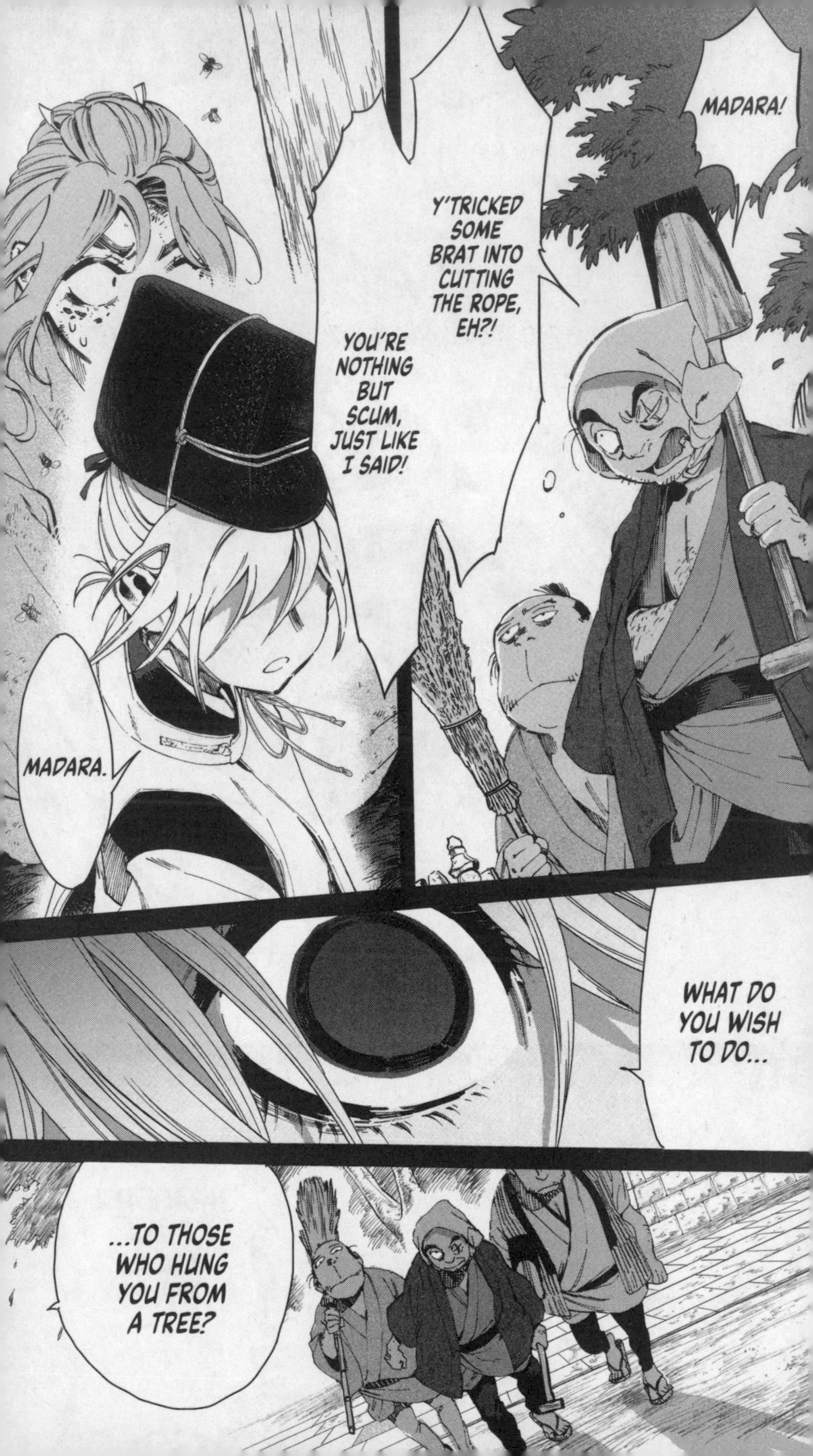
MADARA!
Y'TRICKED SOME BRAT INTO CUTTING THE ROPE, EH?!
YOU'RE NOTHING BUT SCUM, JUST LIKE I SAID!
MADARA.
WHAT DO YOU WISH TO DO...
...TO THOSE WHO HUNG YOU FROM A TREE?

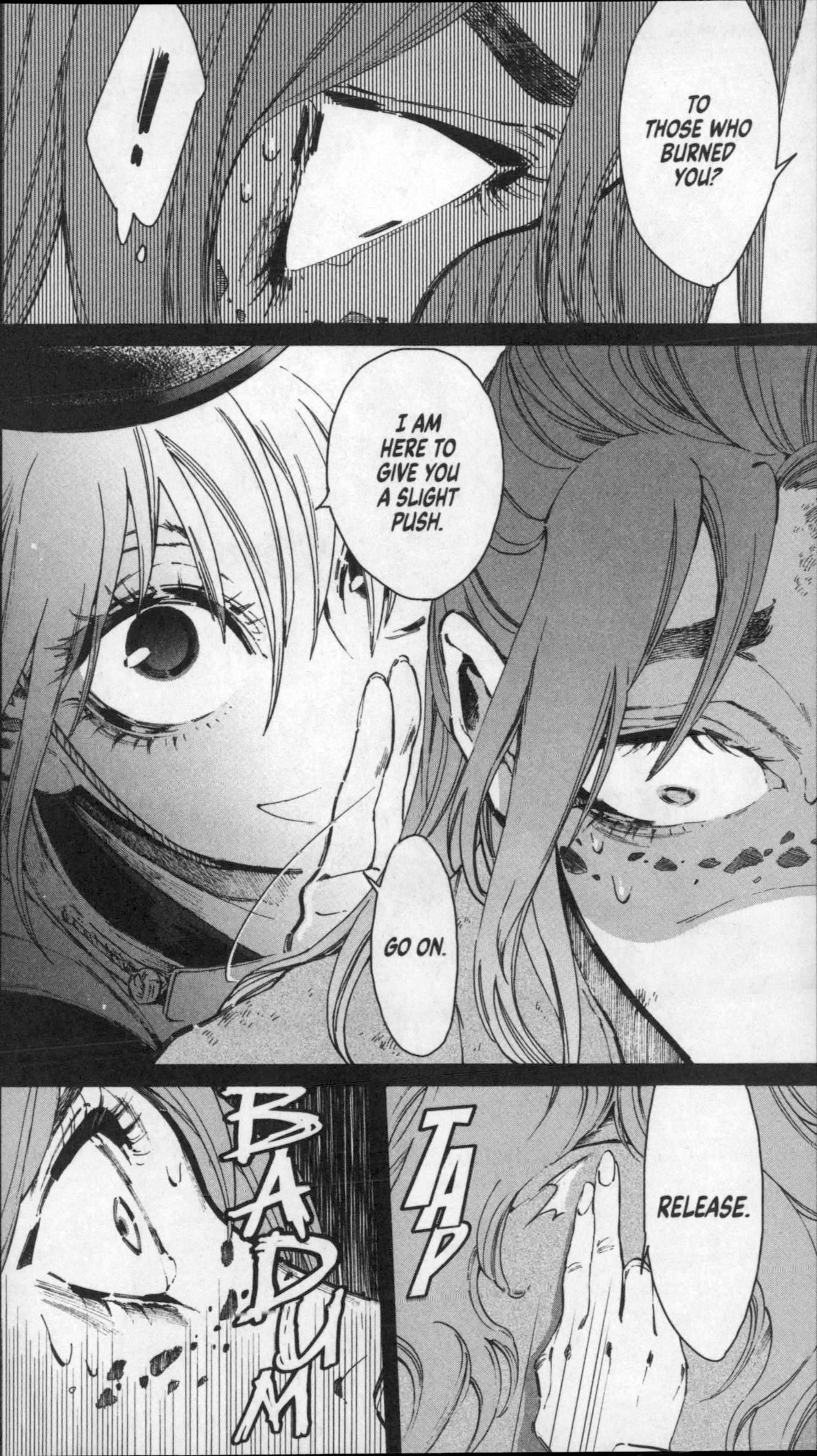
TO THOSE WHO BURNED YOU?
!
I AM HERE TO GIVE YOU A SLIGHT PUSH.
GO ON.
RELEASE.
TAP
BADUM

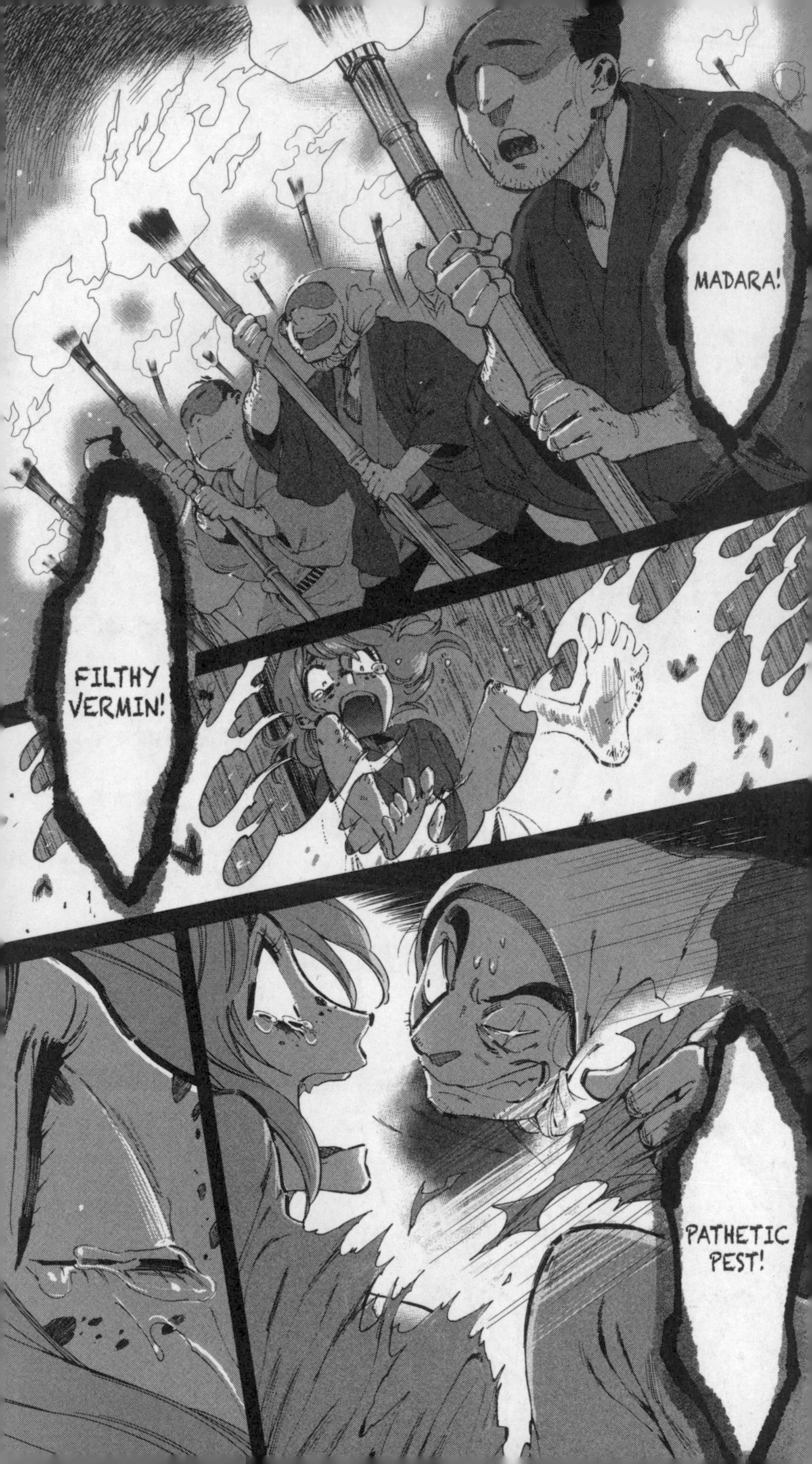
MADARA!
FILTHY VERMIN!
PATHETIC PEST!

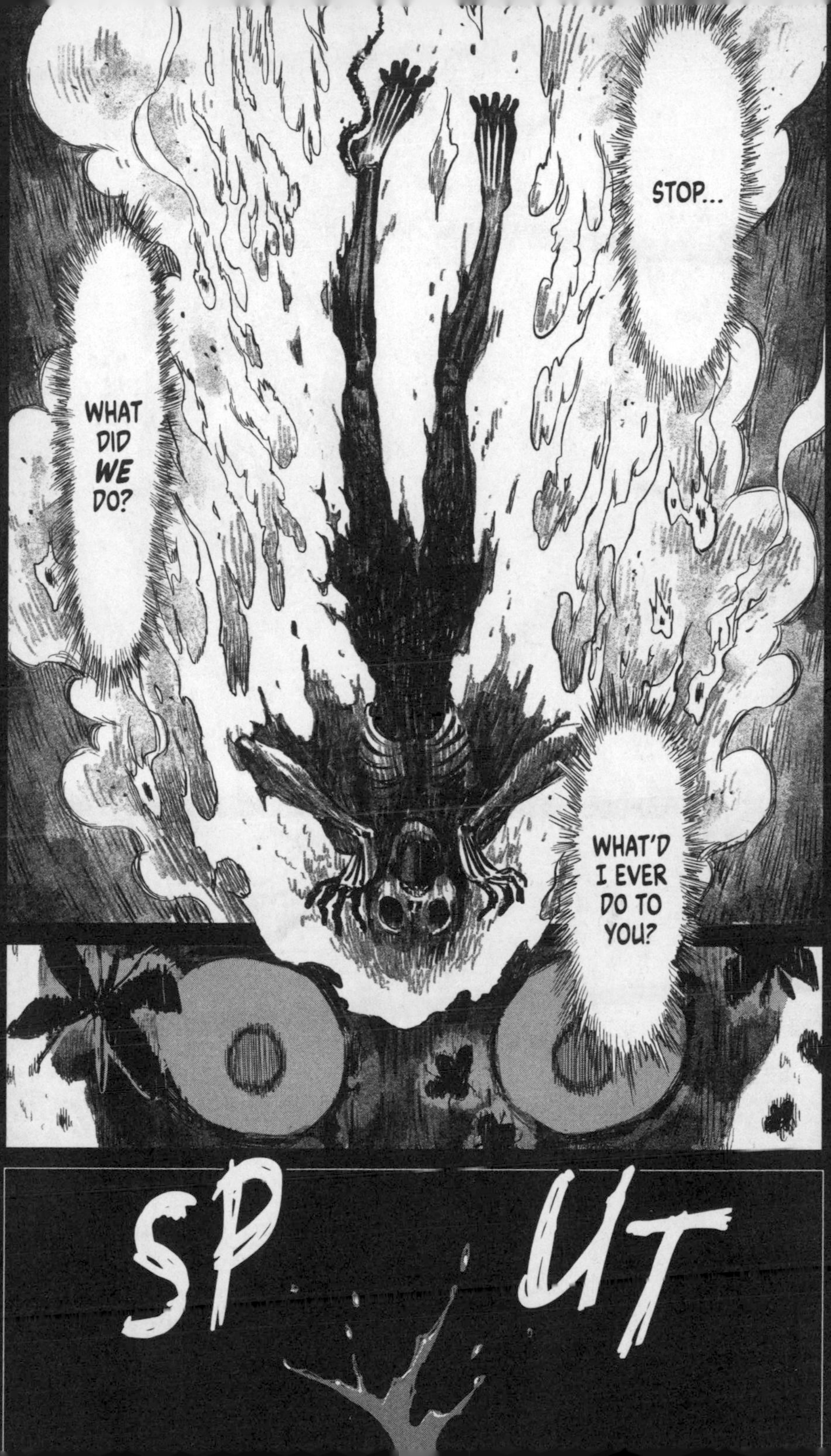
STOP...
WHAT DID WE DO?
WHAT'D I EVER DO TO YOU?
SP UT

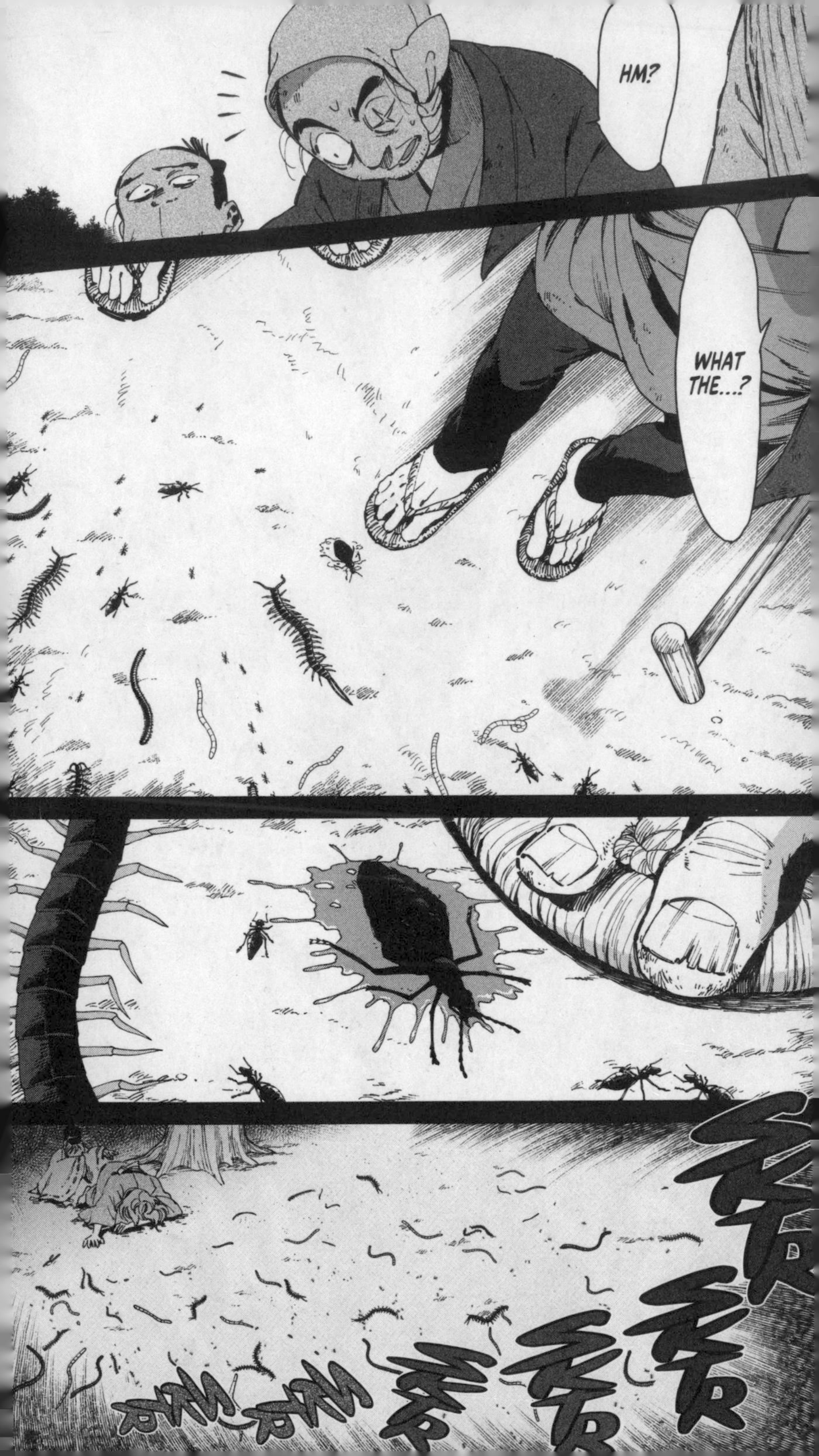
HM?
WHAT THE...?

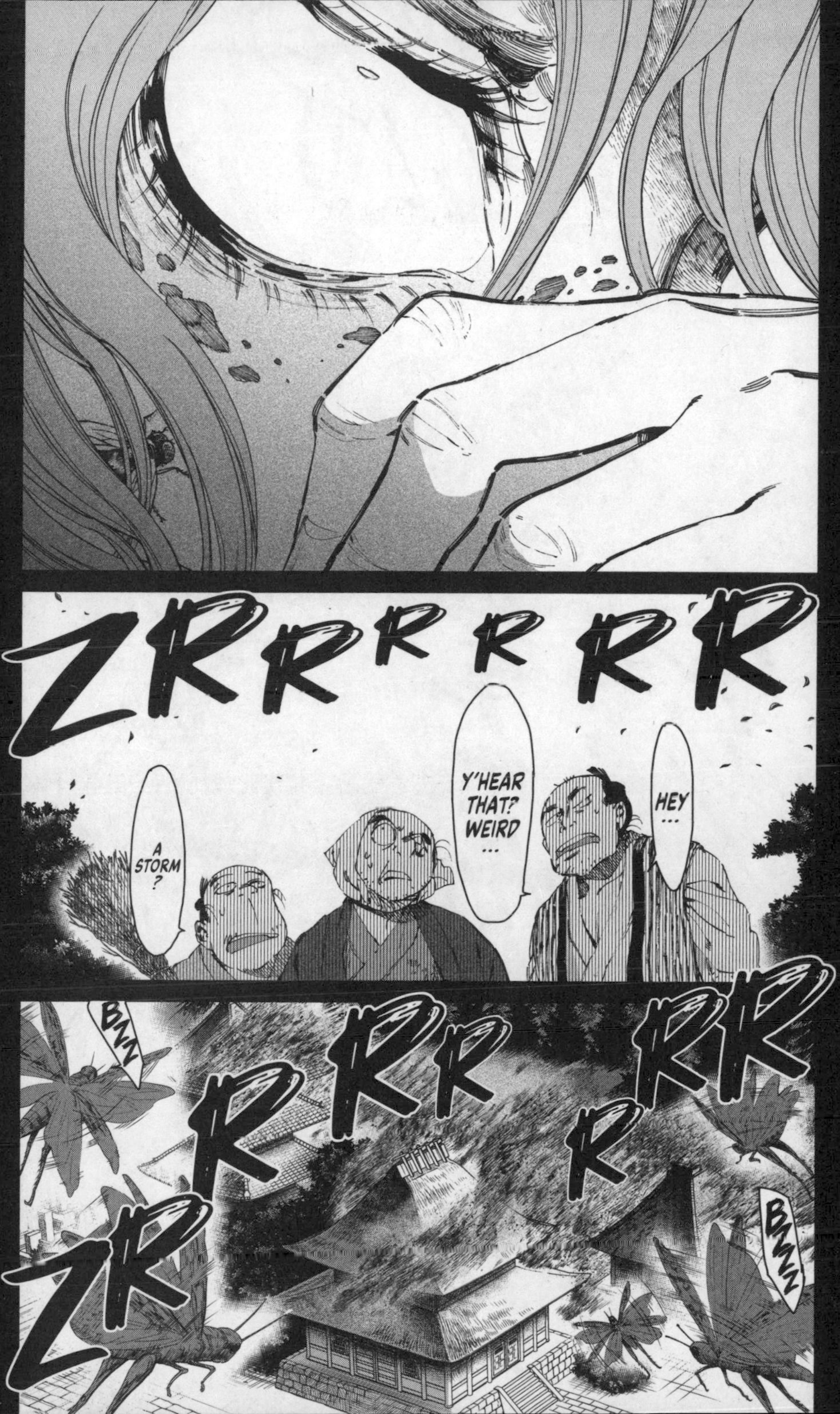
ZRRRRRRR
HEY ...
Y'HEAR THAT? WEIRD ...
A STORM ?
BZZ
ZRRRRRRR
BZZZ

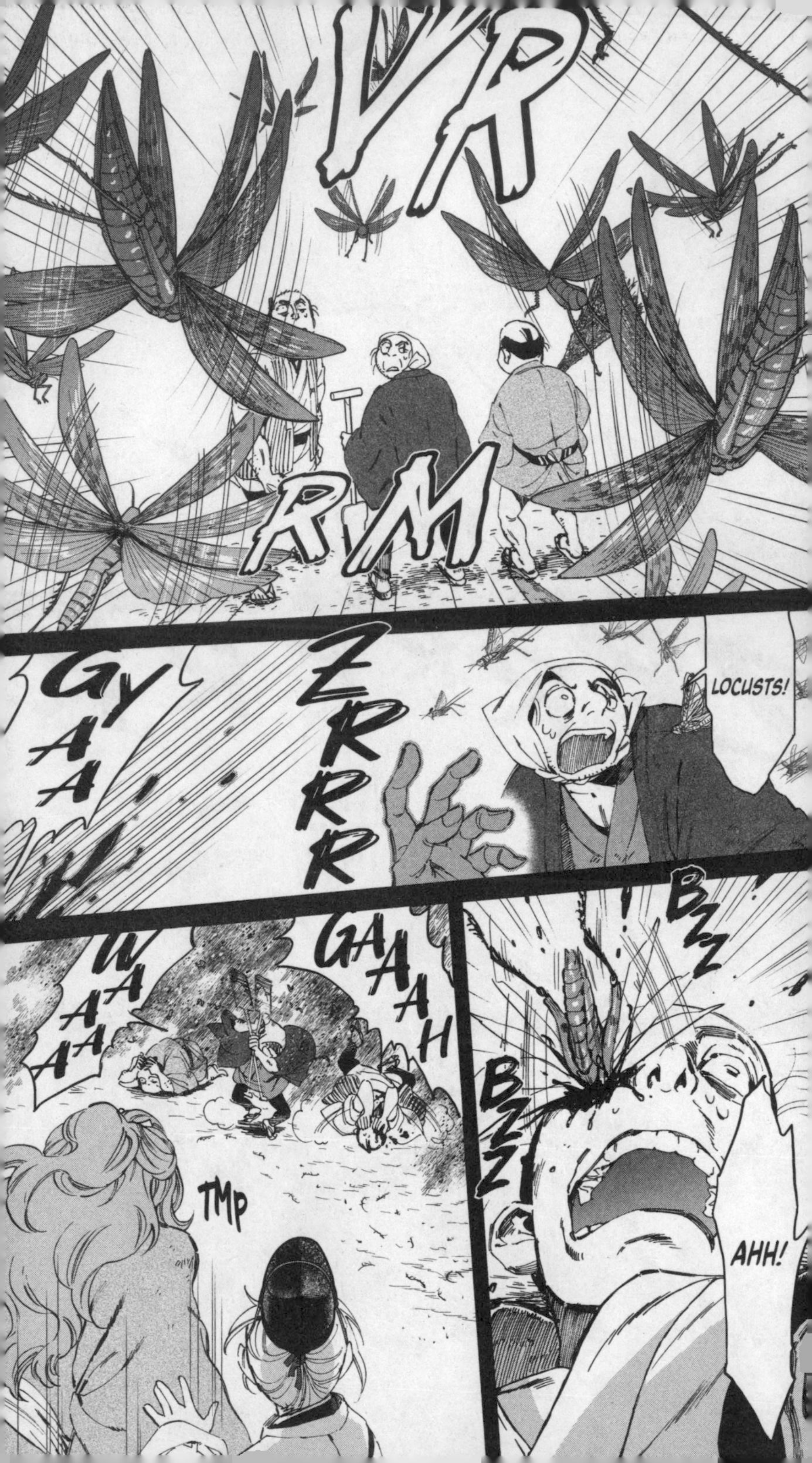
VR
RM
LOCUSTS!
ZRRRR
GyAA
BZZ
BZZZ
AHH!
GAAAH
WAAAAA
TMp

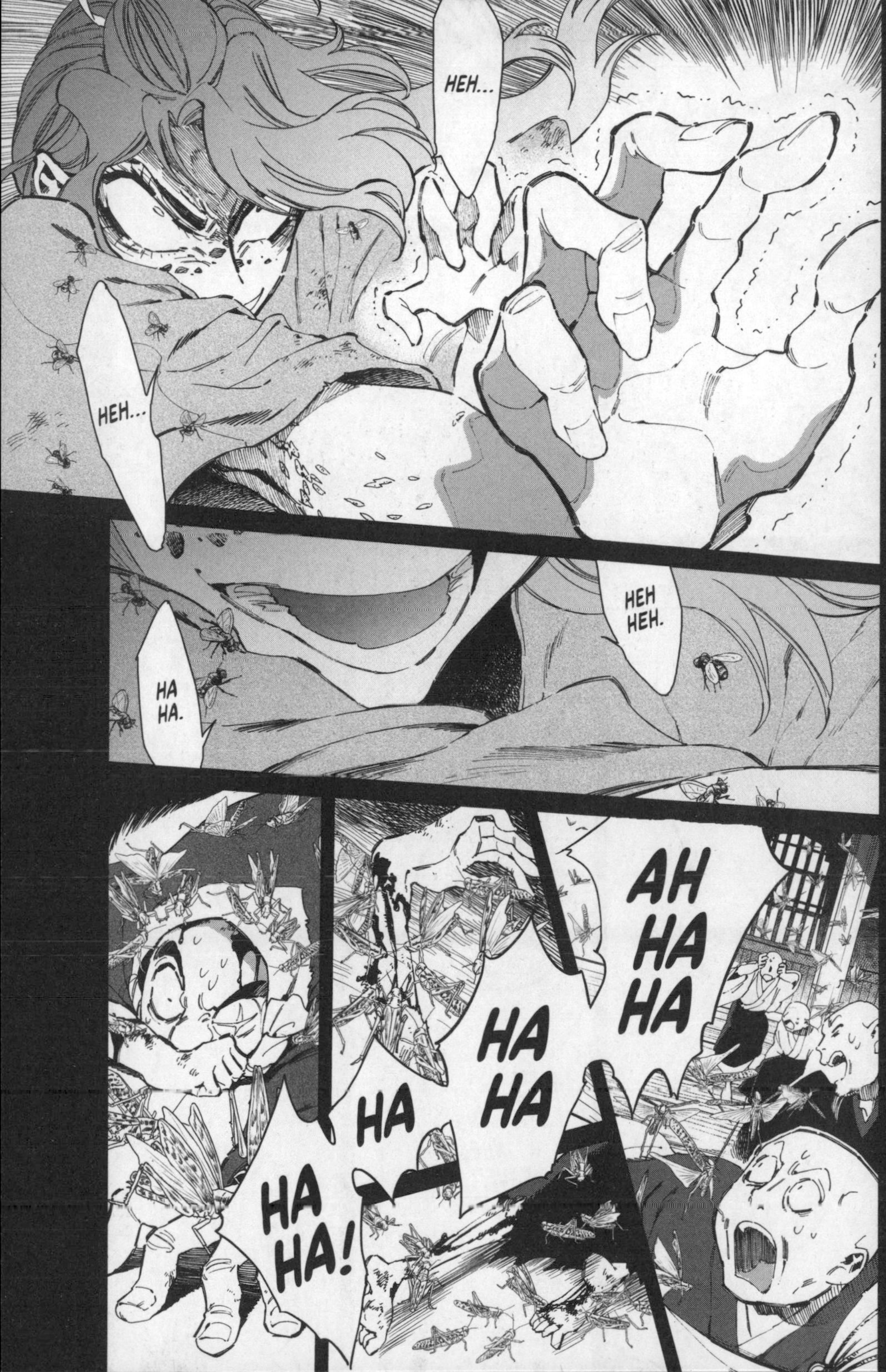
HEH...
HEH...
HEH HEH.
HA HA.
AH HA HA HA
HA HA HA
HA
HA HA!

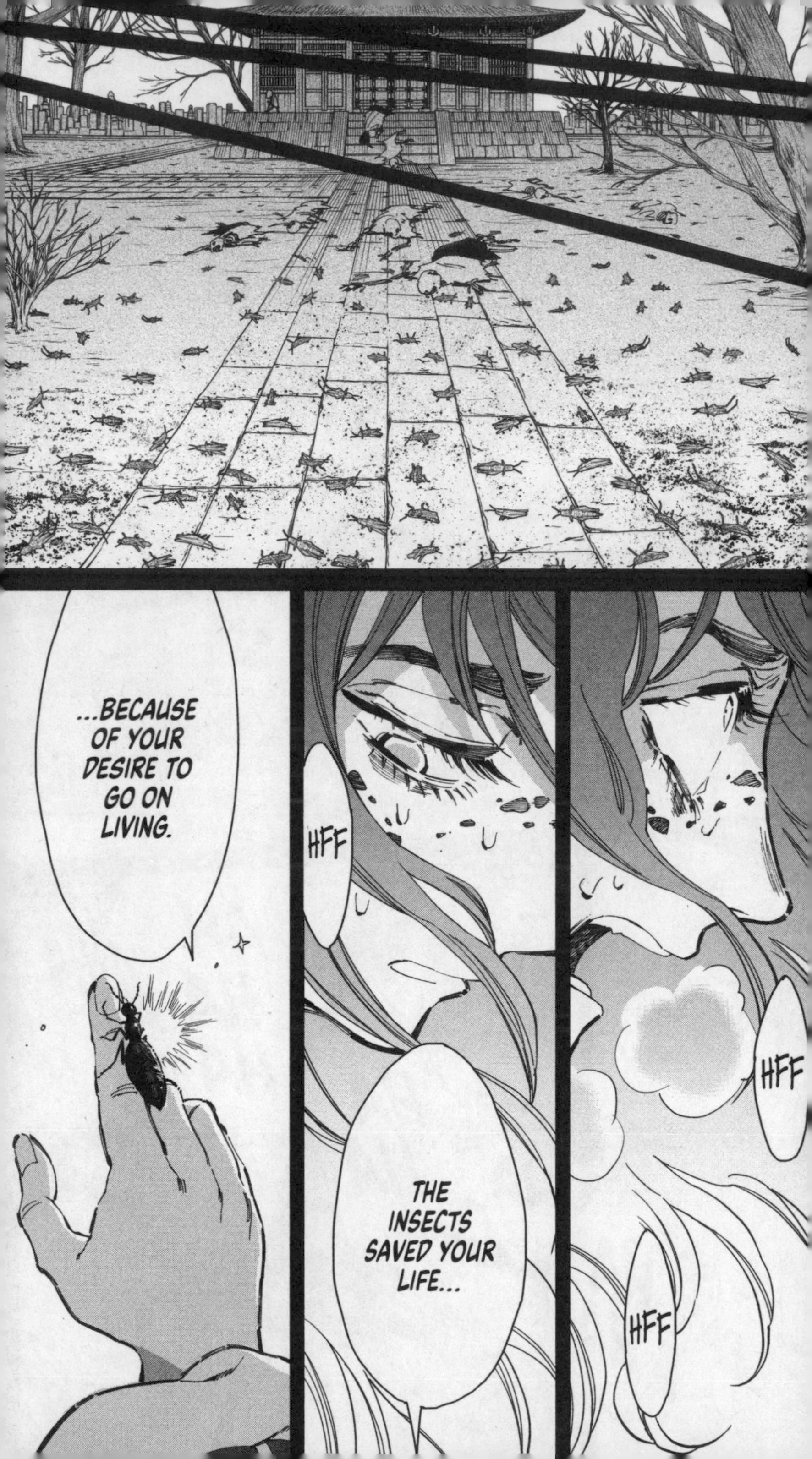

HFF
HFF
HFF
THE INSECTS SAVED YOUR LIFE...
...BECAUSE OF YOUR DESIRE TO GO ON LIVING.

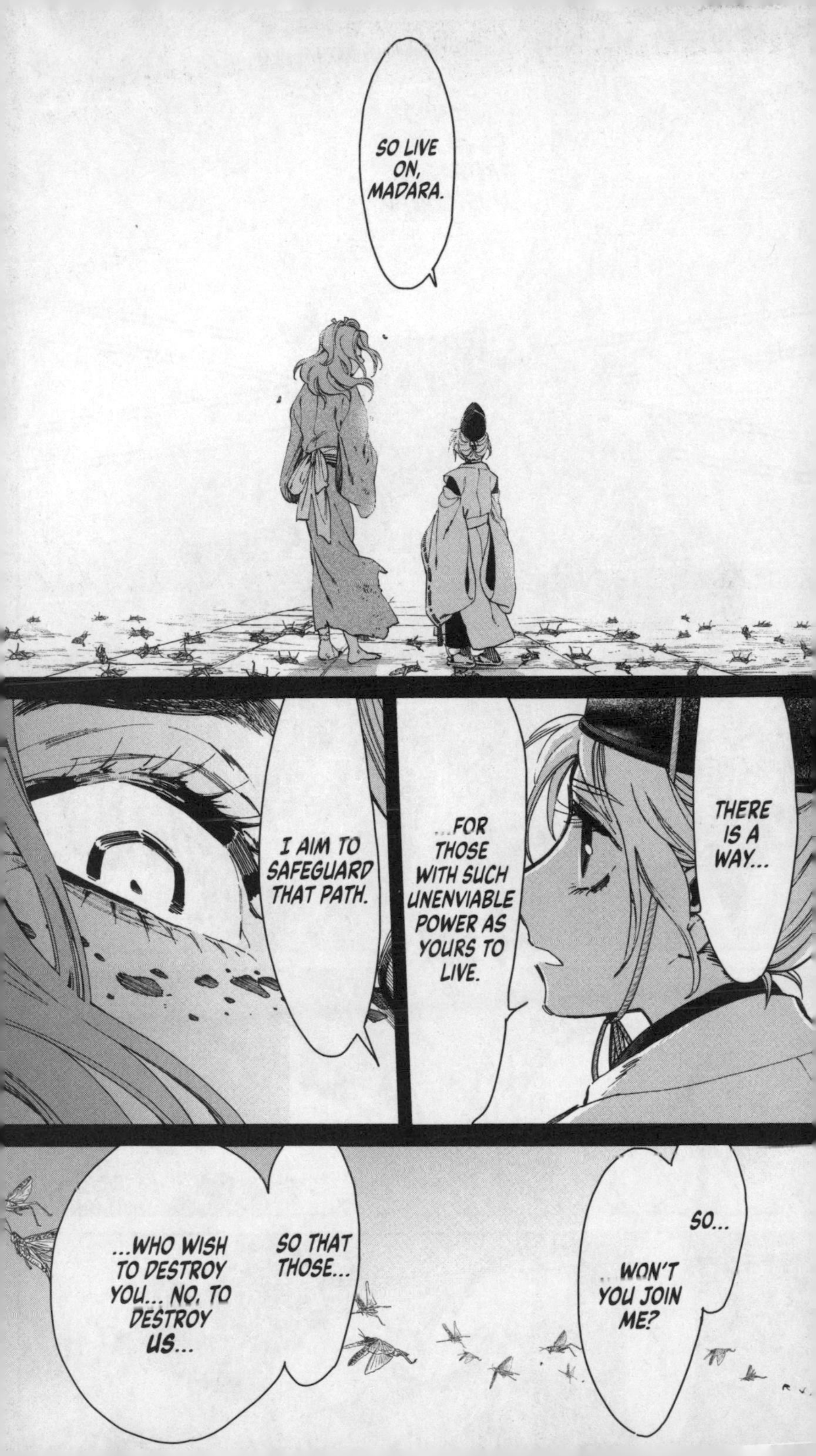
SO LIVE ON, MADARA.
THERE IS A WAY...
...FOR THOSE WITH SUCH UNENVIABLE POWER AS YOURS TO LIVE.
I AIM TO SAFEGUARD THAT PATH.
SO...
WON'T YOU JOIN ME?
SO THAT THOSE...
...WHO WISH TO DESTROY YOU... NO, TO DESTROY US...

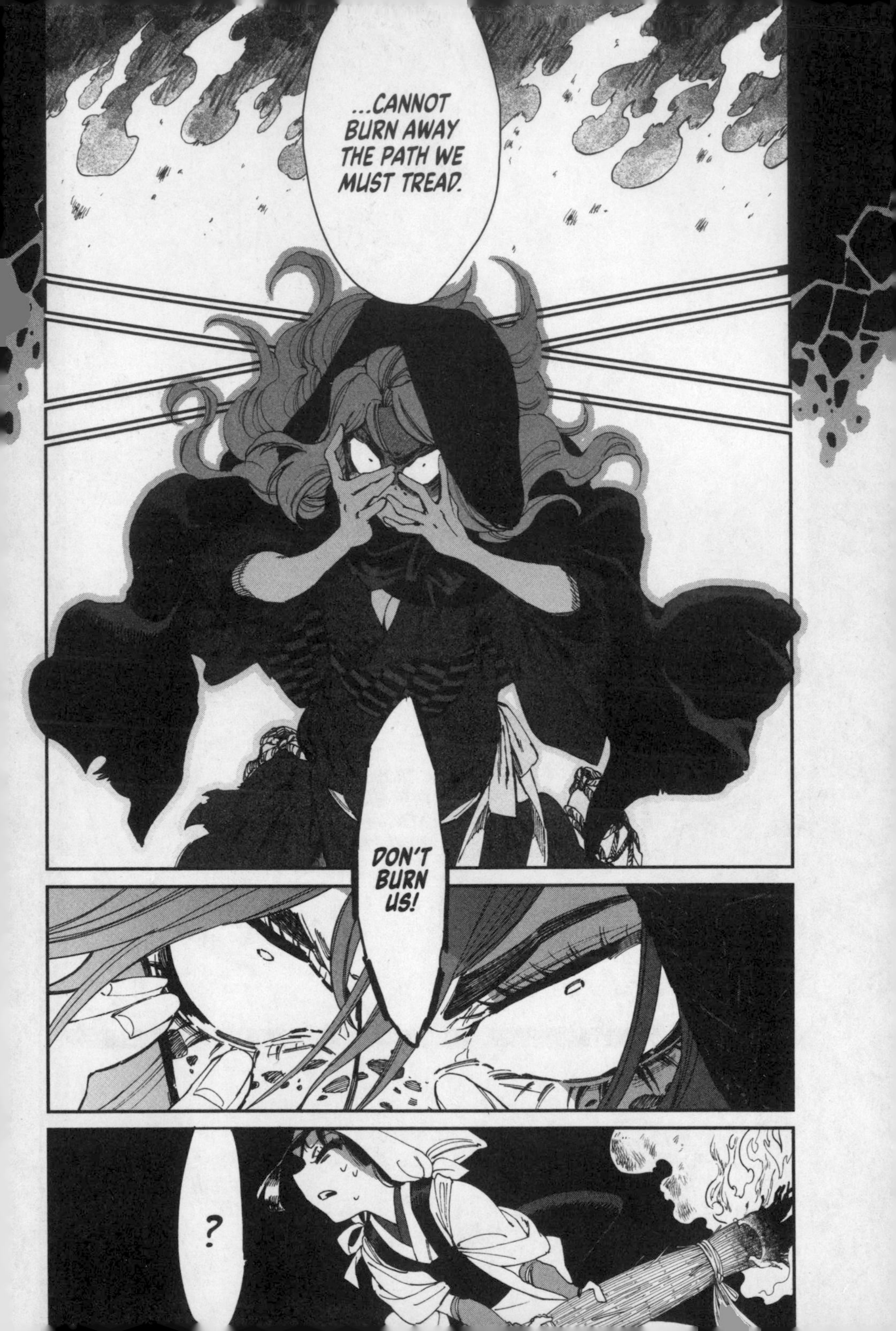
...CANNOT BURN AWAY THE PATH WE MUST TREAD.
DON'T BURN US!
?

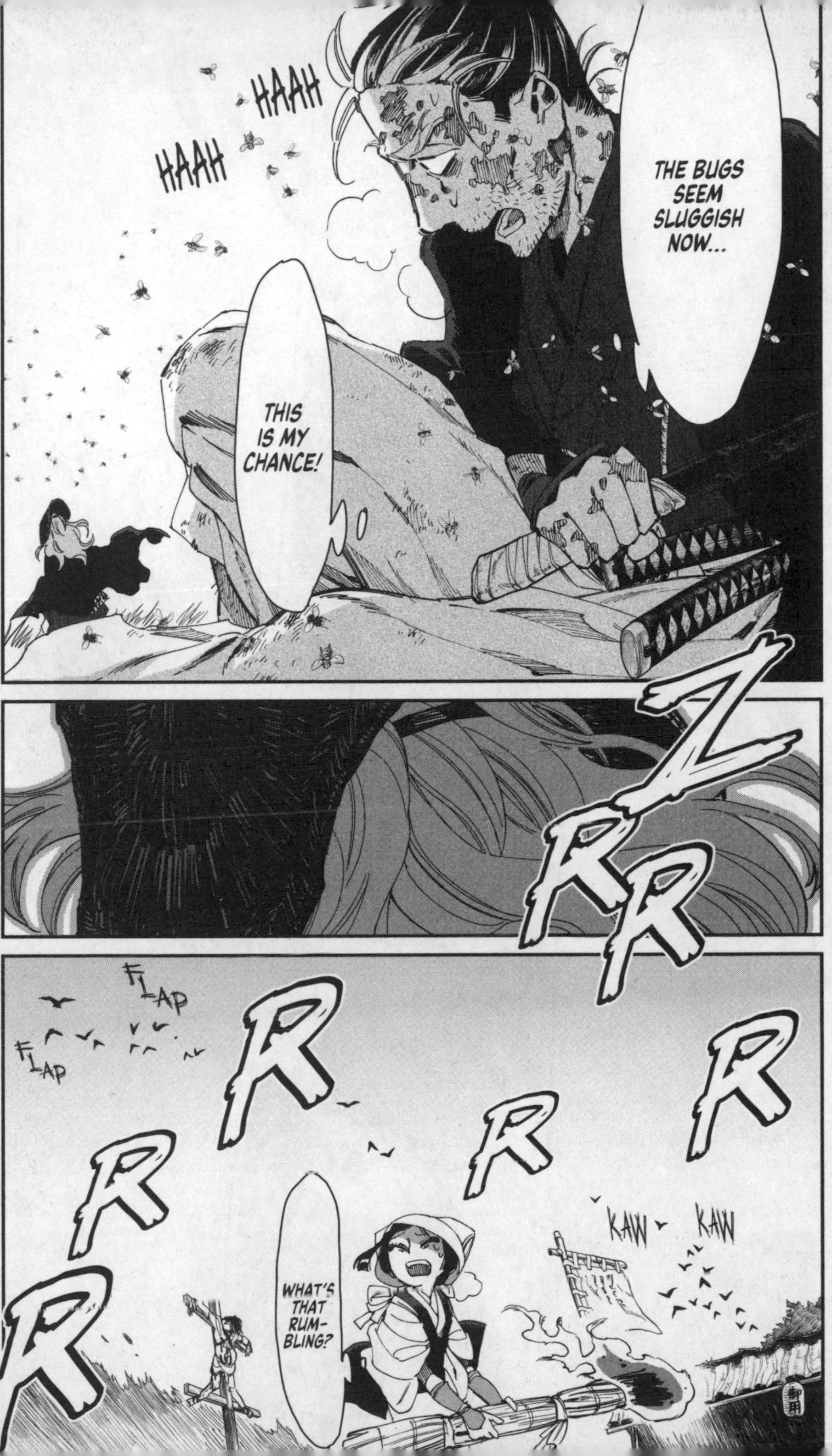
THE BUGS SEEM SLUGGISH NOW...
HAAH
HAAH
THIS IS MY CHANCE!
ZRR
RRRRR
FLAP
FLAP
KAW KAW
WHAT'S THAT RUM-BLING?

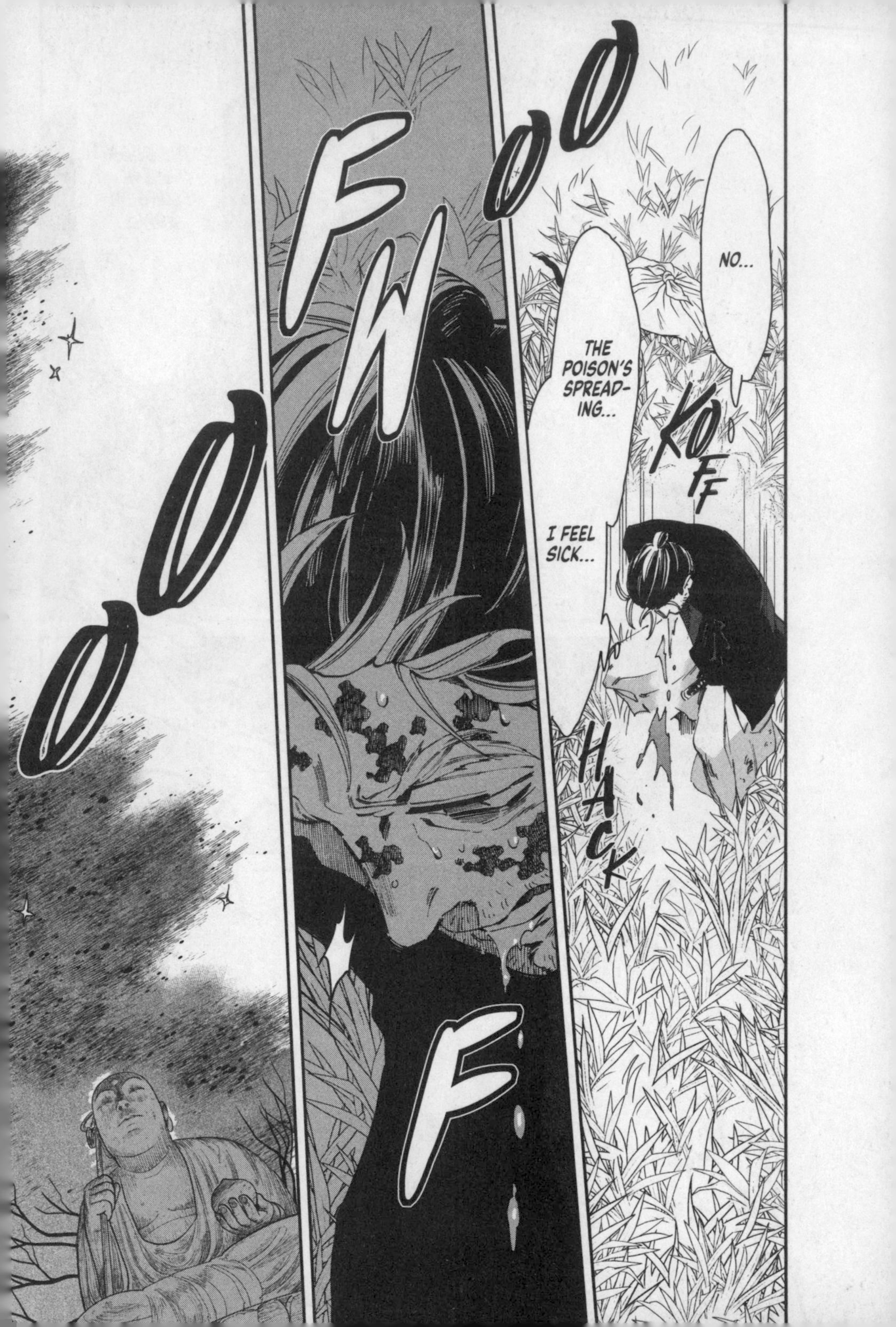

NO...
THE POISON'S SPREAD-ING...
KOFF
I FEEL SICK...
HACK
FWOOOOOOOOF

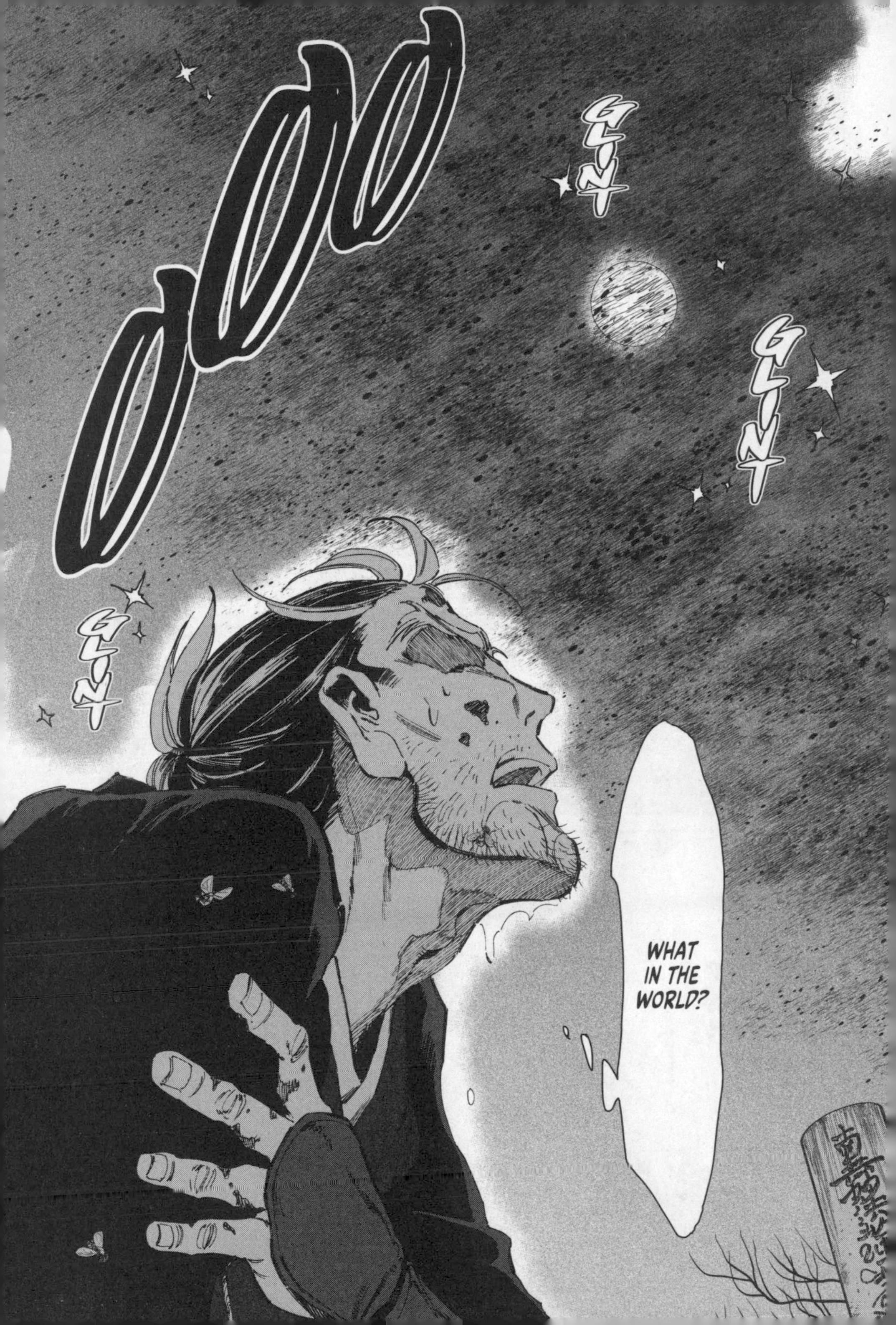
GLINT
GLINT
WHAT IN THE WORLD?
GLINT

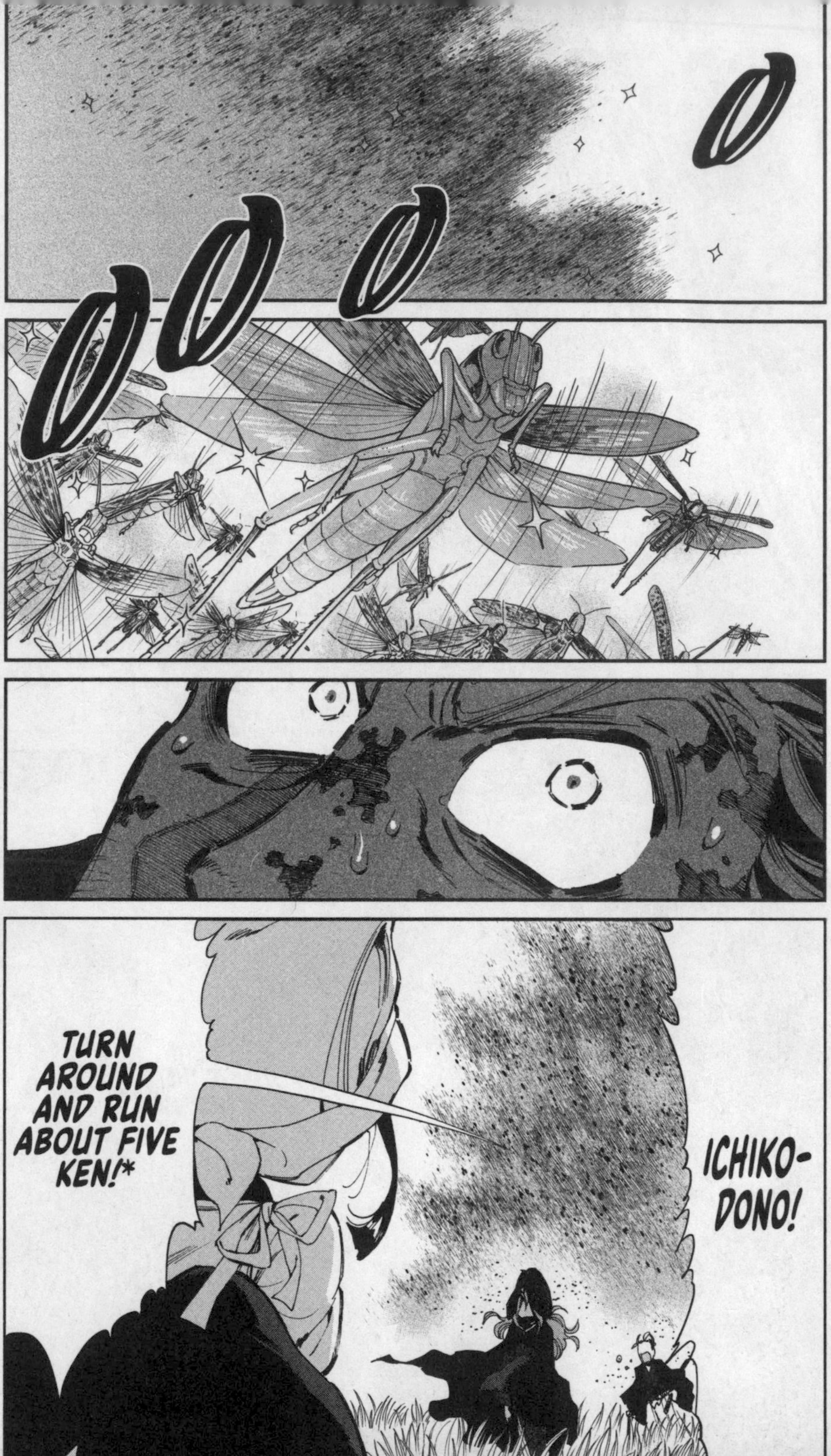
ICHIKO-DONO!
TURN AROUND AND RUN ABOUT FIVE KEN!*

*ABOUT NINE METERS

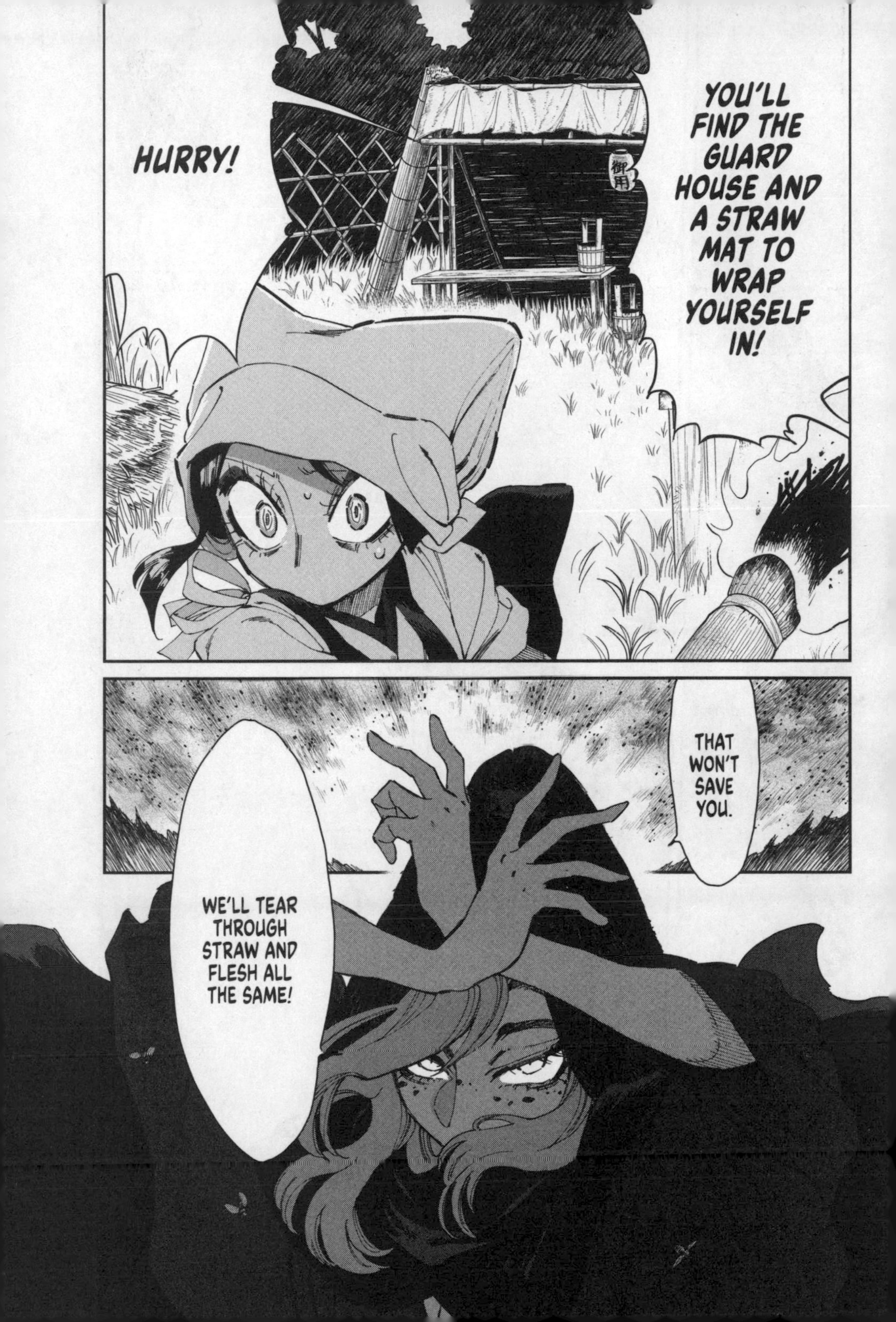
YOU'LL FIND THE GUARD HOUSE AND A STRAW MAT TO WRAP YOURSELF IN!
HURRY!
御用
THAT WON'T SAVE YOU.
WE'LL TEAR THROUGH STRAW AND FLESH ALL THE SAME!

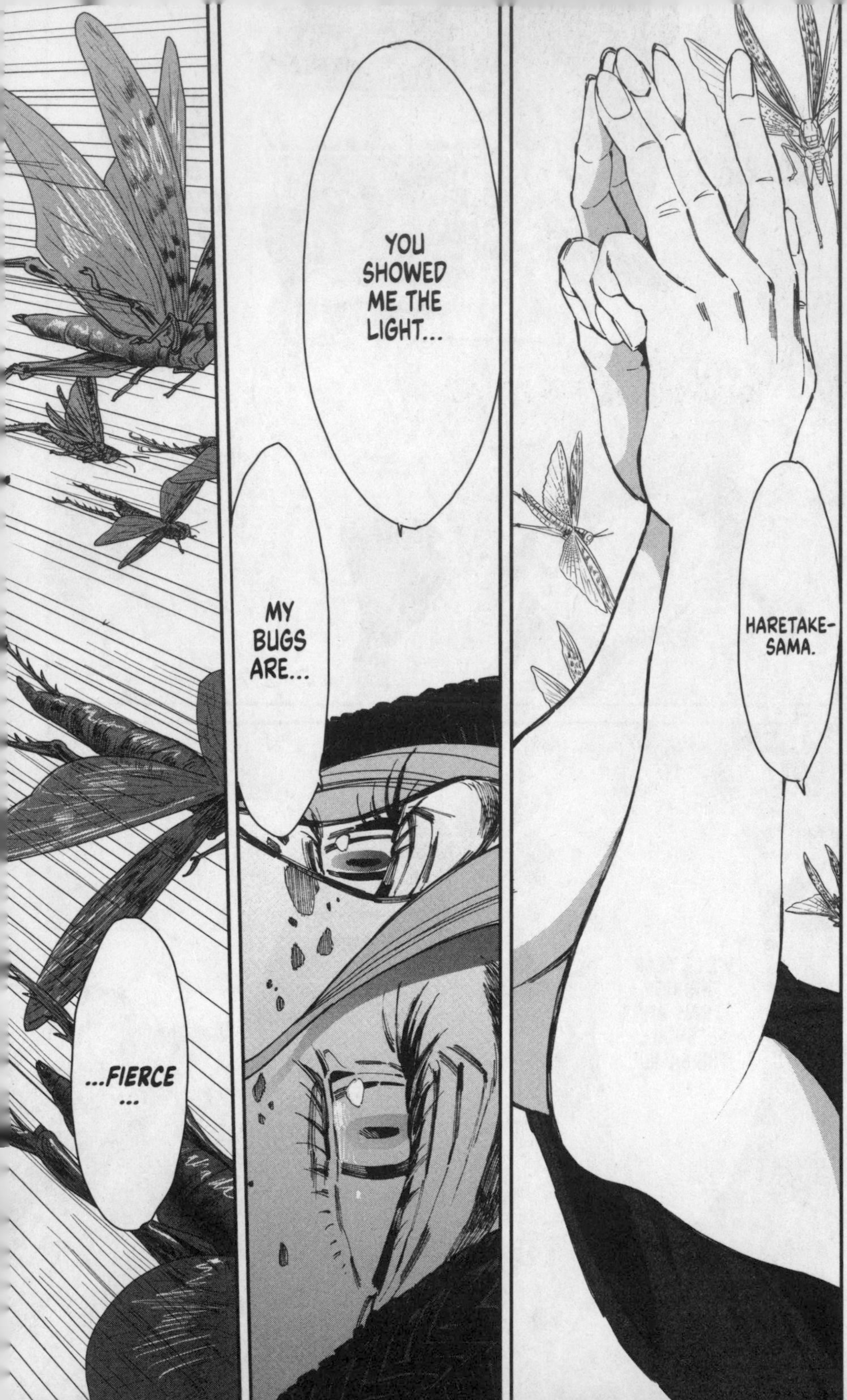
HARETAKE-SAMA.
YOU SHOWED ME THE LIGHT...
MY BUGS ARE...
...FIERCE ...

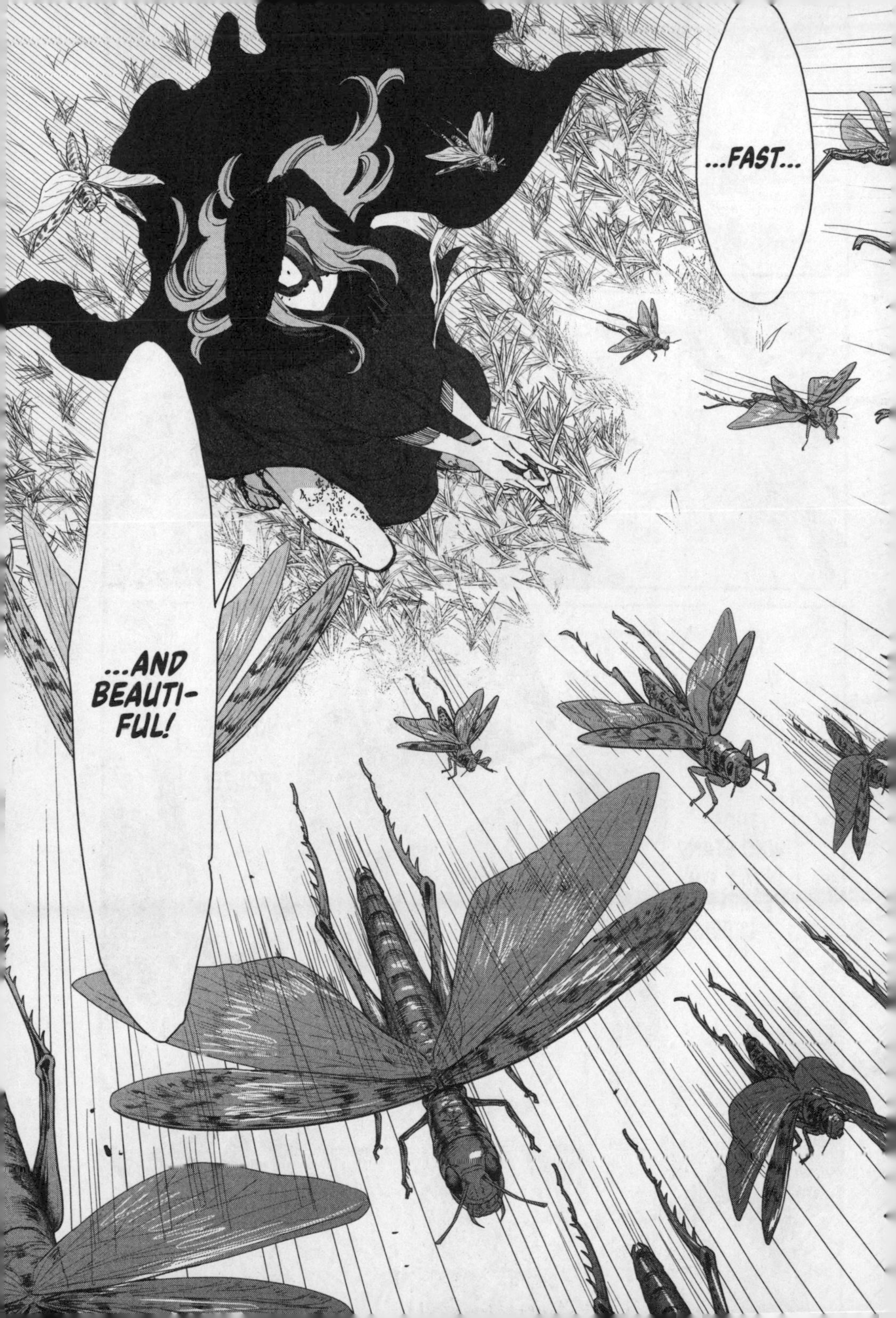
...FAST...
...AND BEAUTI-FUL!

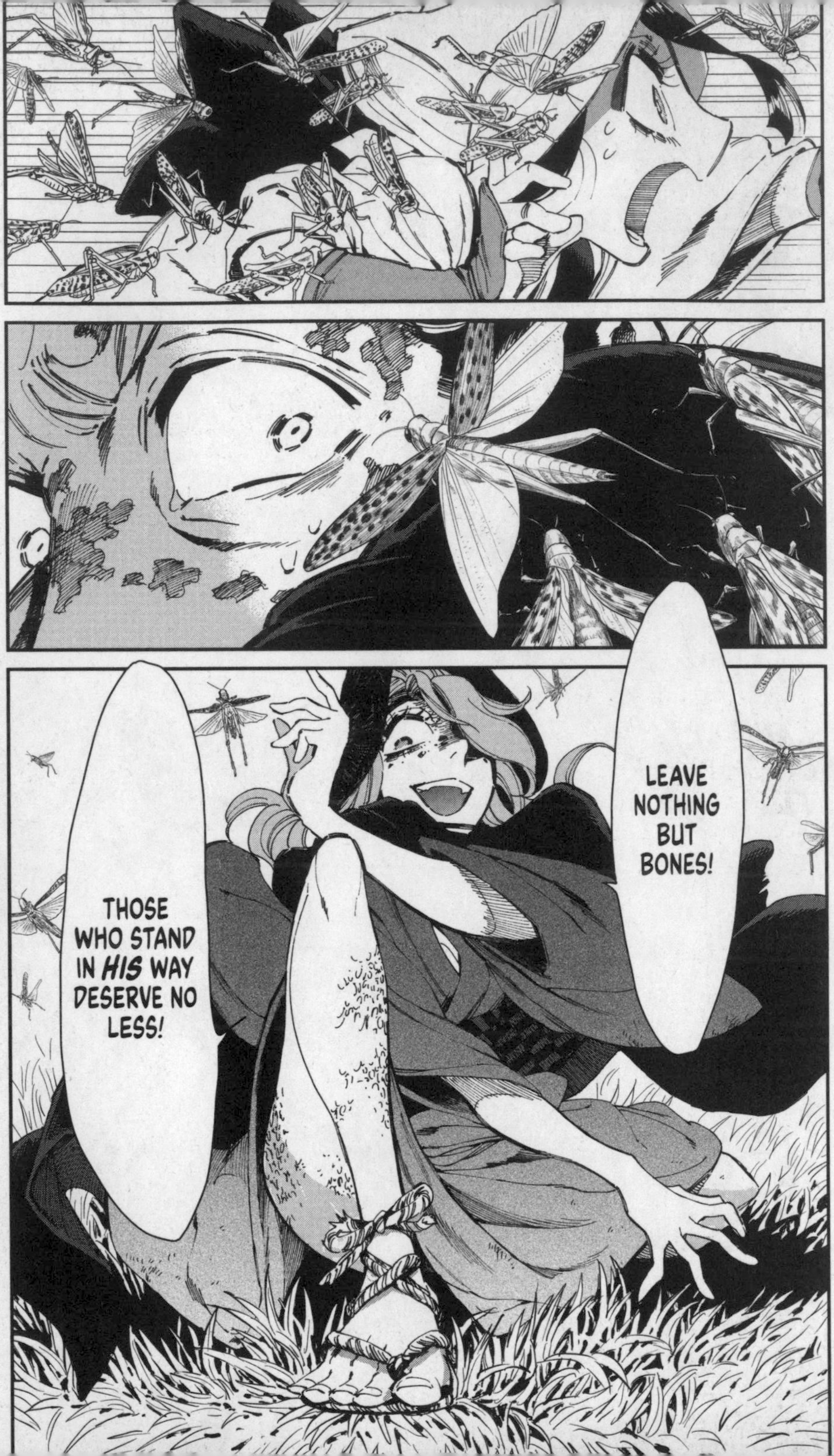
LEAVE NOTHING BUT BONES!
THOSE WHO STAND IN *HIS* WAY DESERVE NO LESS!

STEEL of the CELESTIAL SHADOWS

Trivia of the Celestial Shadows #③

Manzai Performer

o Around the New Year, they traveled around, putting on celebratory performances.

o Usually a two-person team, with one playing the *Tayu* role and the other the *Saizo* role.

o Since they could trace their roots back to the *shomoji* performers (lower class, civilian onmyoji) of the middle ages, at least in some regions, they wound up falling under control of the Tsuchimikado Clan, which oversaw all onmyoji in the early modern period (Azuchi-Momoyama to the end of the Edo Period).

° The origin of modern-day manzai comedy performances.

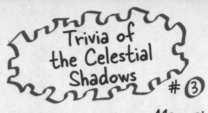

I'm the Tayu here!

The manzai practiced in modern times (like Mikawa-style manzai) involves performances that even people nowadays find delightful!

I hope these traditions stick around for a long time.

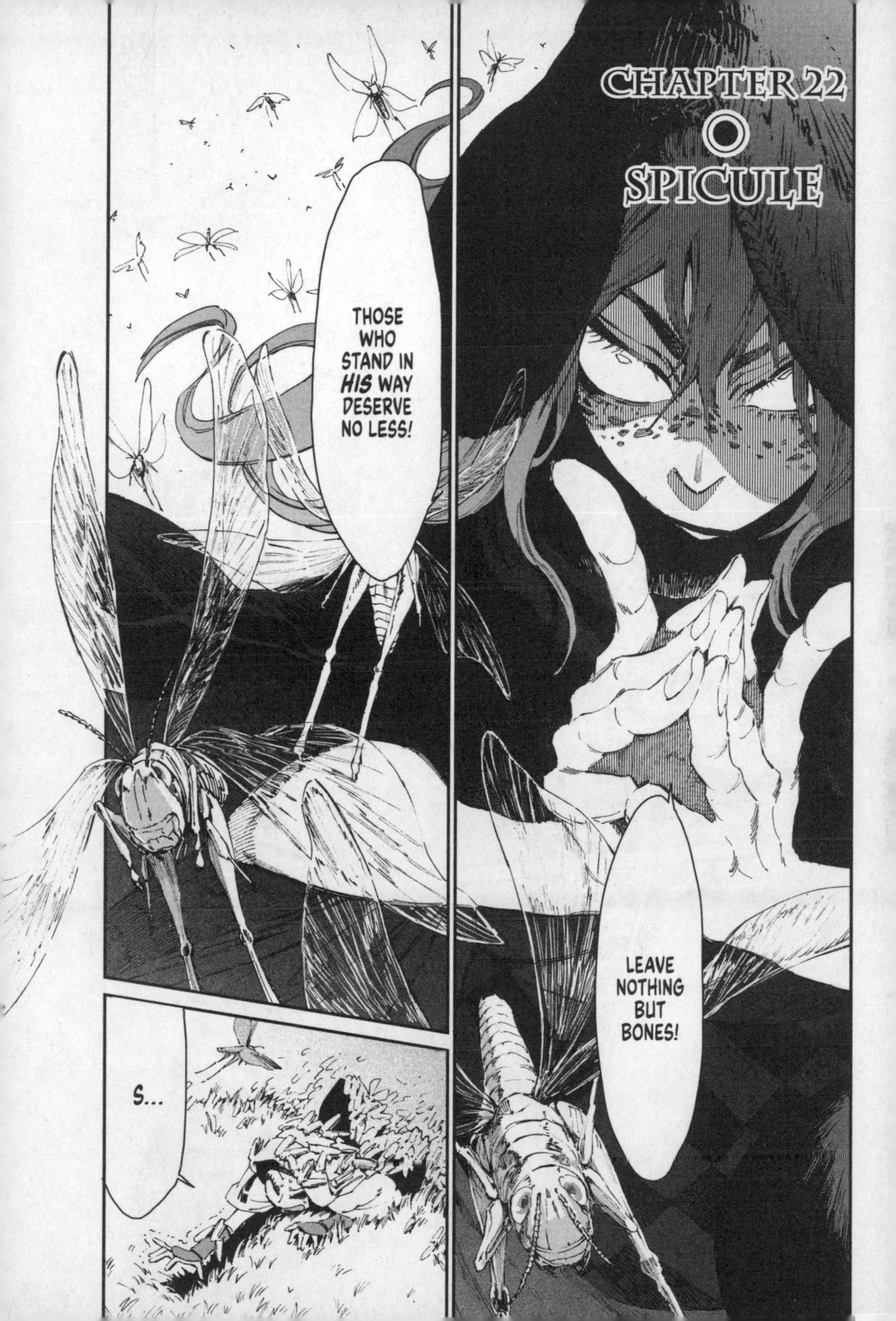
CHAPTER 22
O SPICULE
LEAVE NOTHING BUT BONES!
THOSE WHO STAND IN HIS WAY DESERVE NO LESS!
S...

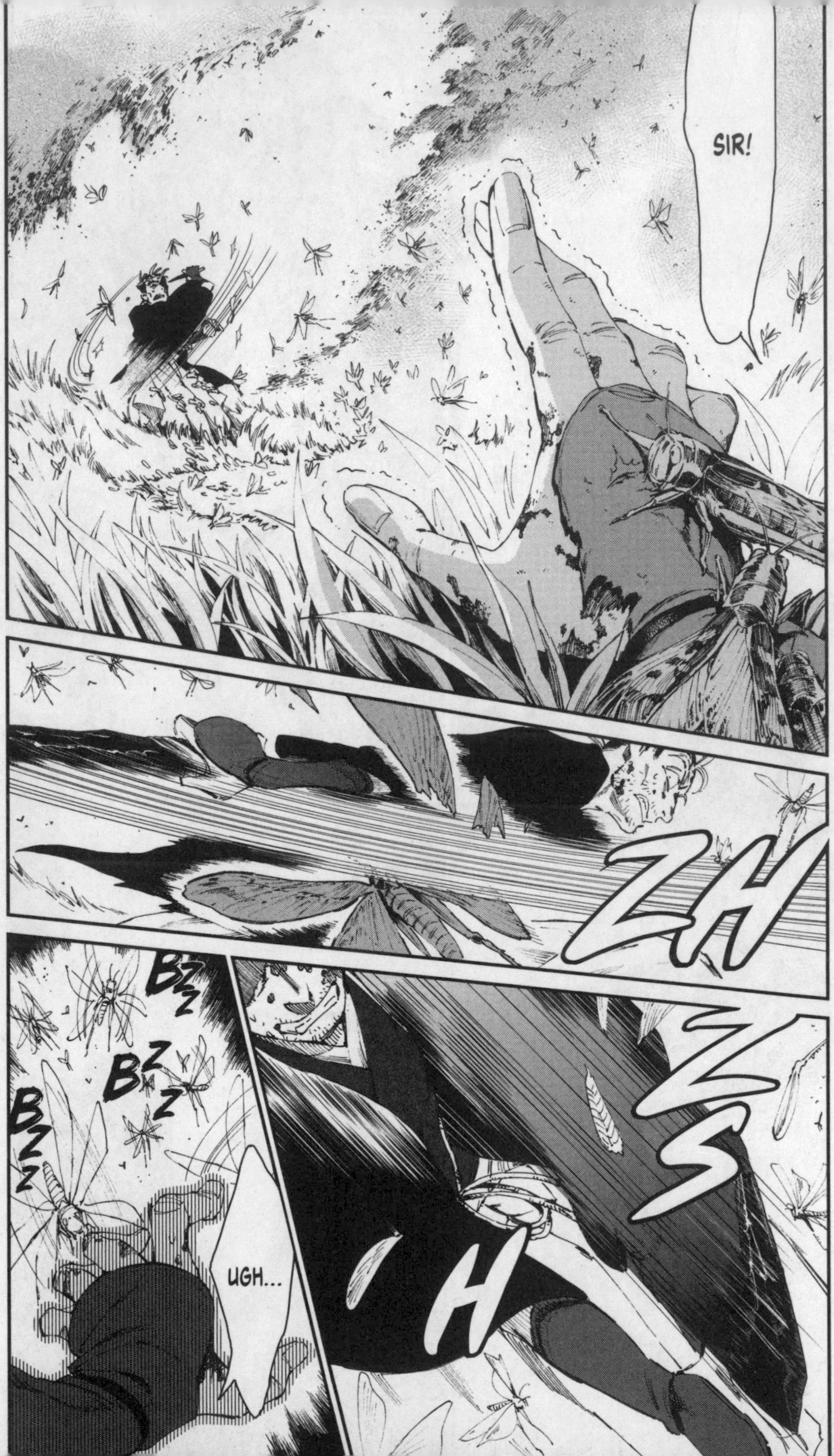
SIR!
ZH
ZWSH
BZZ
BZZZ
BZZ
UGH...

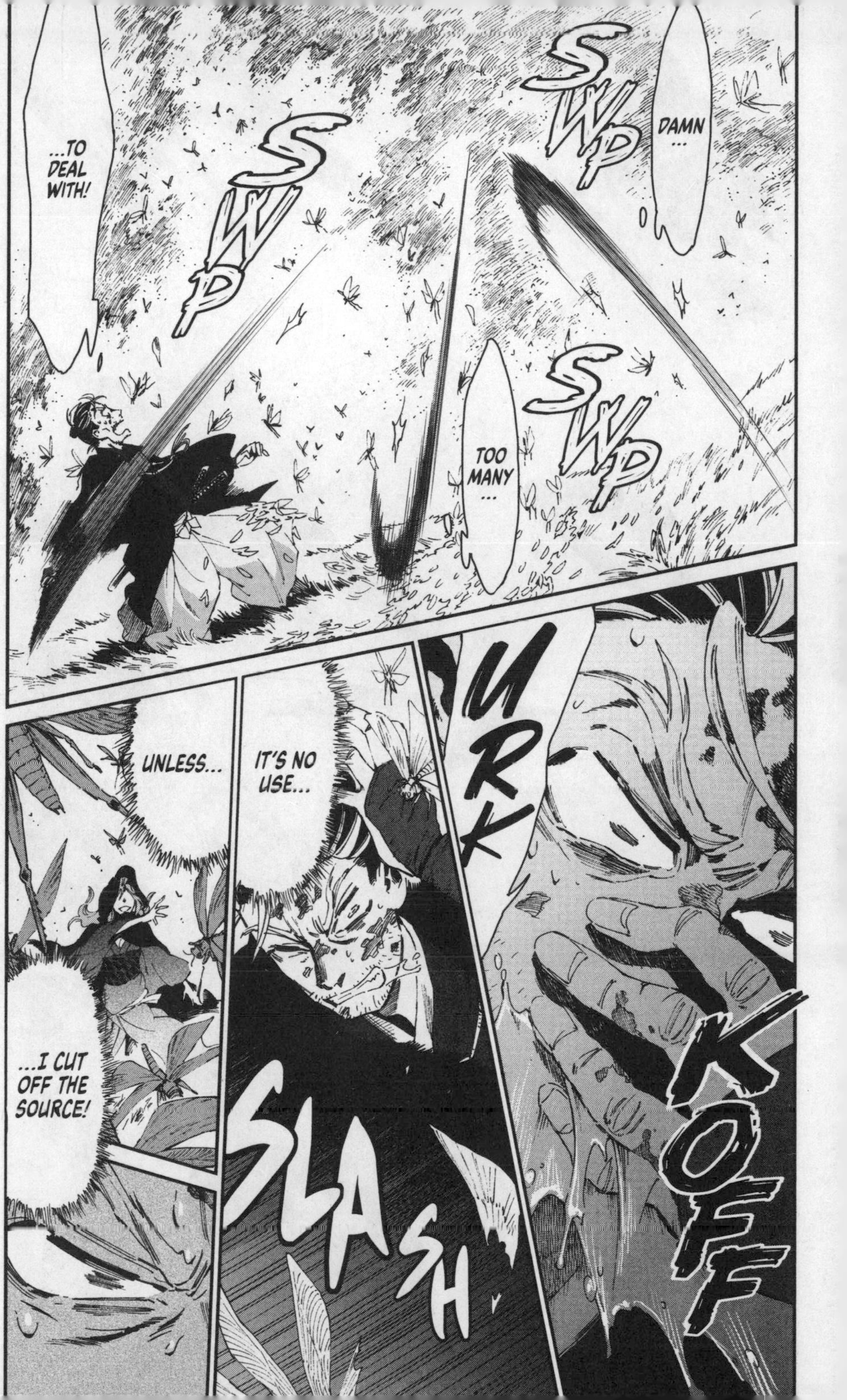
SWP
DAMN...
TOO MANY...
SWP
SWP
...TO DEAL WITH!
URK
KOFF
IT'S NO USE...
SLASH
UNLESS...
...I CUT OFF THE SOURCE!

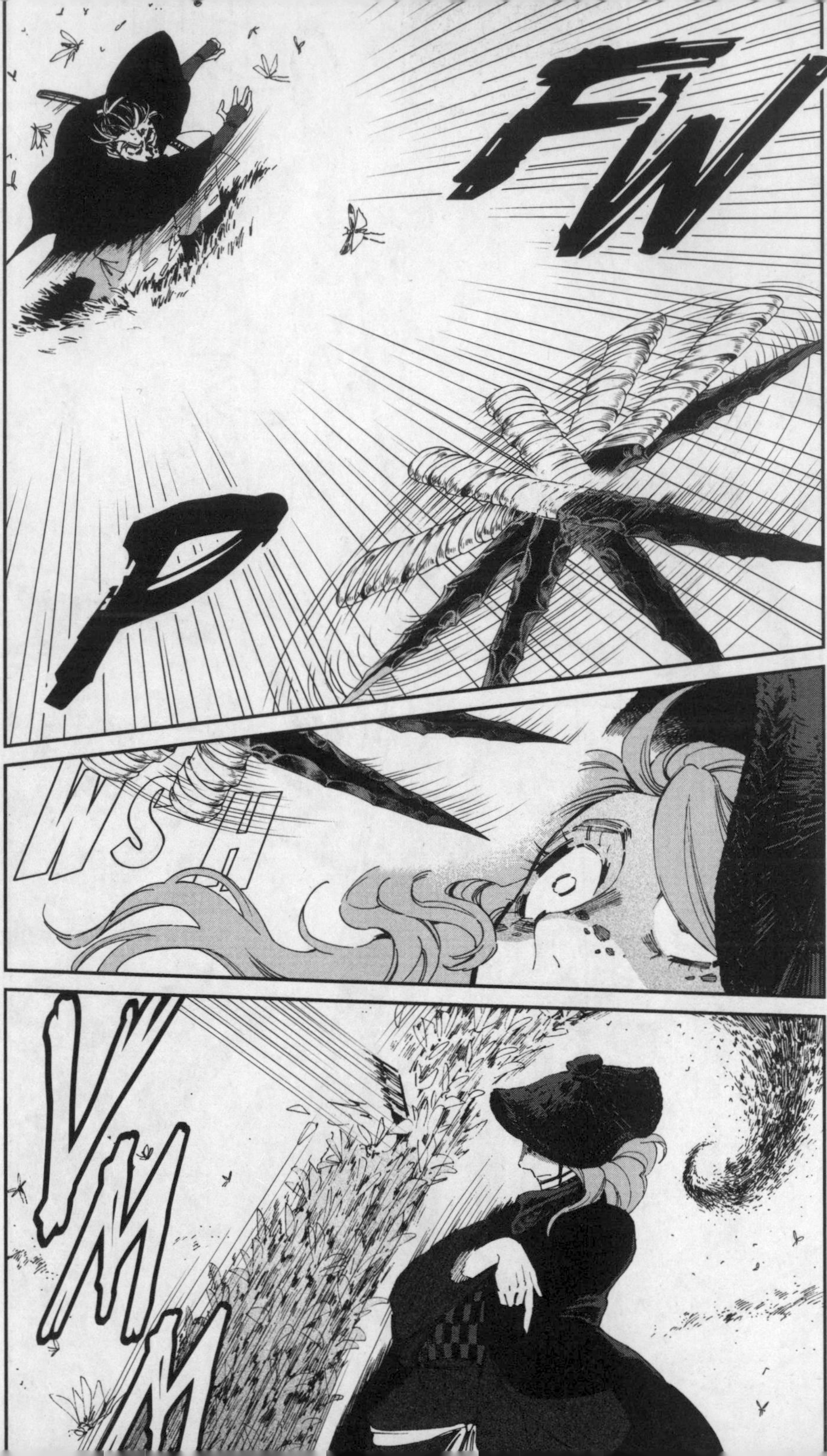
FW
P
WSH
VMM

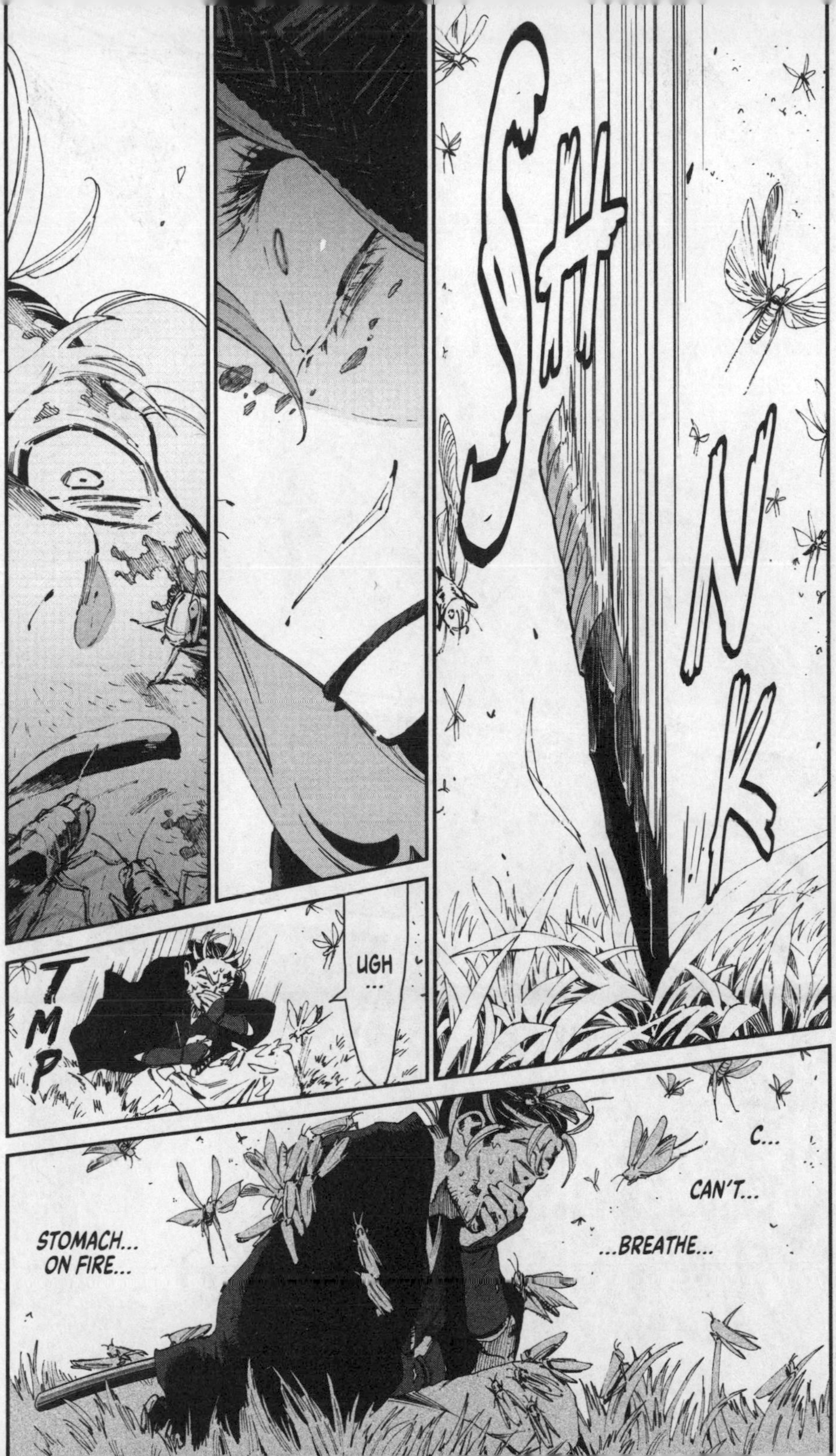
SHNK
UGH...
TMP
C...
CAN'T...
...BREATHE...
STOMACH... ON FIRE...

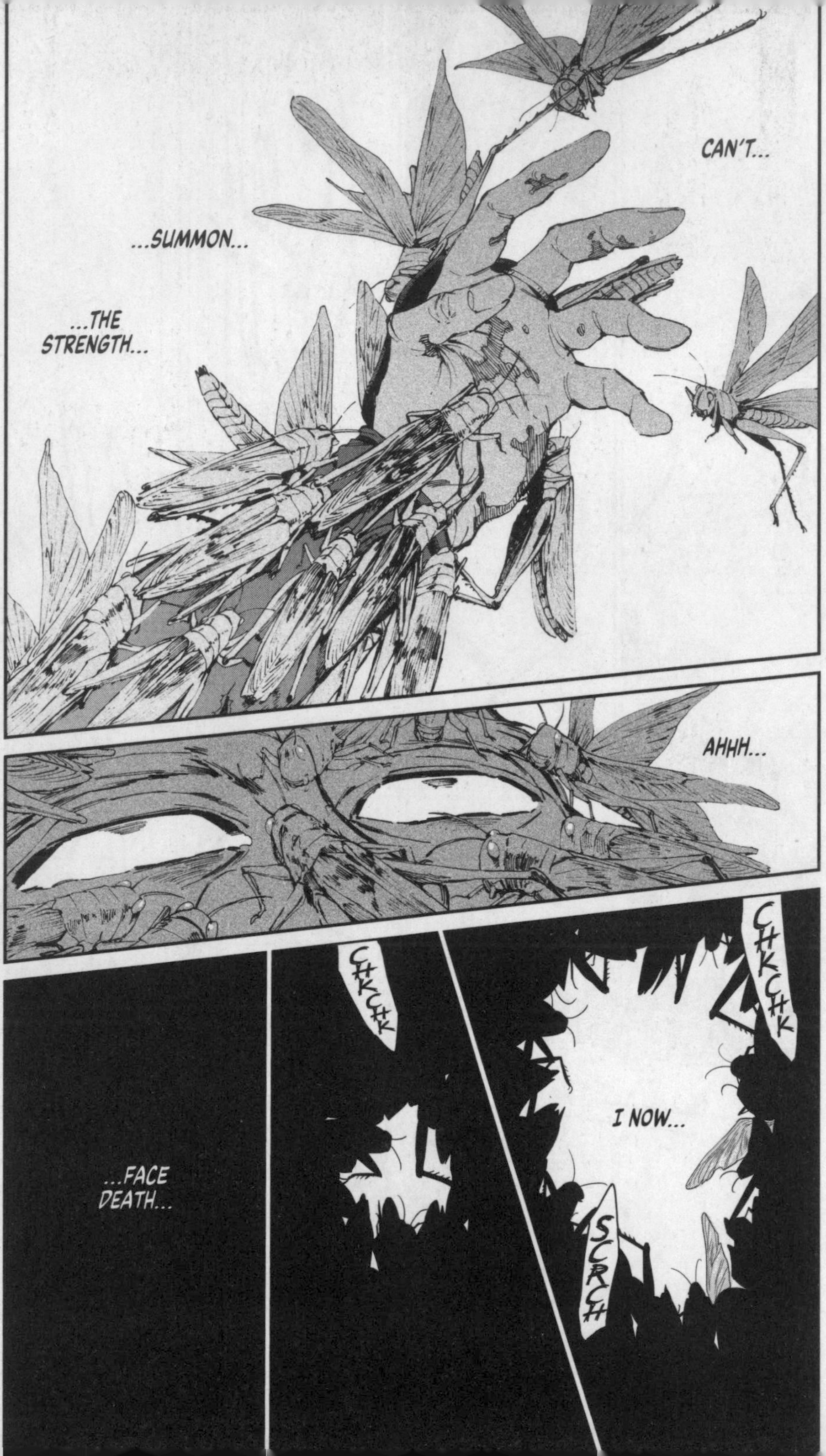
CAN'T...
...SUMMON...
...THE STRENGTH...
AHHH...
CHKCHK
I NOW...
SCRCH
CHKCHK
...FACE DEATH...

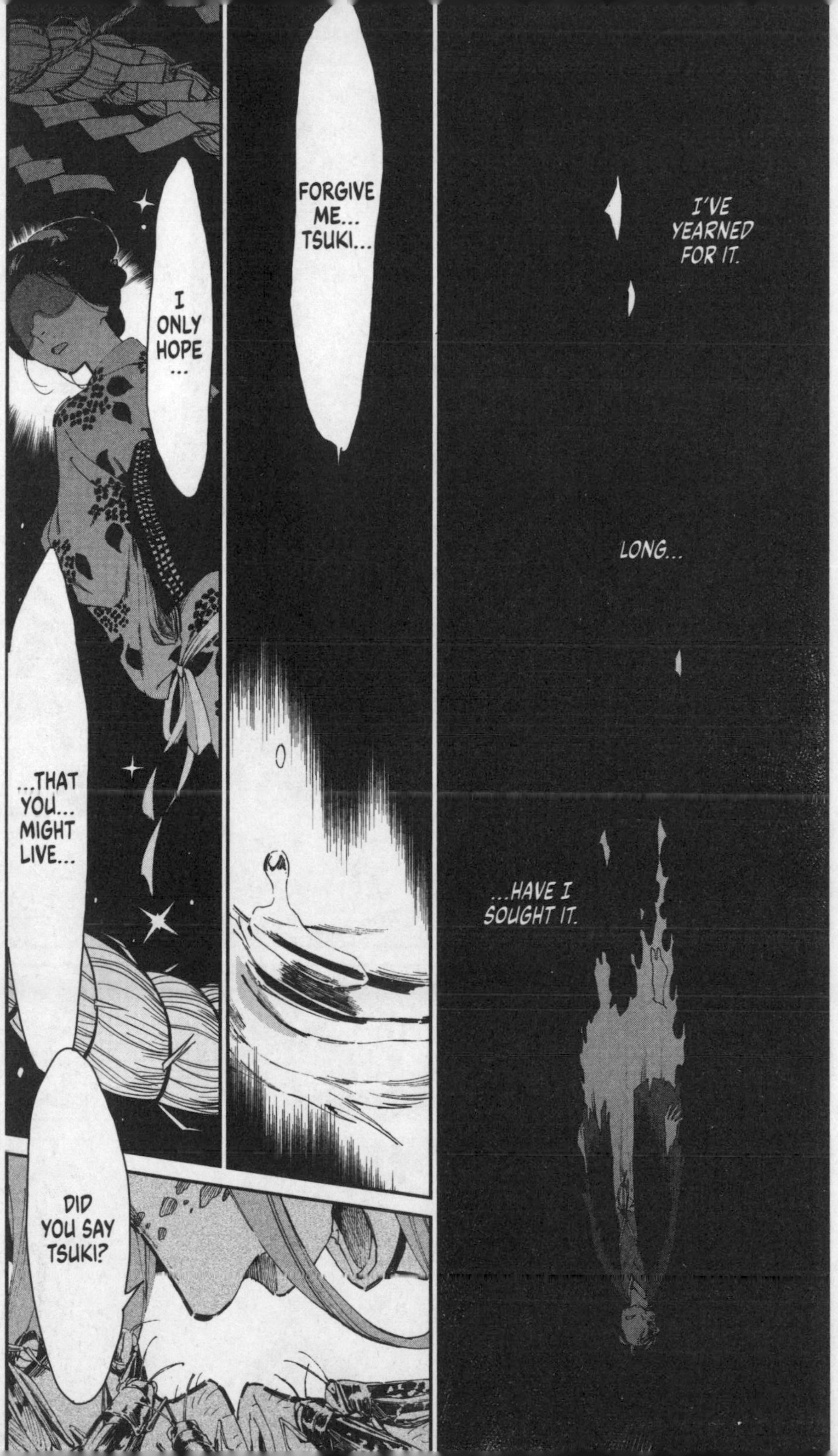
I'VE YEARNED FOR IT.
LONG...
...HAVE I SOUGHT IT.
FORGIVE ME... TSUKI...
I ONLY HOPE...
...THAT YOU... MIGHT LIVE...
DID YOU SAY TSUKI?

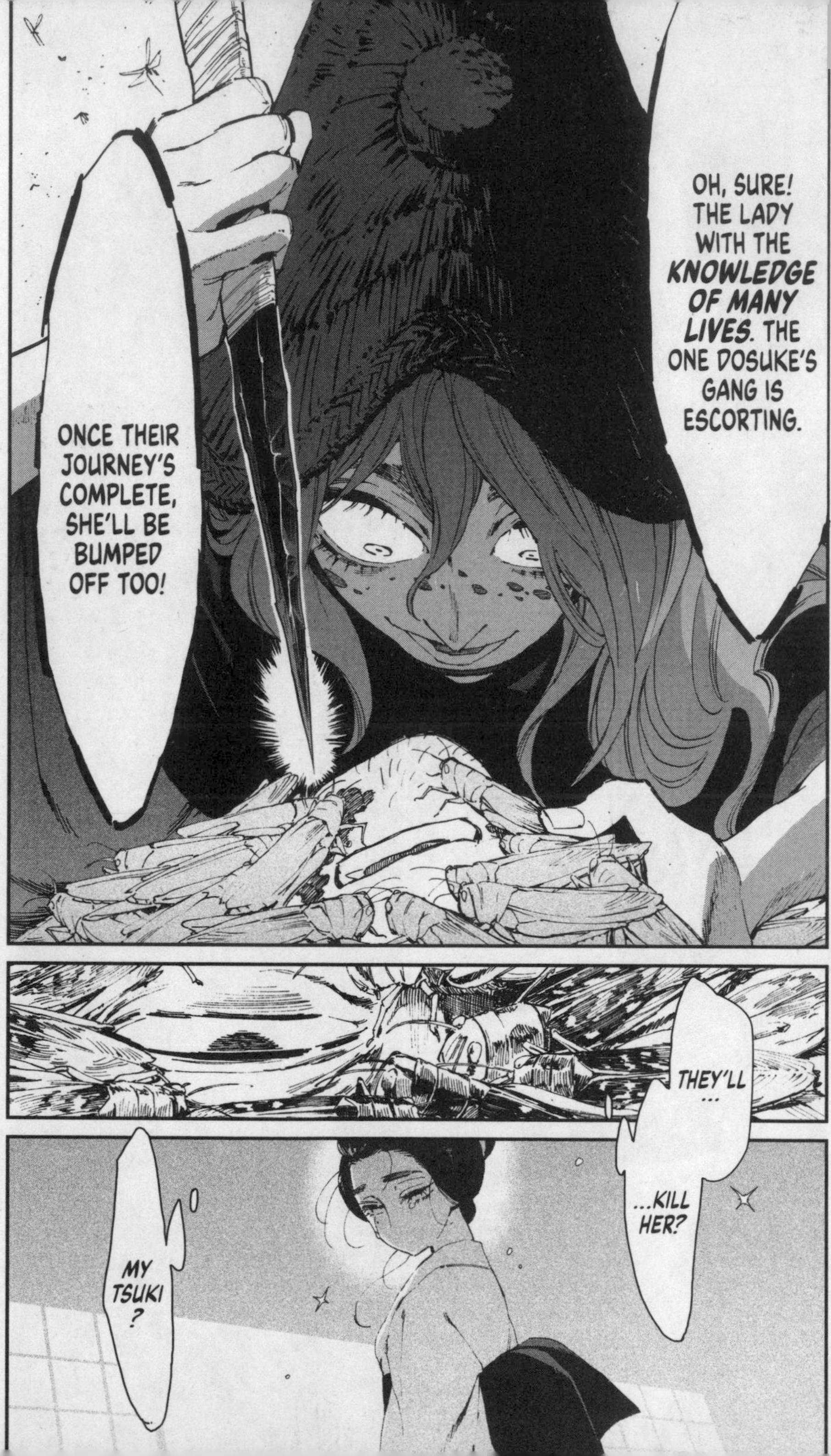
OH, SURE! THE LADY WITH THE *KNOWLEDGE OF MANY LIVES*. THE ONE DOSUKE'S GANG IS ESCORTING.
ONCE THEIR JOURNEY'S COMPLETE, SHE'LL BE BUMPED OFF TOO!
THEY'LL ...
...KILL HER?
MY TSUKI ?

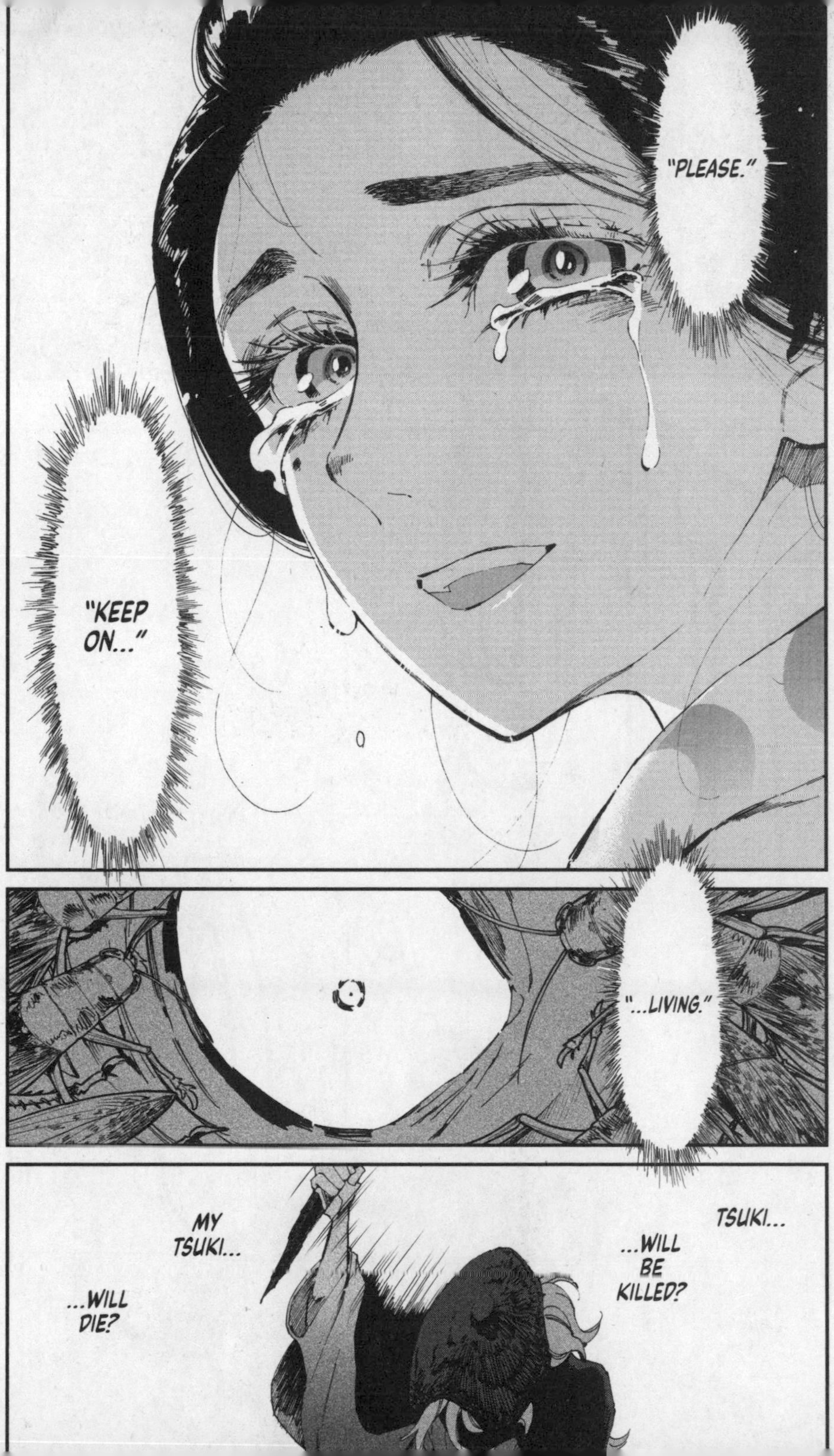
"PLEASE."
"KEEP ON..."
"...LIVING."
TSUKI...
...WILL BE KILLED?
MY TSUKI...
...WILL DIE?

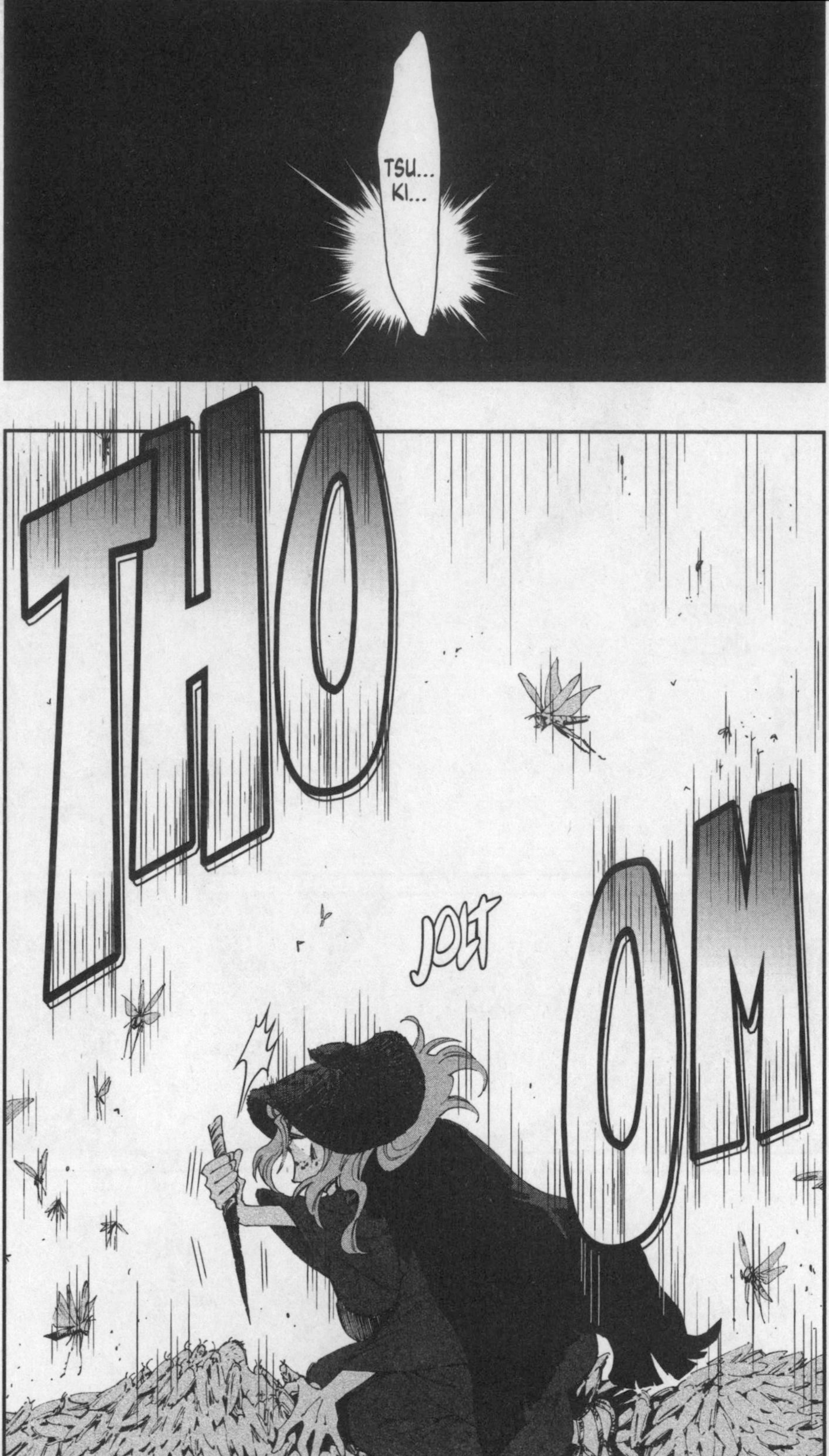
TSU... KI...
THOOM
JOLT

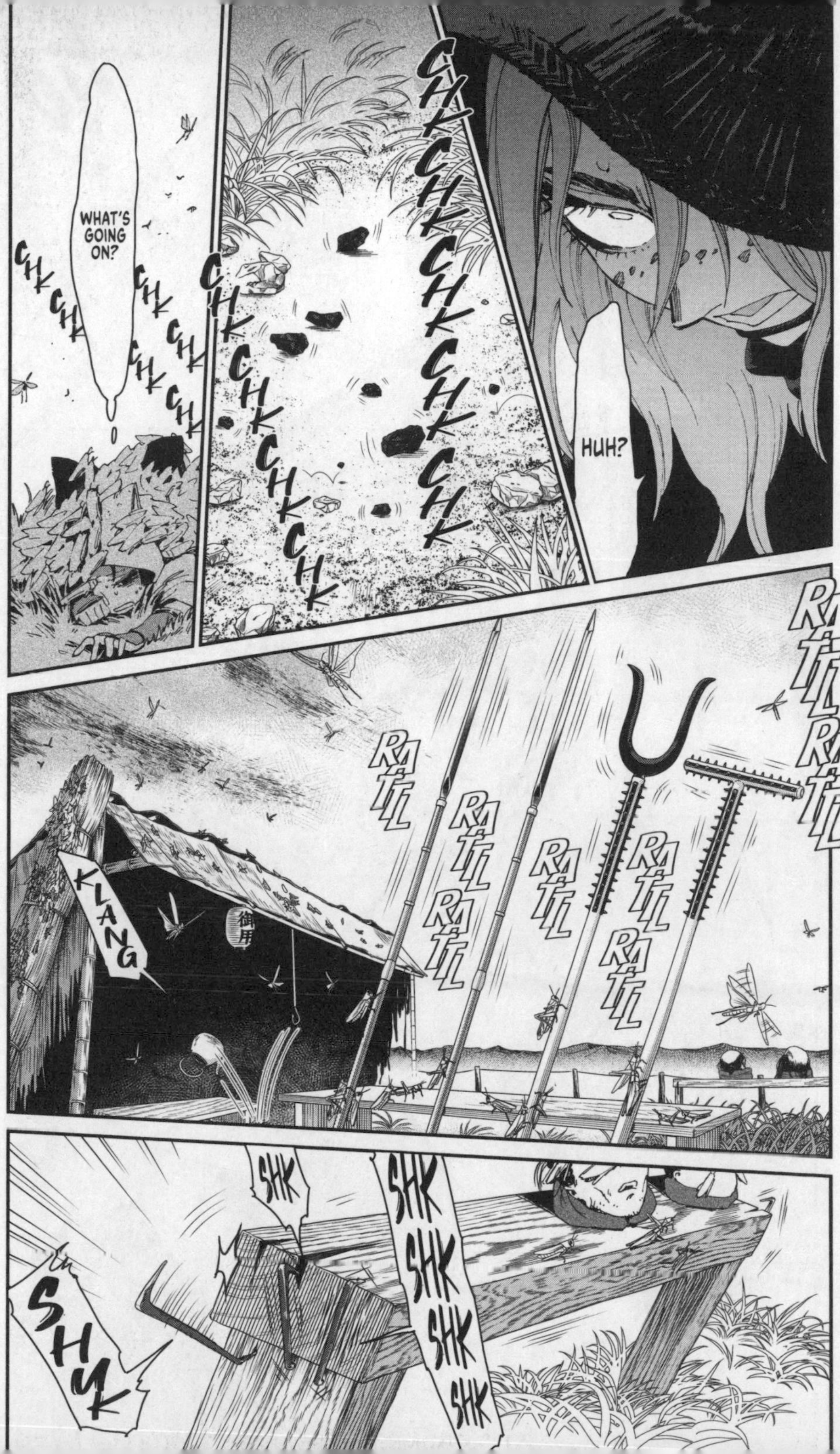
HUH?
CHKCHKCHKCHKCHK
CHKCHKCHKCHK
WHAT'S GOING ON?
CHKCHK
CHKCHK
CHKCHK
RATTLRATTL
RATTL
RATTL
RATTLRATTL
RATTLRATTL
RATTL
KLANG
御用
SHK
SHK SHK SHK SHK
SHUK

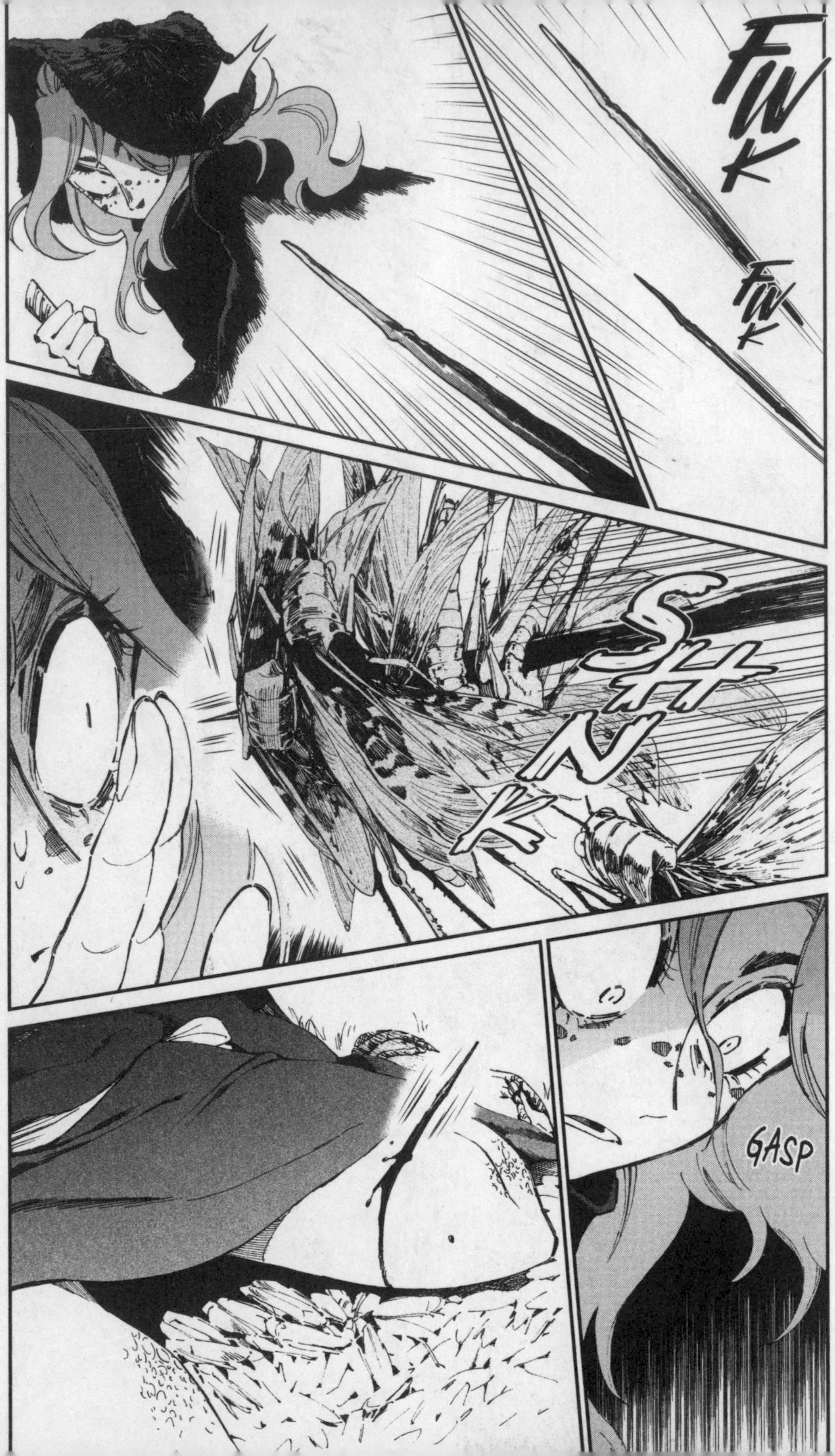
FWNK
FWNK
SHNK
GASP

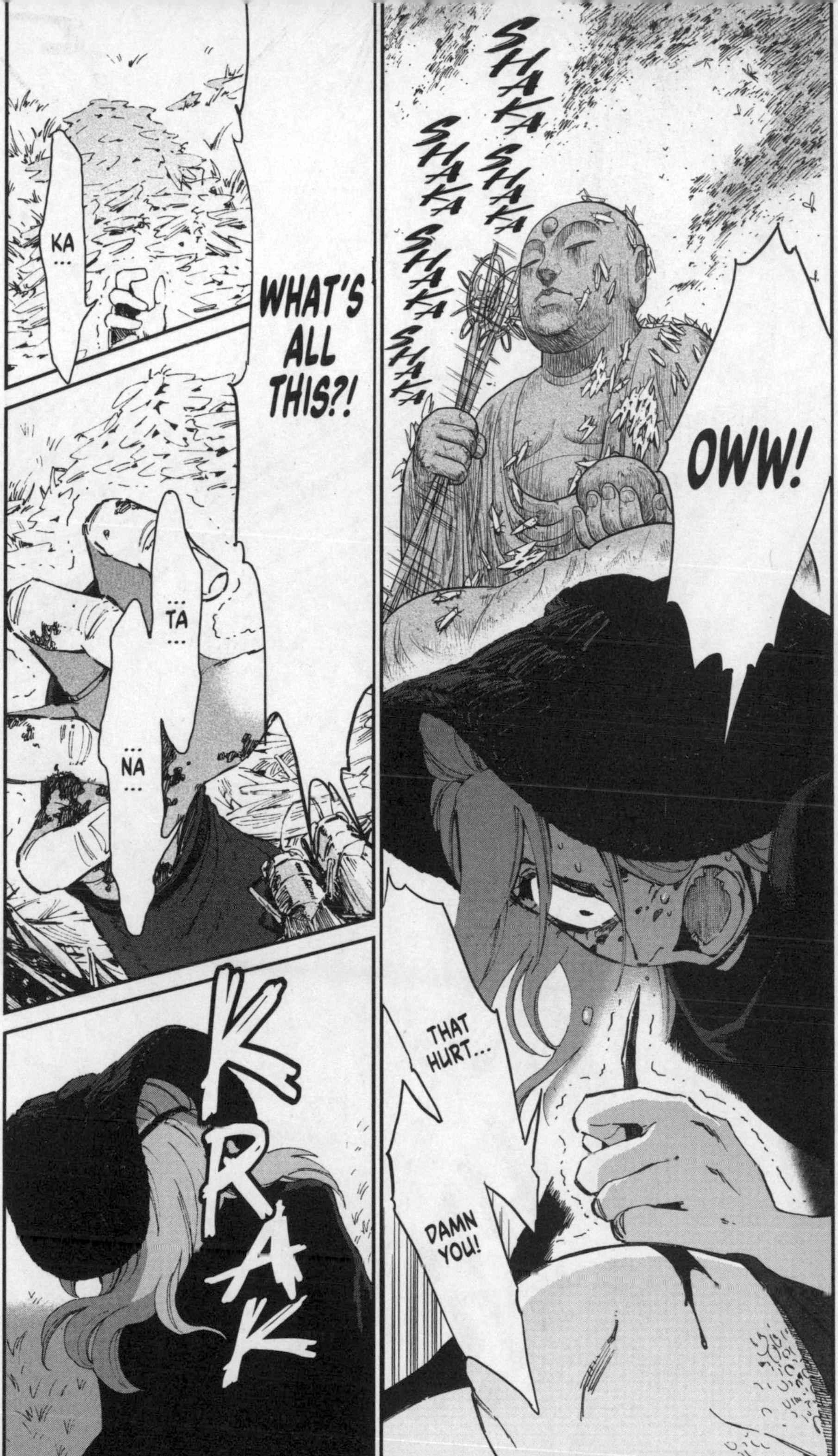
SHAKA SHAKA
SHAKA SHAKA SHAKA
OWW!
THAT HURT...
DAMN YOU!
KA...
WHAT'S ALL THIS?!
...TA...
...NA...
KRAK

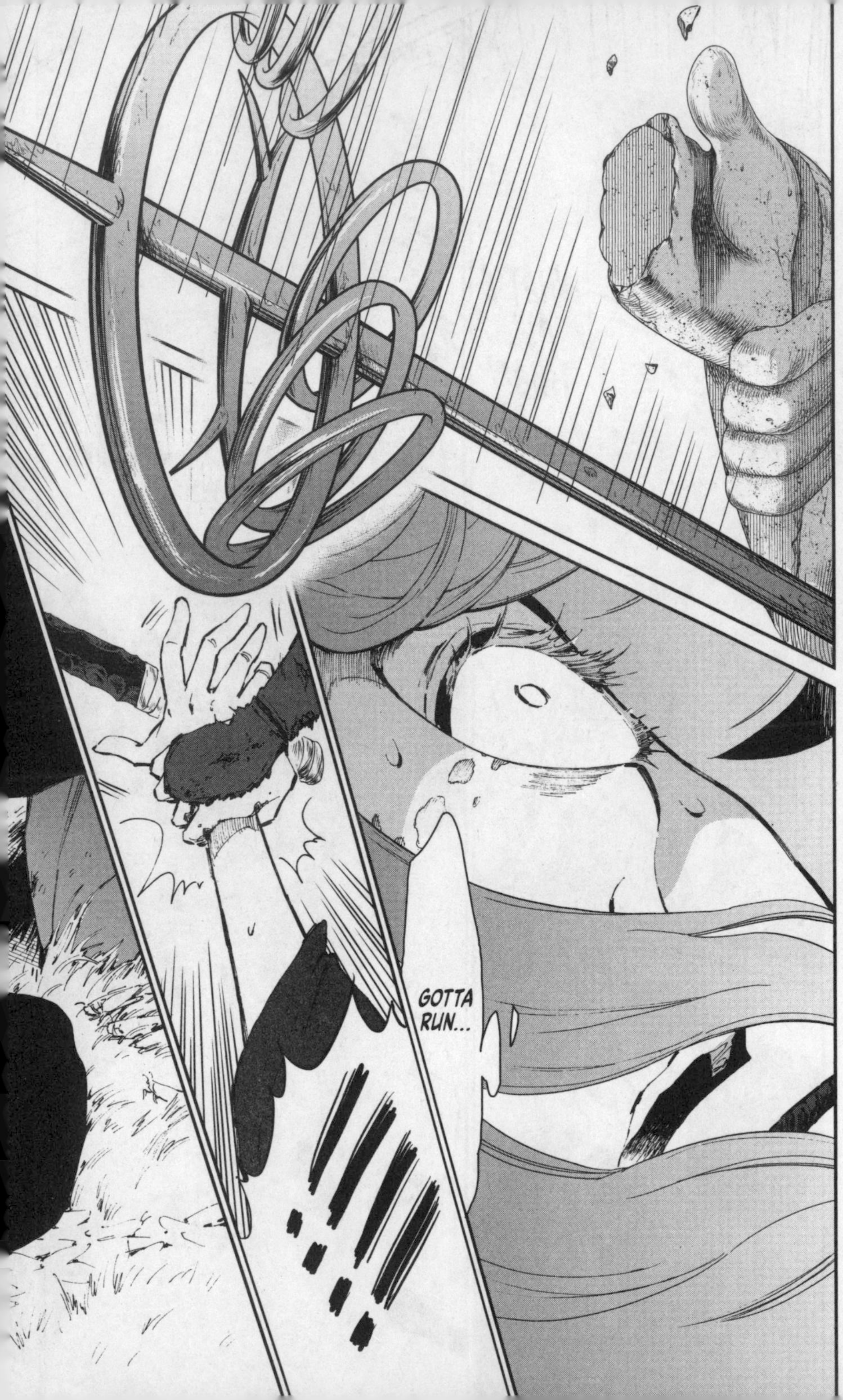
GOTTA RUN...

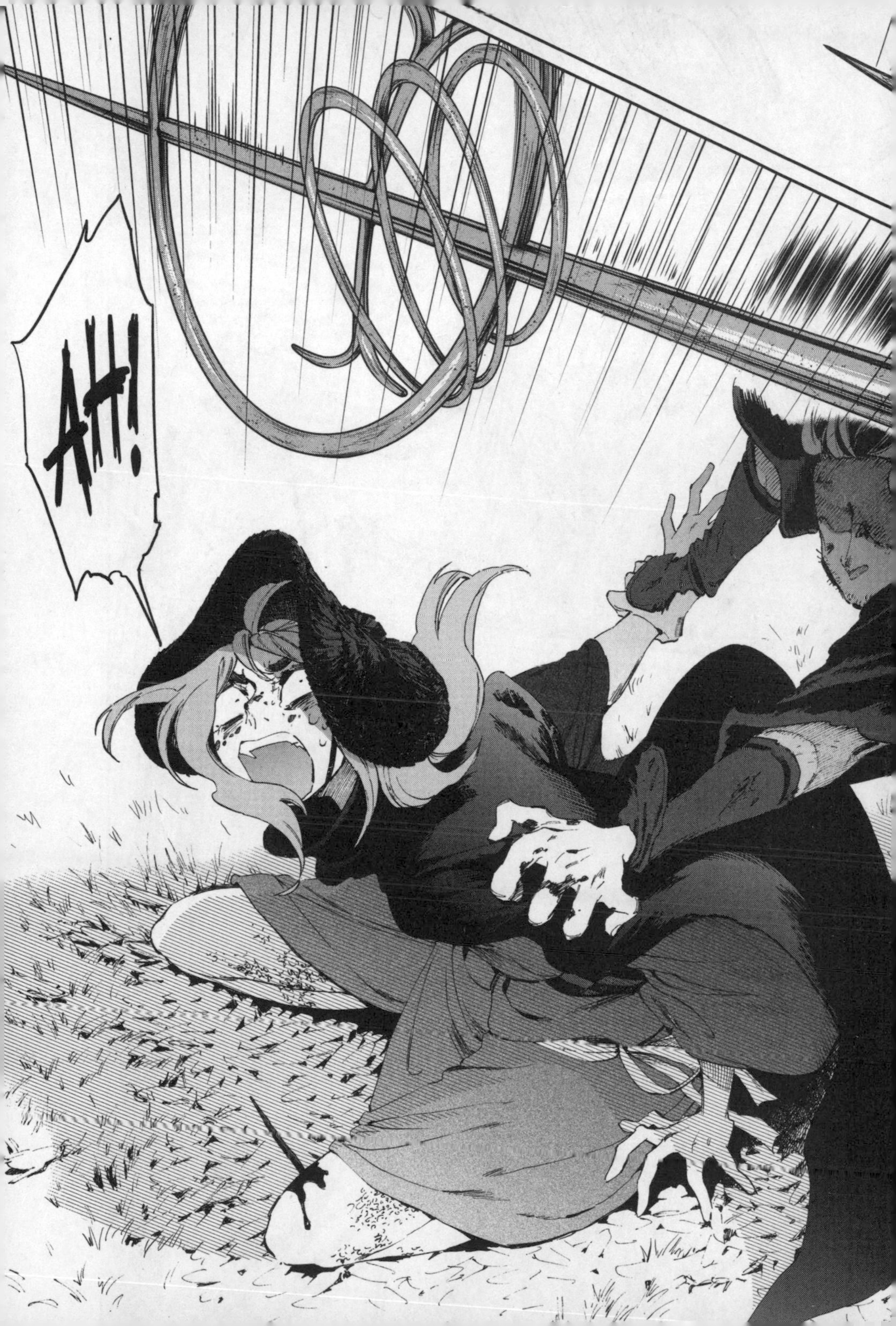
AH!

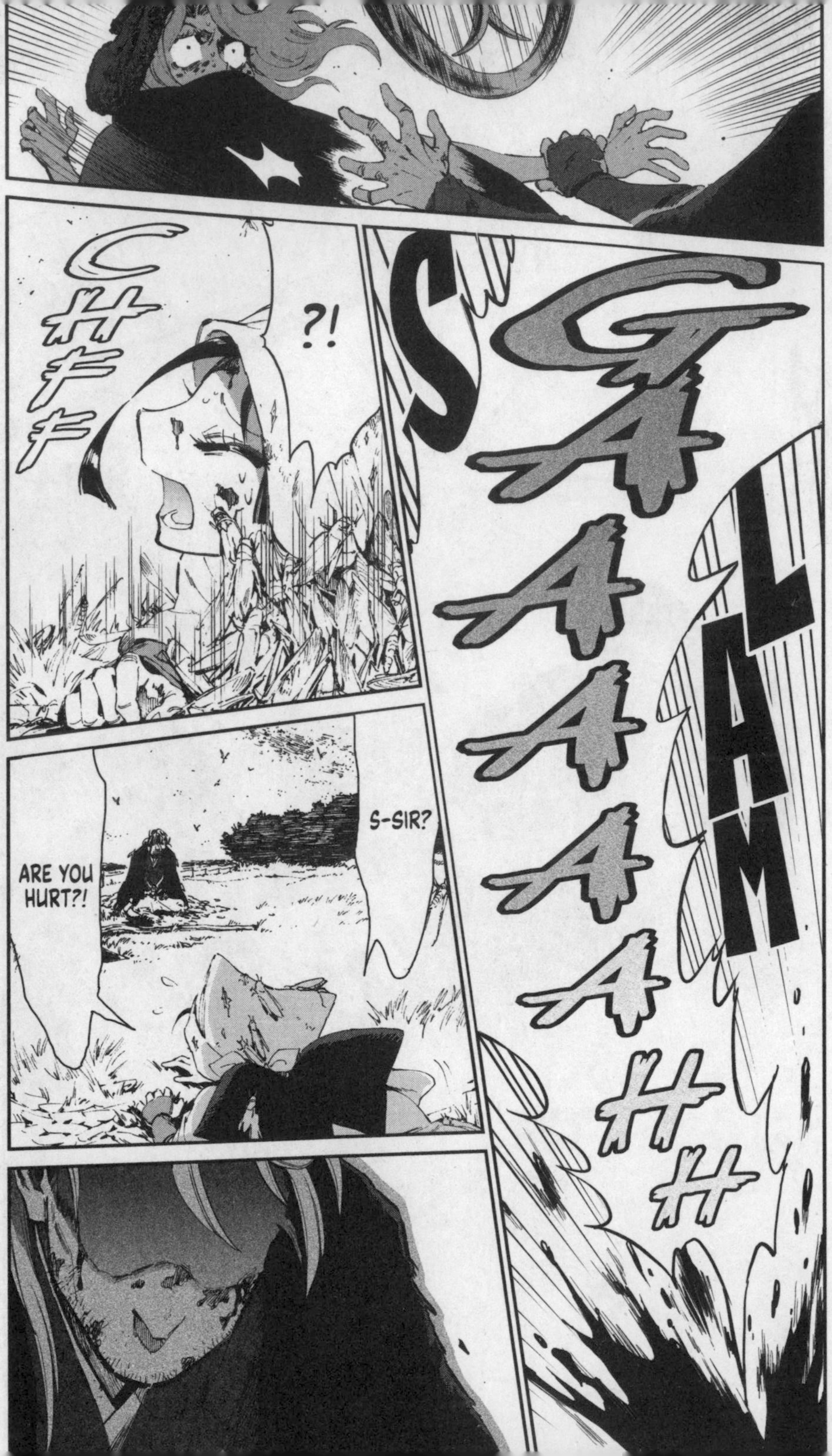
SLAM
GAAAAAHH
?!
CHFF
S-SIR?
ARE YOU HURT?!

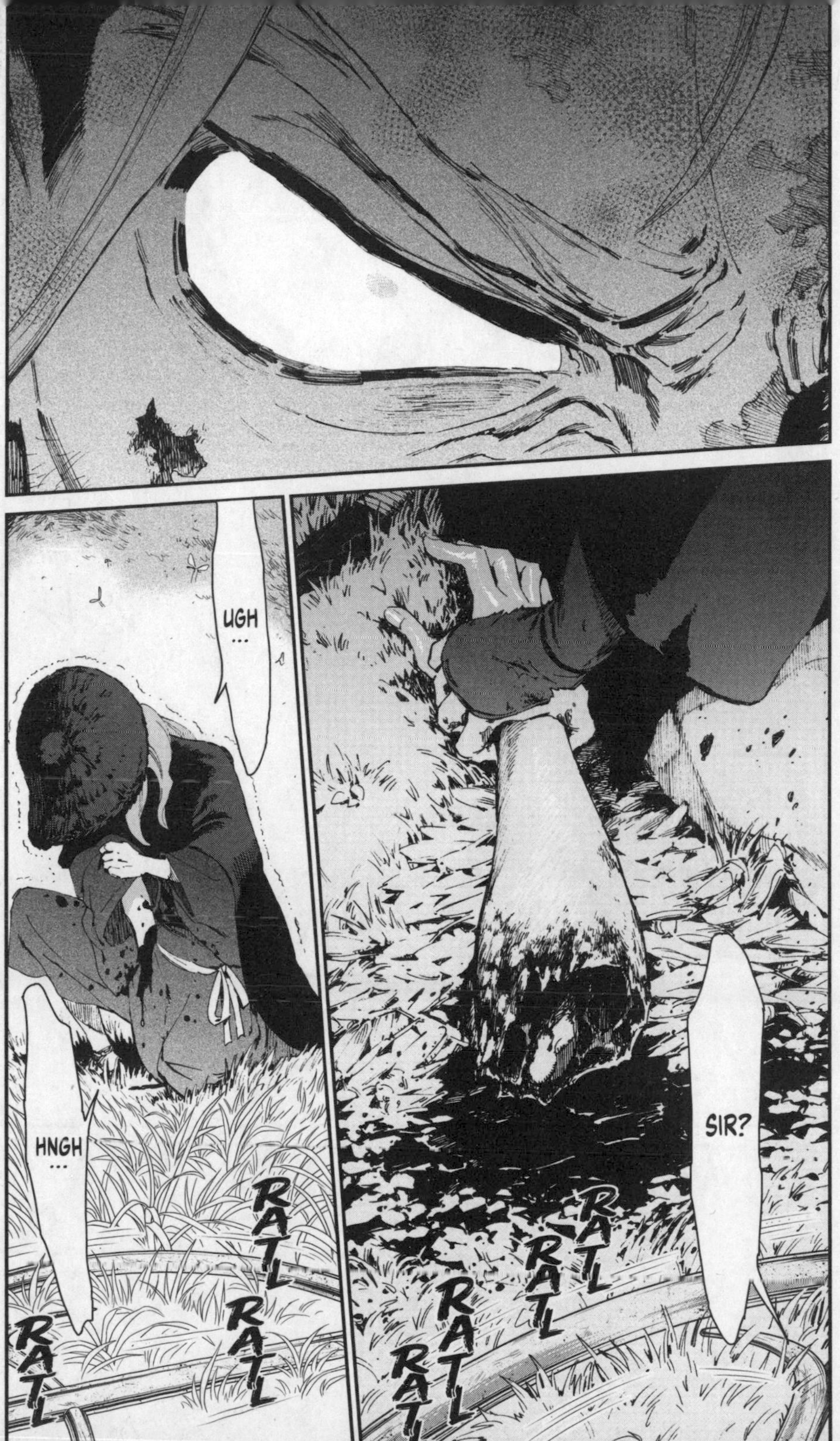
SIR?
RATTL
RATTL
RATTL
UGH...
HNGH...
RATTL
RATTL
RATTL

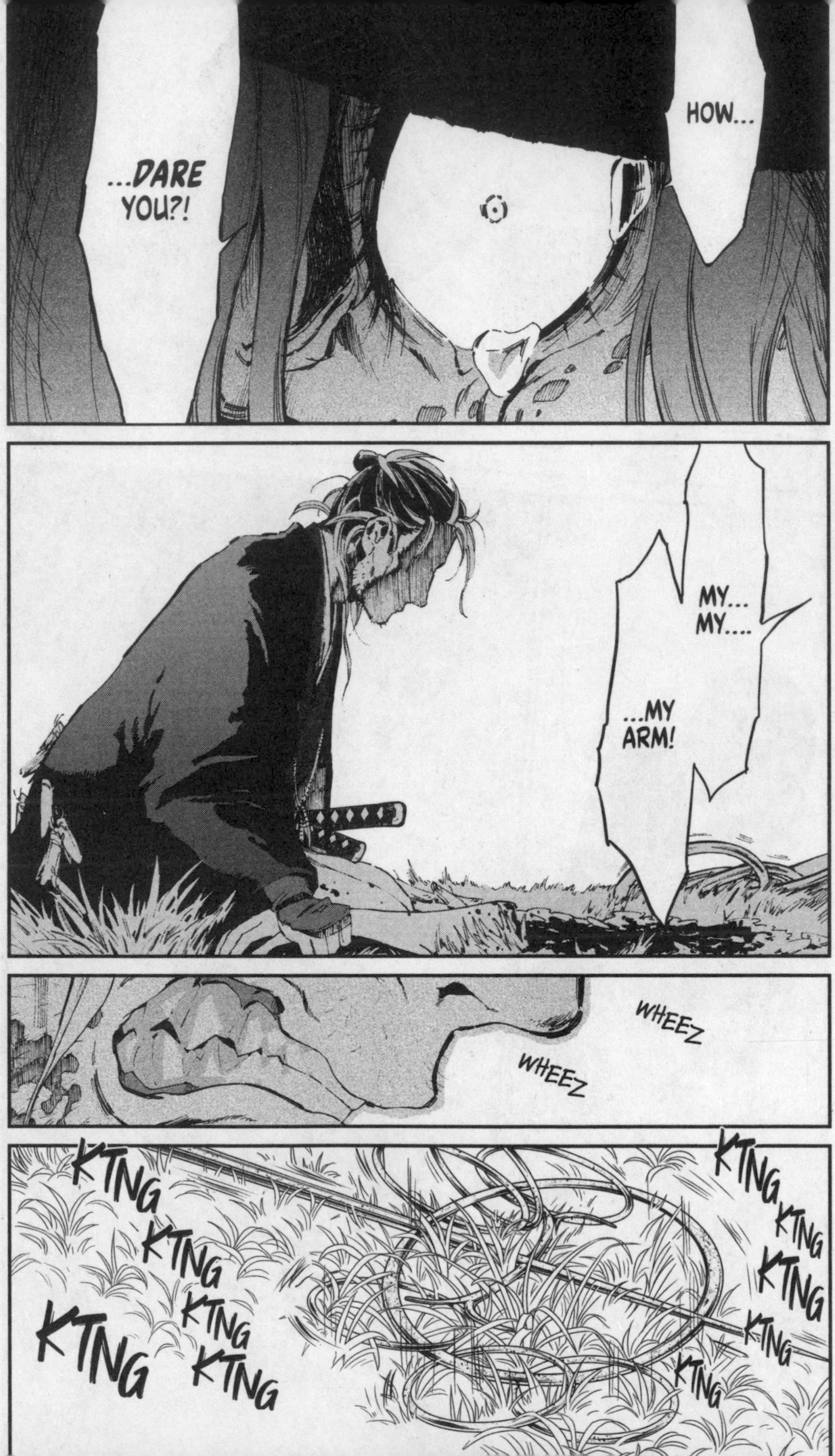
HOW...
...DARE YOU?!
MY... MY....
...MY ARM!
WHEEZ
WHEEZ
KTNG KTNG KTNG KTNG KTNG KTNG
KTNG KTNG KTNG KTNG KTNG KTNG

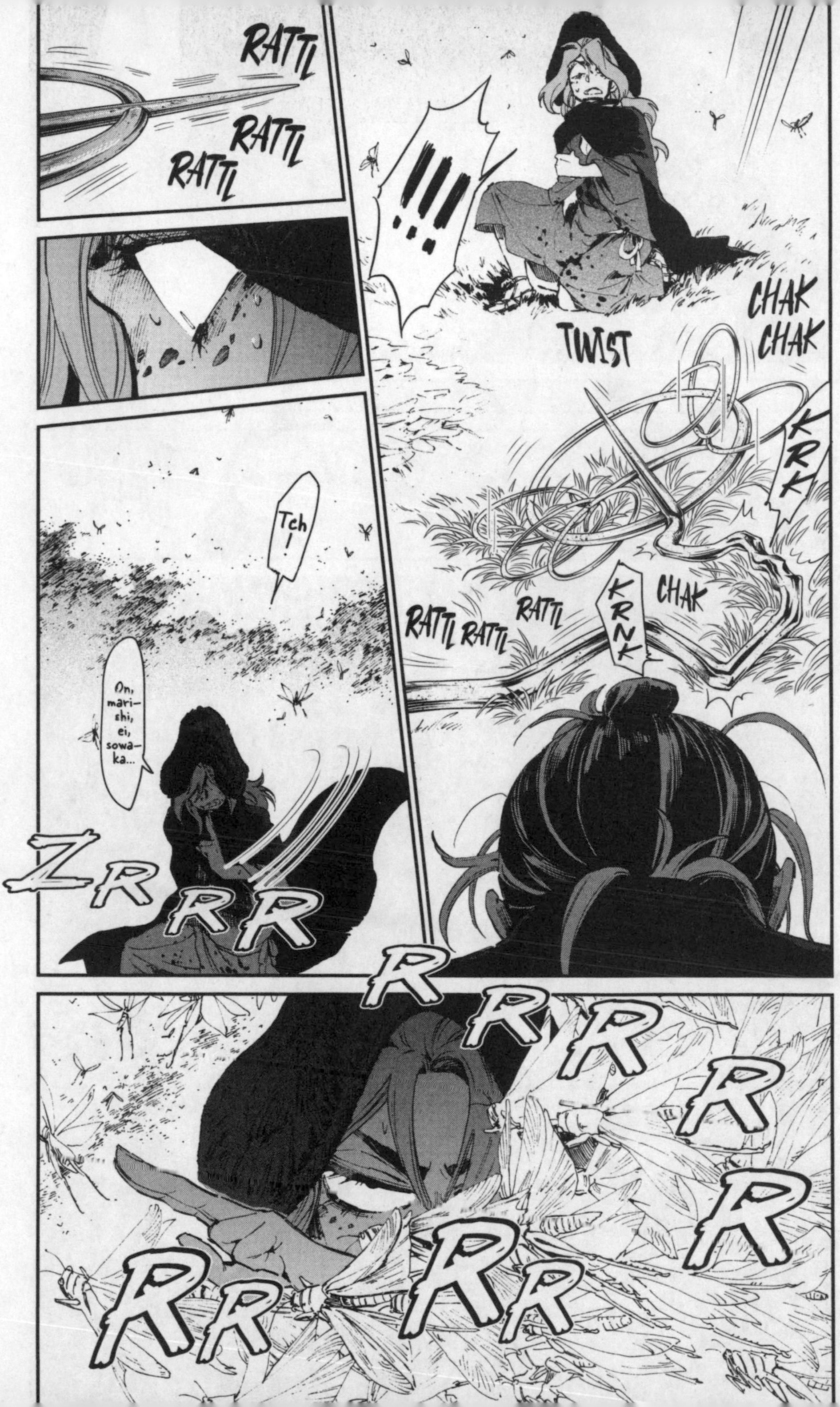
!!!
RATTL
RATTL
RATTL
CHAK
CHAK
TWIST
KRK
CHAK
KRNK
RATTL
RATTL RATTL
Tch!
On, marishi, ei, sowaka...
ZRRRRRRRRRRRRRR

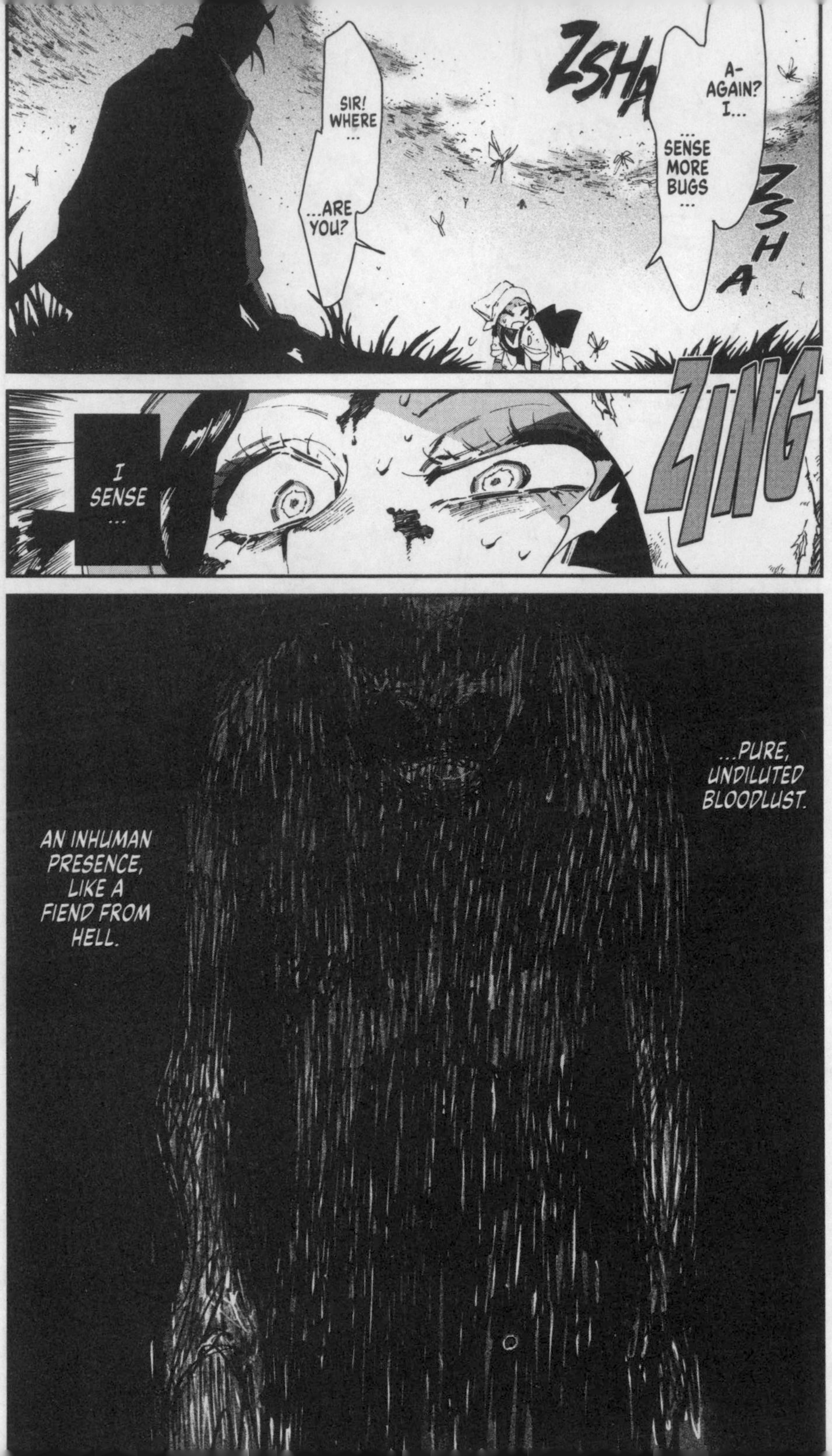
ZSHA
A- AGAIN? I... ...SENSE MORE BUGS...
ZSHA
SIR! WHERE...
...ARE YOU?
ZING
I SENSE...
...PURE, UNDILUTED BLOODLUST.
AN INHUMAN PRESENCE, LIKE A FIEND FROM HELL.

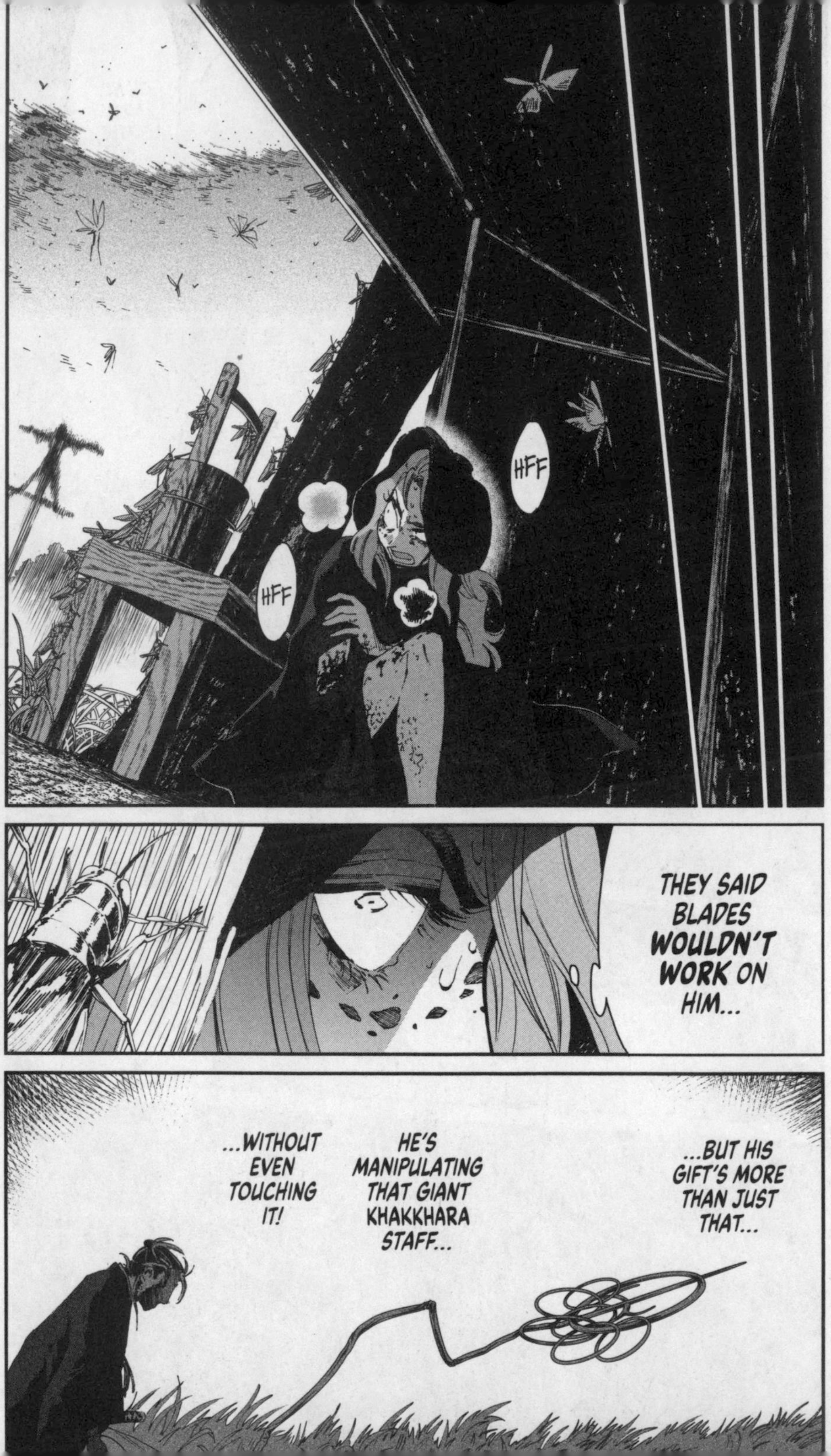
HFF
HFF
THEY SAID BLADES WOULDN'T WORK ON HIM...
...BUT HIS GIFT'S MORE THAN JUST THAT...
HE'S MANIPULATING THAT GIANT KHAKKHARA STAFF...
...WITHOUT EVEN TOUCHING IT!

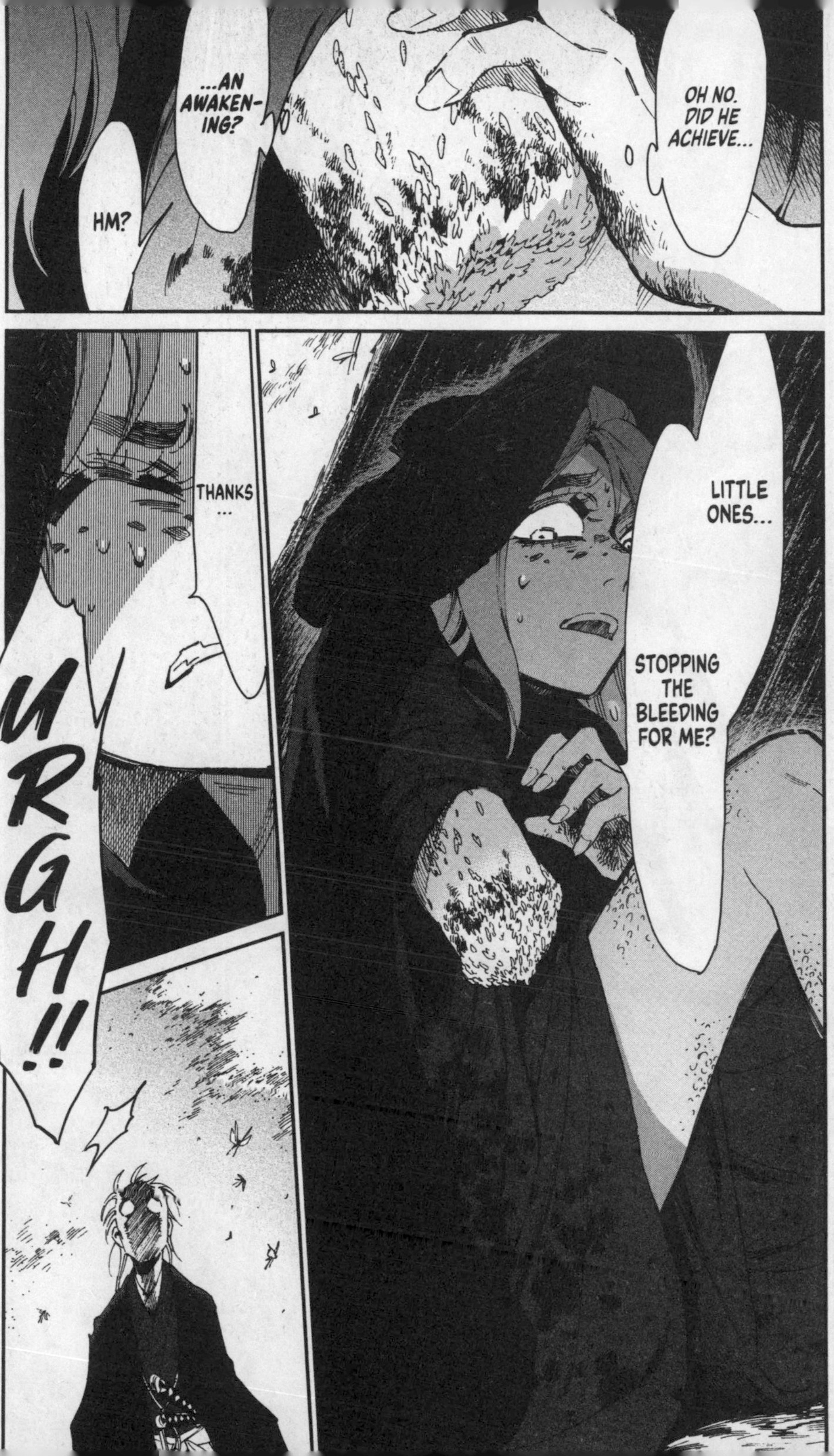
OH NO. DID HE ACHIEVE...
...AN AWAKEN-ING?
HM?
LITTLE ONES...
STOPPING THE BLEEDING FOR ME?
THANKS...
URGH!!

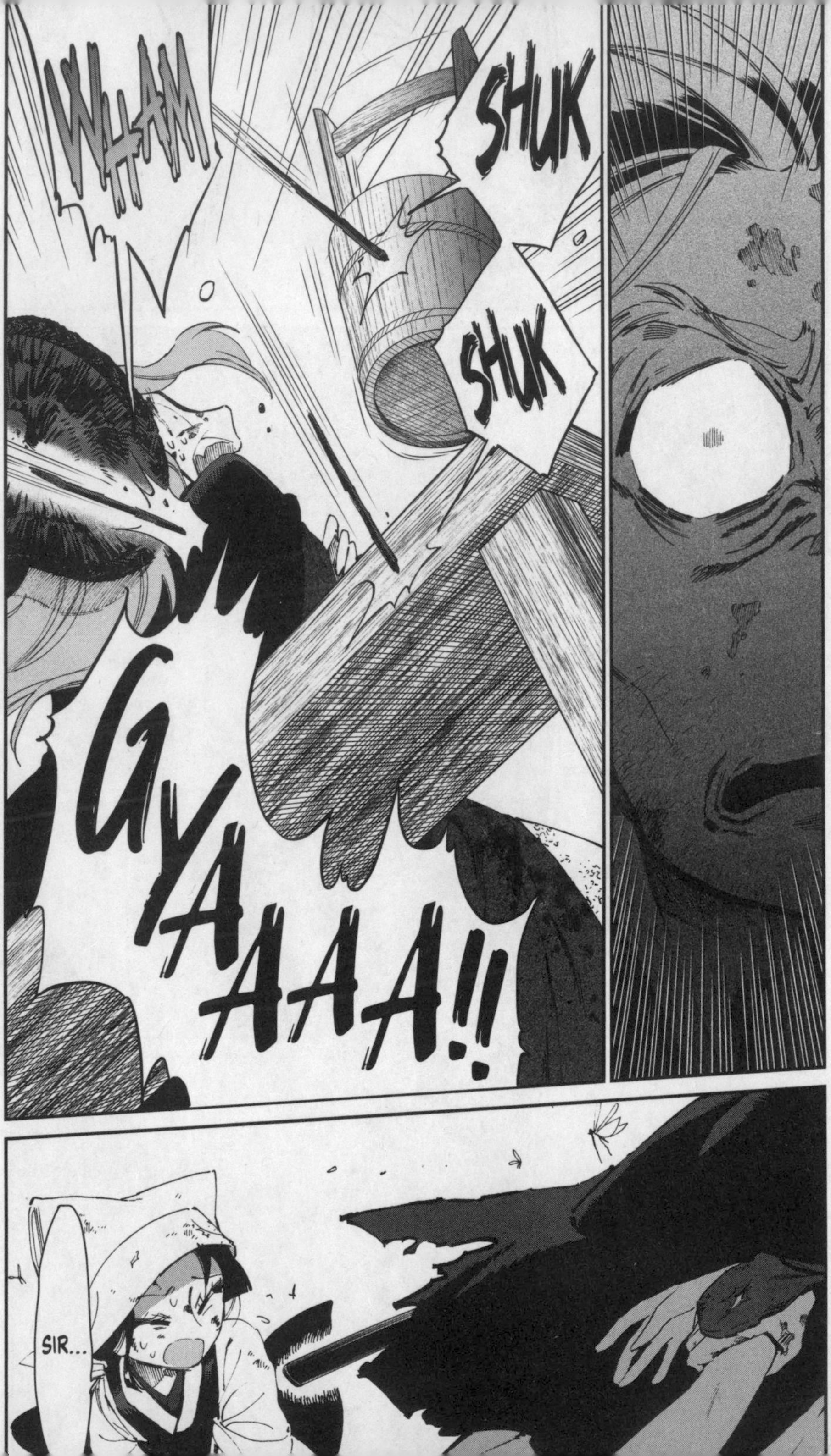
SHUK
SHUK
WHAM
GYAAAAA!!
SIR...

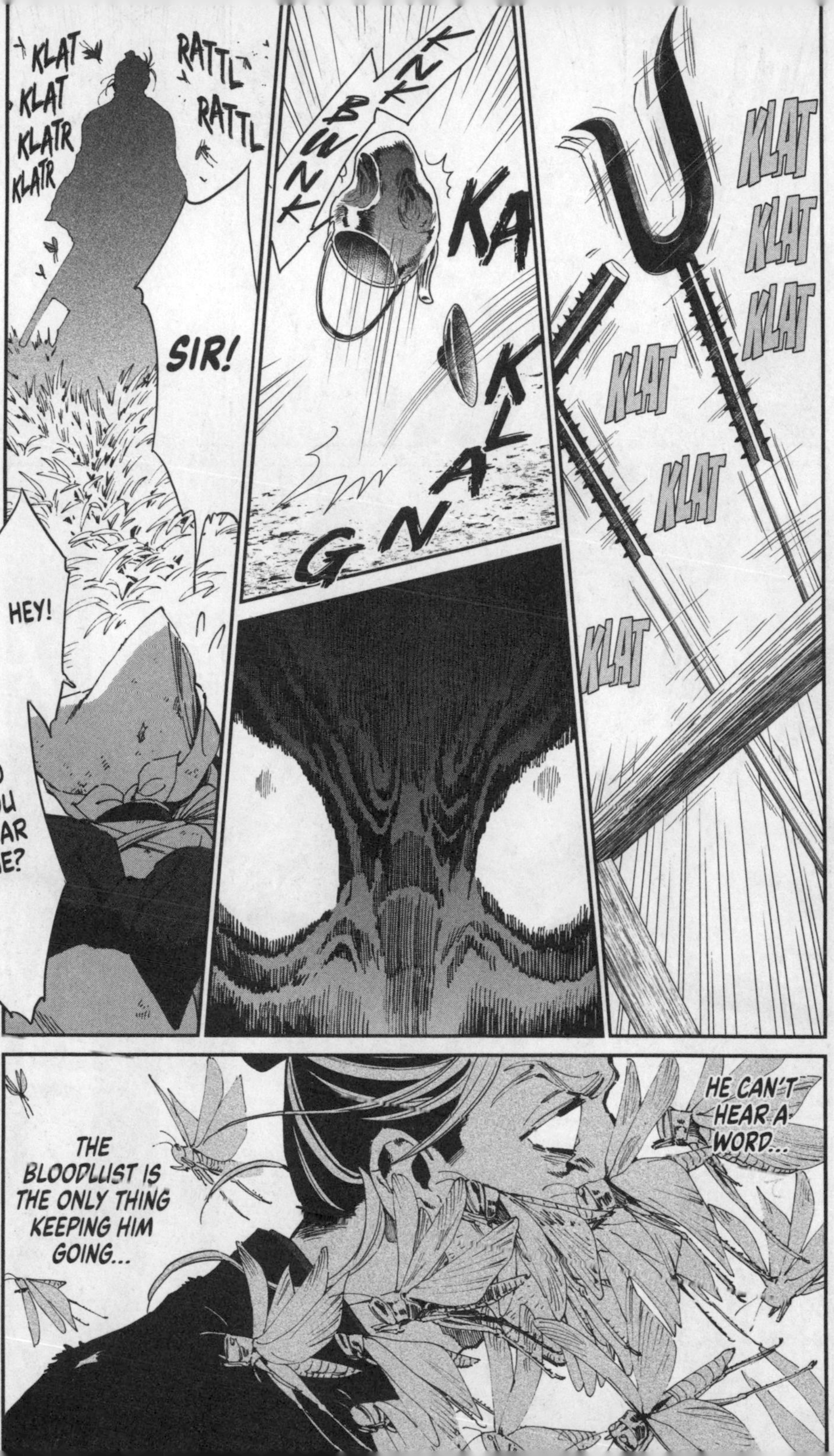
KLAT
KLAT
KLAT
KLAT
KLAT
KLAT
KLAT
KNK
BWNK
KA
KLANG
KLAT
KLAT
KLATR
KLATR
RATTL
RATTL
SIR!
HEY!
DO YOU HEAR ME?
HE CAN'T HEAR A WORD...
THE BLOODLUST IS THE ONLY THING KEEPING HIM GOING...

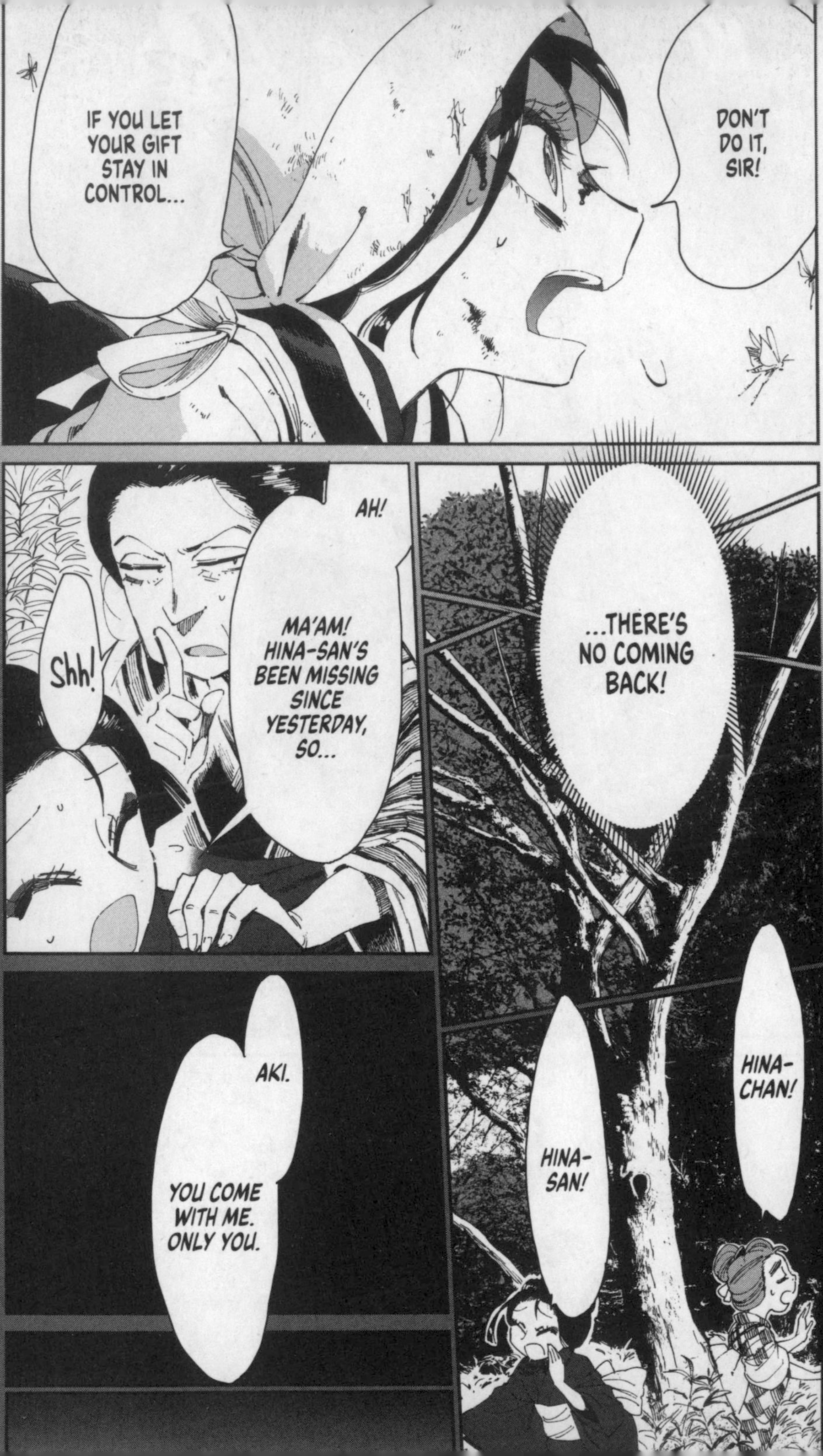
DON'T DO IT, SIR!
IF YOU LET YOUR GIFT STAY IN CONTROL...
...THERE'S NO COMING BACK!
HINA-CHAN!
HINA-SAN!
AH!
MA'AM! HINA-SAN'S BEEN MISSING SINCE YESTERDAY, SO...
Shh!
AKI.
YOU COME WITH ME. ONLY YOU.

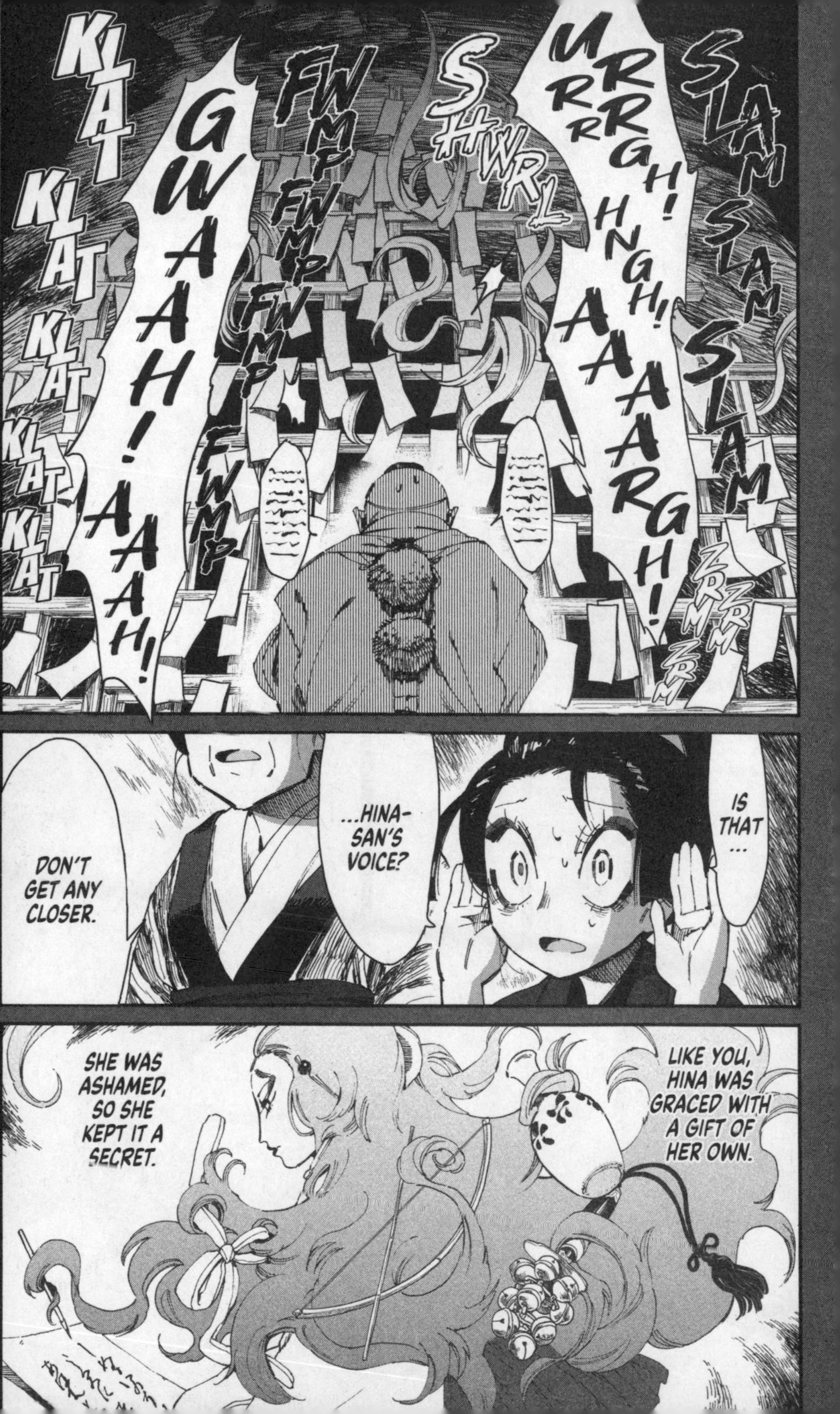
SLAM SLAM SLAM
ZRMM ZRMM ZRMM
URRRRRGH! HNGH HNGH! AAAAARGH!
SHWRL
FWMP FWMP FWMP FWMP
GWAAAH! AAAAH!
KLAT KLAT KLAT KLAT KLAT KLAT
IS THAT...
...HINA-SAN'S VOICE?
DON'T GET ANY CLOSER.
LIKE YOU, HINA WAS GRACED WITH A GIFT OF HER OWN.
SHE WAS ASHAMED, SO SHE KEPT IT A SECRET.

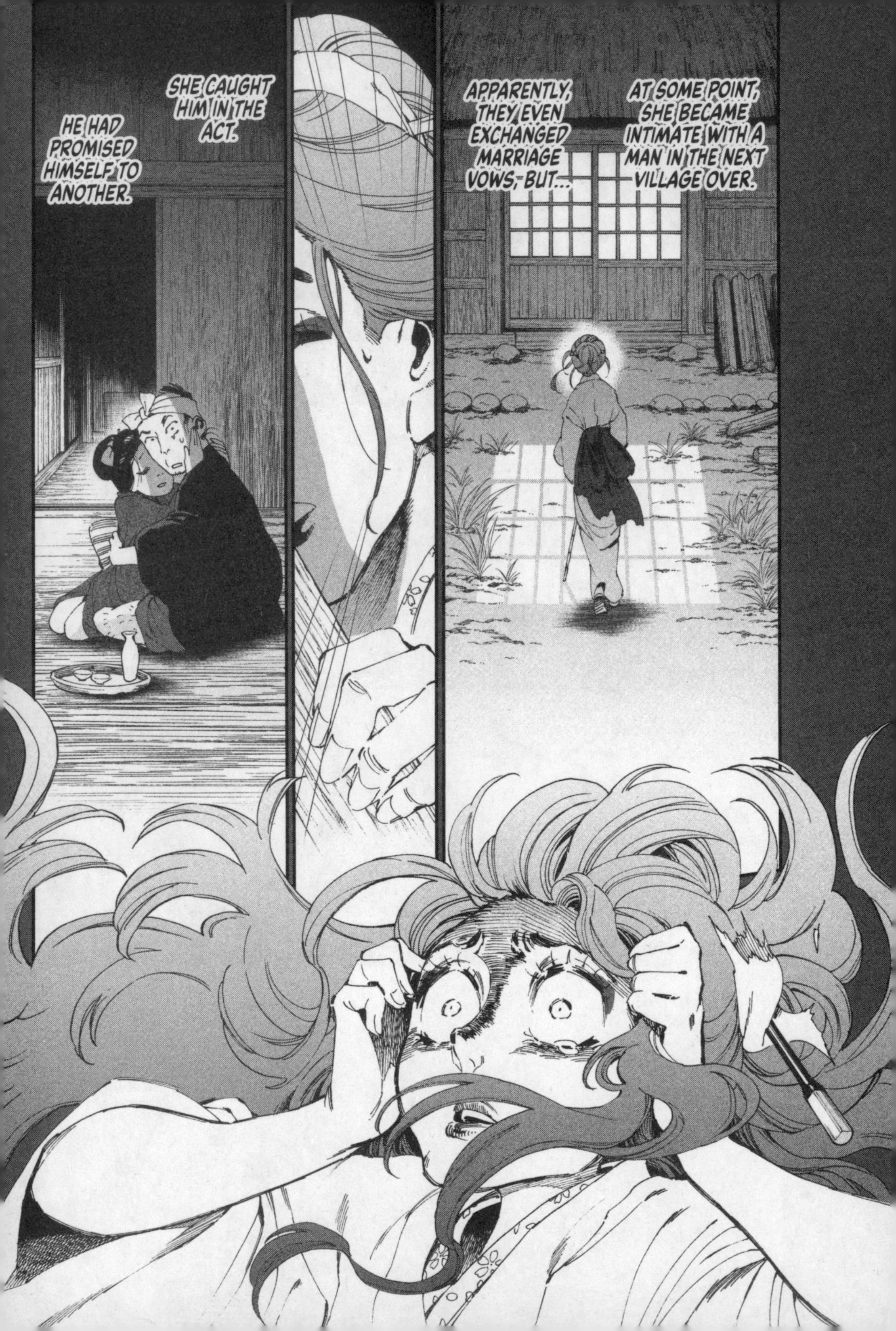
AT SOME POINT, SHE BECAME INTIMATE WITH A MAN IN THE NEXT VILLAGE OVER.
APPARENTLY, THEY EVEN EXCHANGED MARRIAGE VOWS, BUT...
SHE CAUGHT HIM IN THE ACT.
HE HAD PROMISED HIMSELF TO ANOTHER.

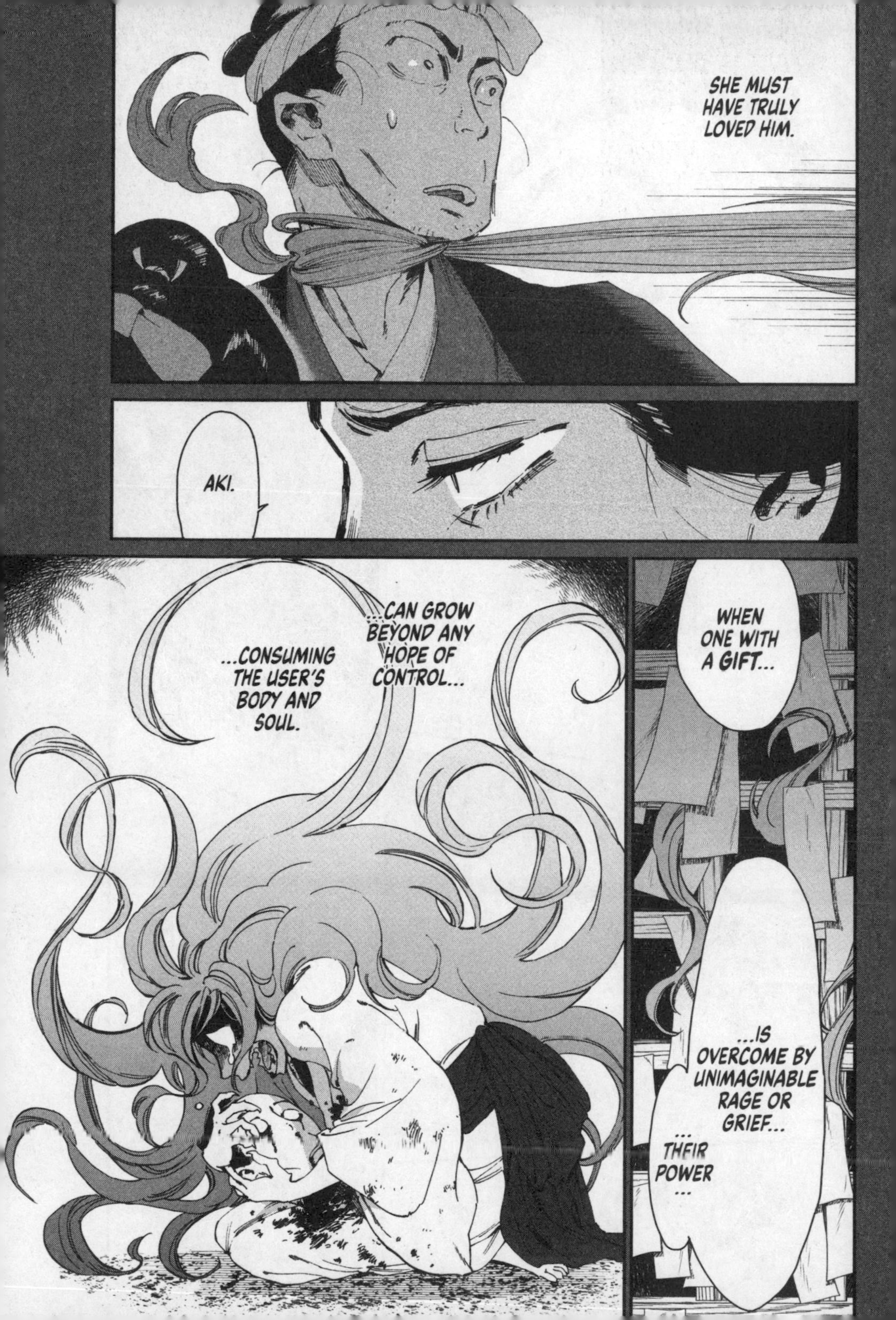
SHE MUST HAVE TRULY LOVED HIM.
AKI.
WHEN ONE WITH A GIFT...
...IS OVERCOME BY UNIMAGINABLE RAGE OR GRIEF...
...THEIR POWER...
...CAN GROW BEYOND ANY HOPE OF CONTROL...
...CONSUMING THE USER'S BODY AND SOUL.

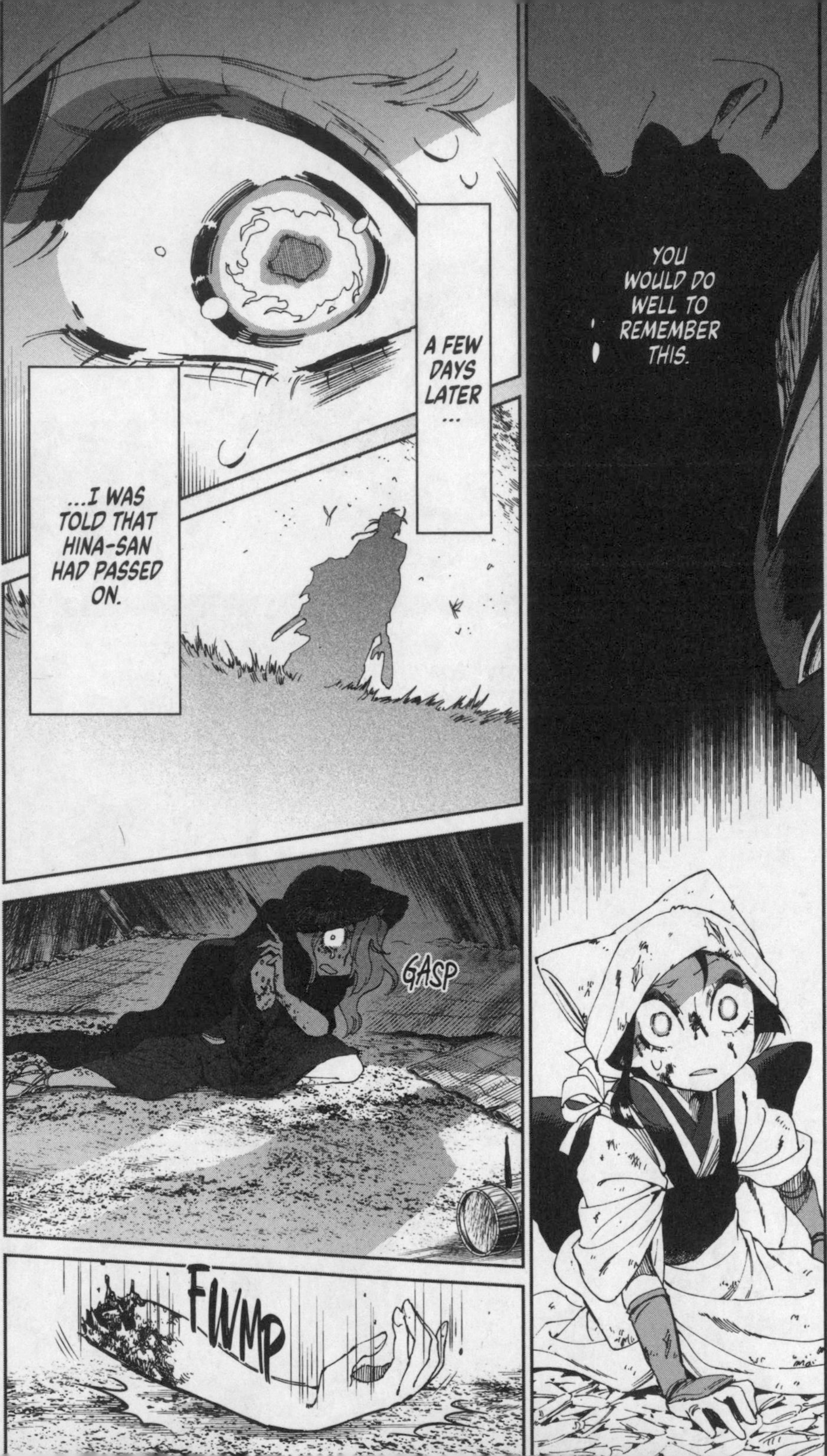
YOU WOULD DO WELL TO REMEMBER THIS.
A FEW DAYS LATER ...
...I WAS TOLD THAT HINA-SAN HAD PASSED ON.
GASP
FWMP

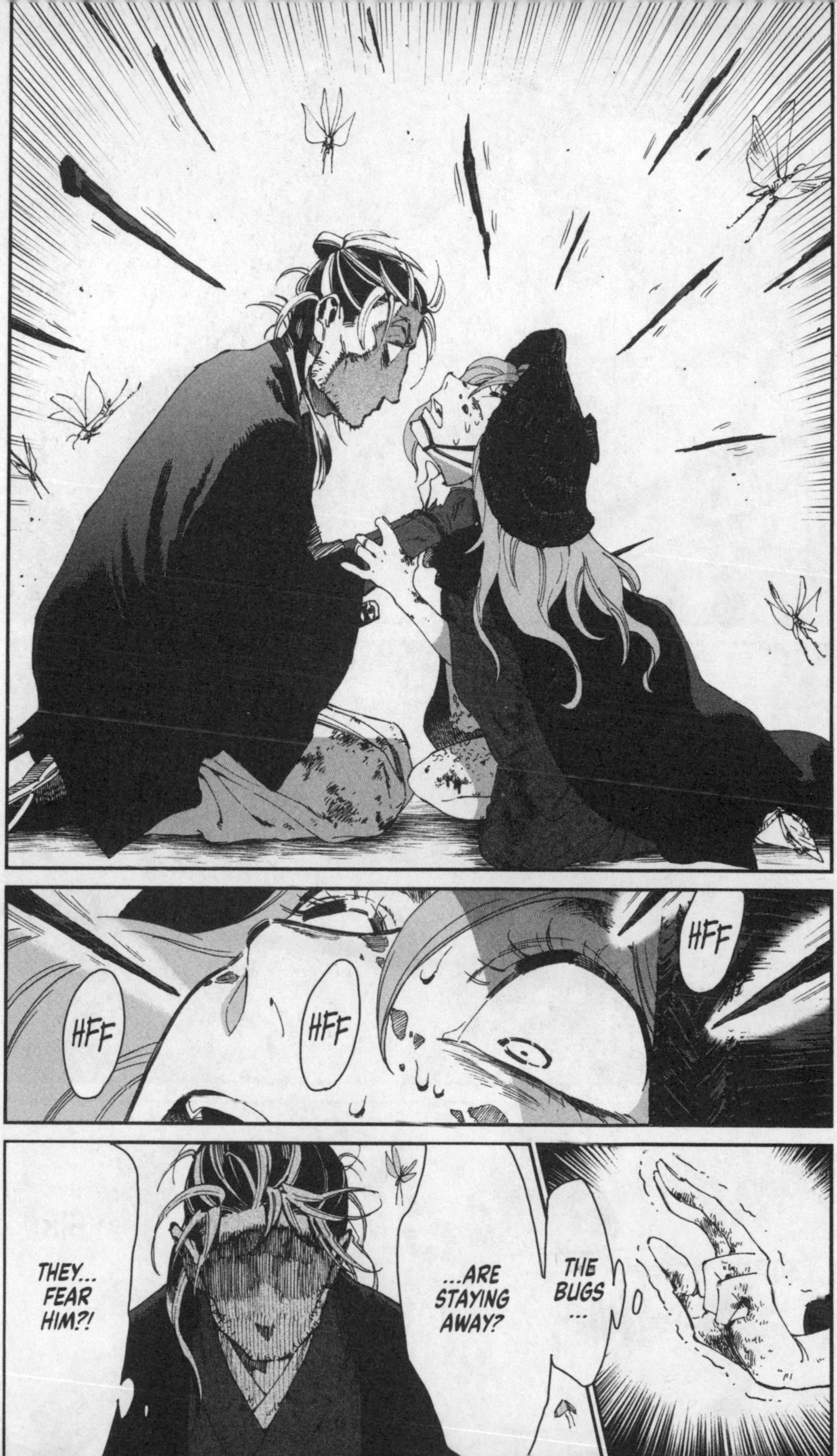
HFF
HFF
HFF
THE BUGS...
...ARE STAYING AWAY?
THEY... FEAR HIM?!

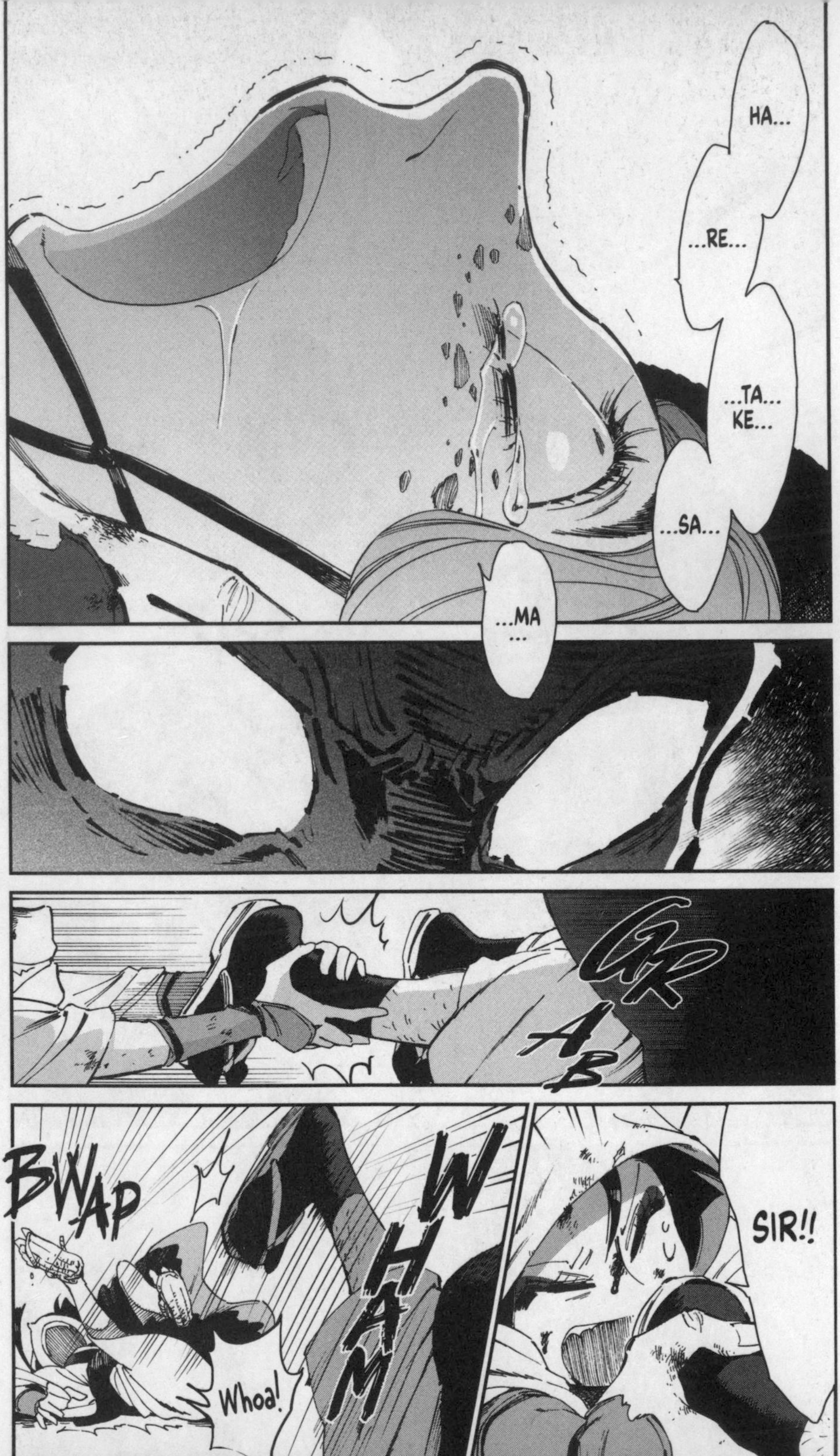
HA...
...RE...
...TA...
KE...
...SA...
...MA
...
GRAB
SIR!!
WHAM
BWAP
Whoa!

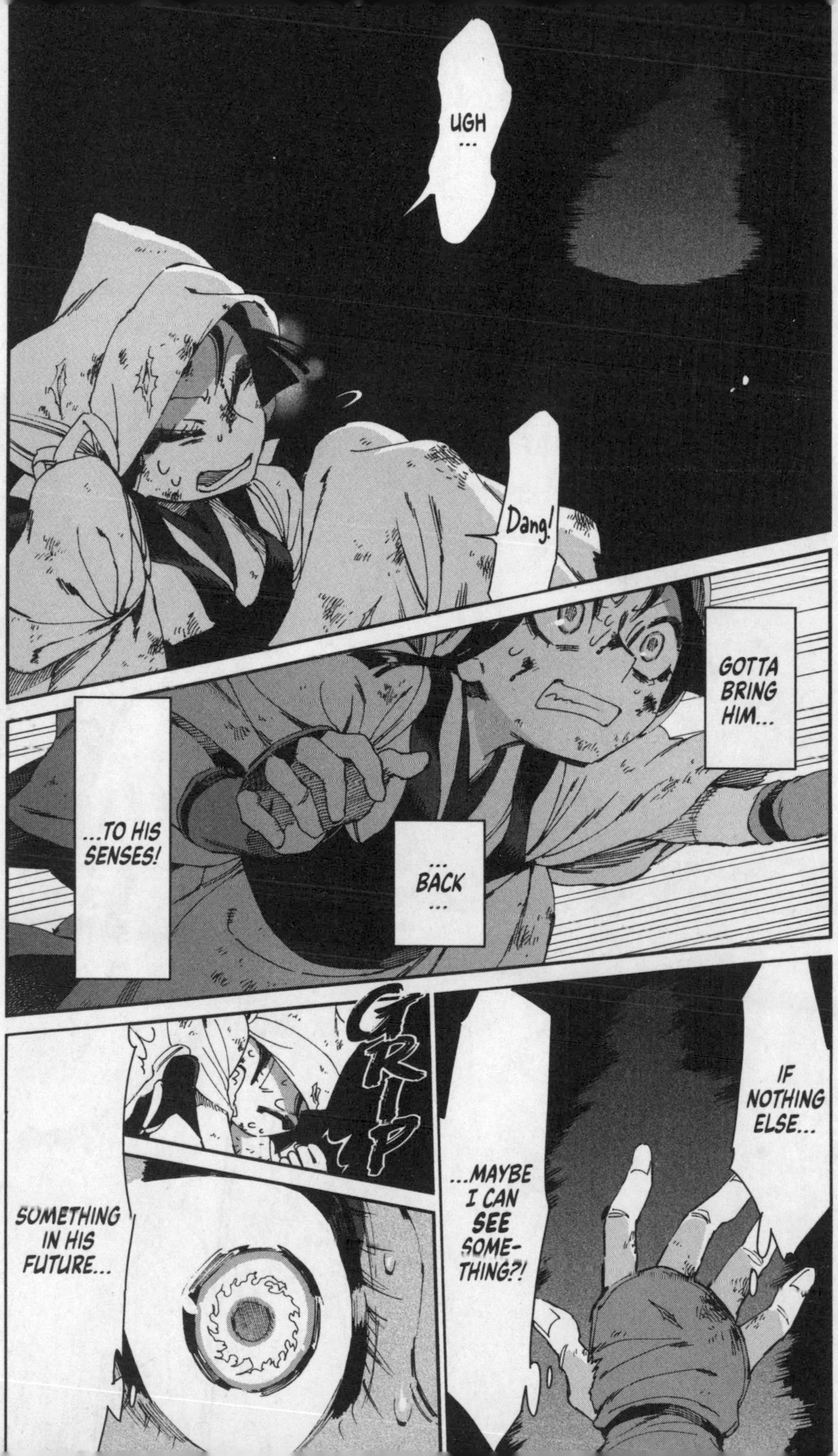
UGH ...
Dang!
GOTTA BRING HIM...
... BACK ...
...TO HIS SENSES!
GRIP
IF NOTHING ELSE...
...MAYBE I CAN SEE SOME-THING?!
SOMETHING IN HIS FUTURE...

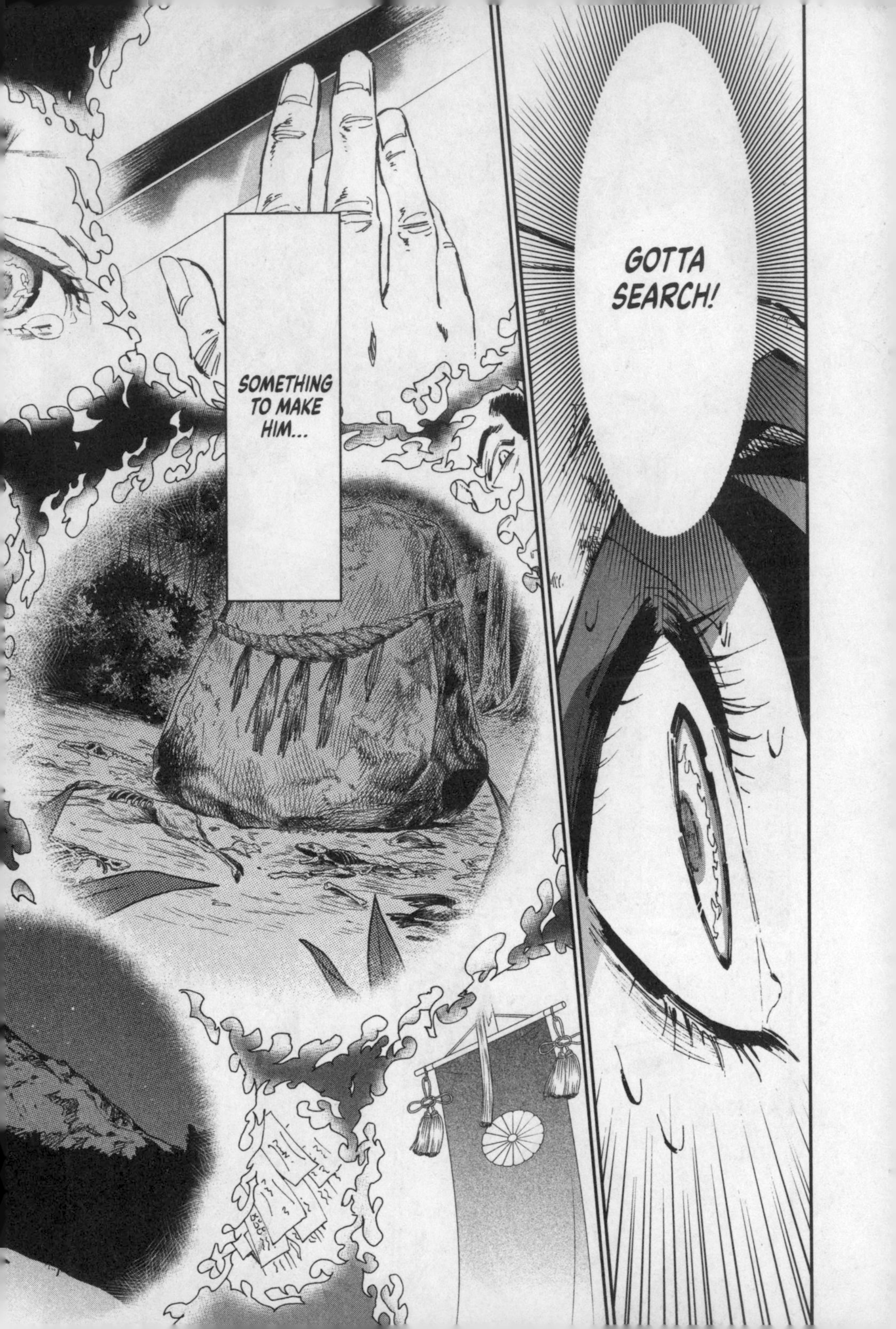
GOTTA SEARCH!
SOMETHING TO MAKE HIM...

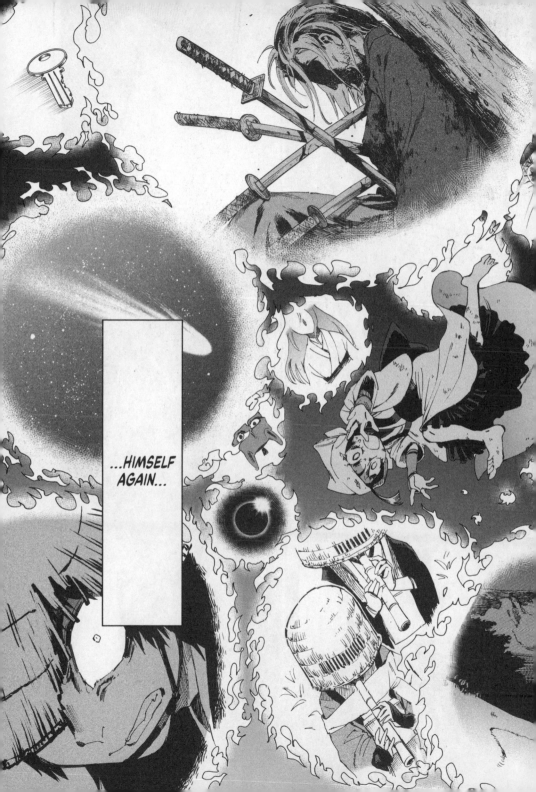

...HIMSELF
AGAIN...

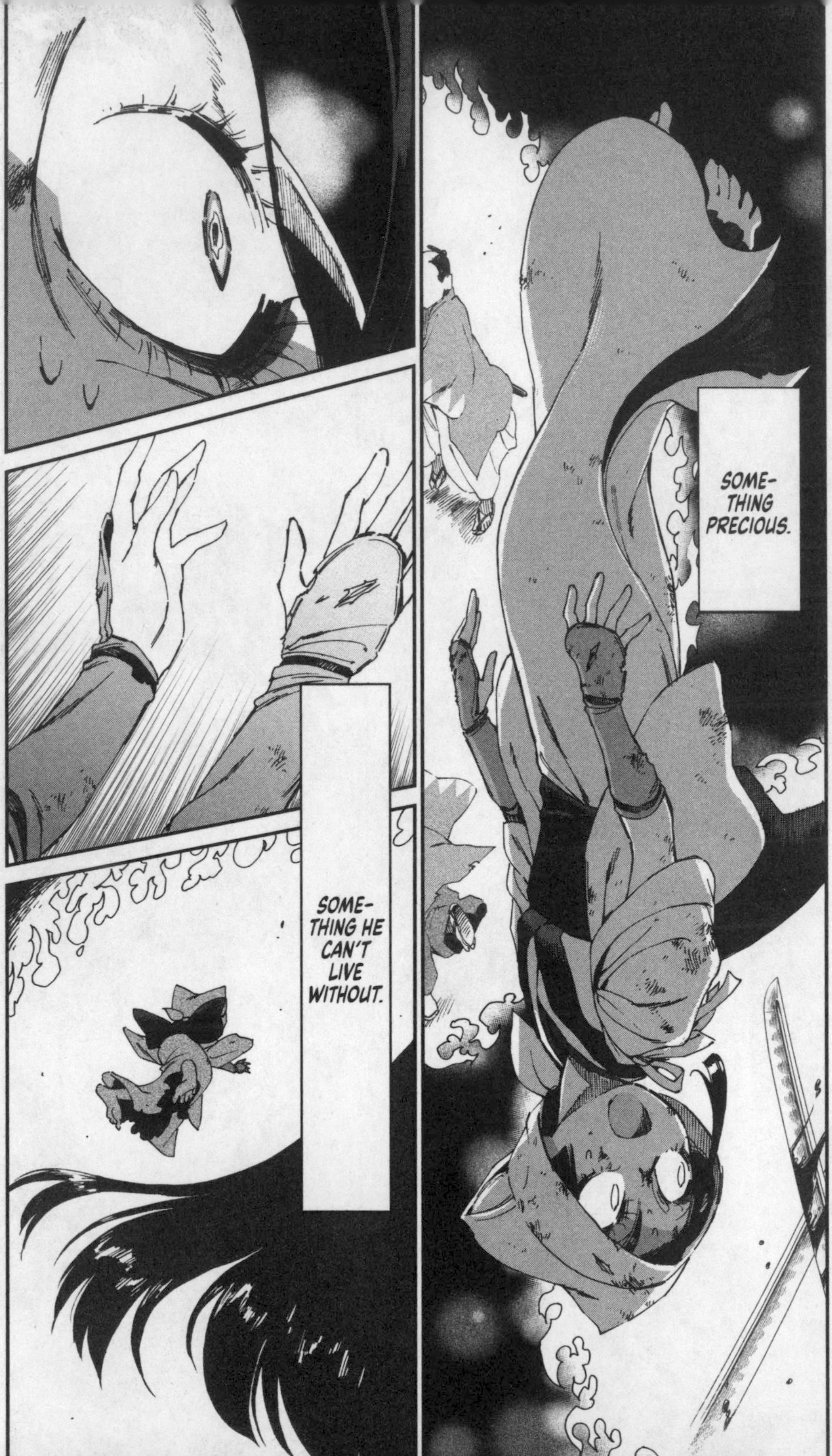
SOME-THING PRECIOUS.
SOME-THING HE CAN'T LIVE WITHOUT.

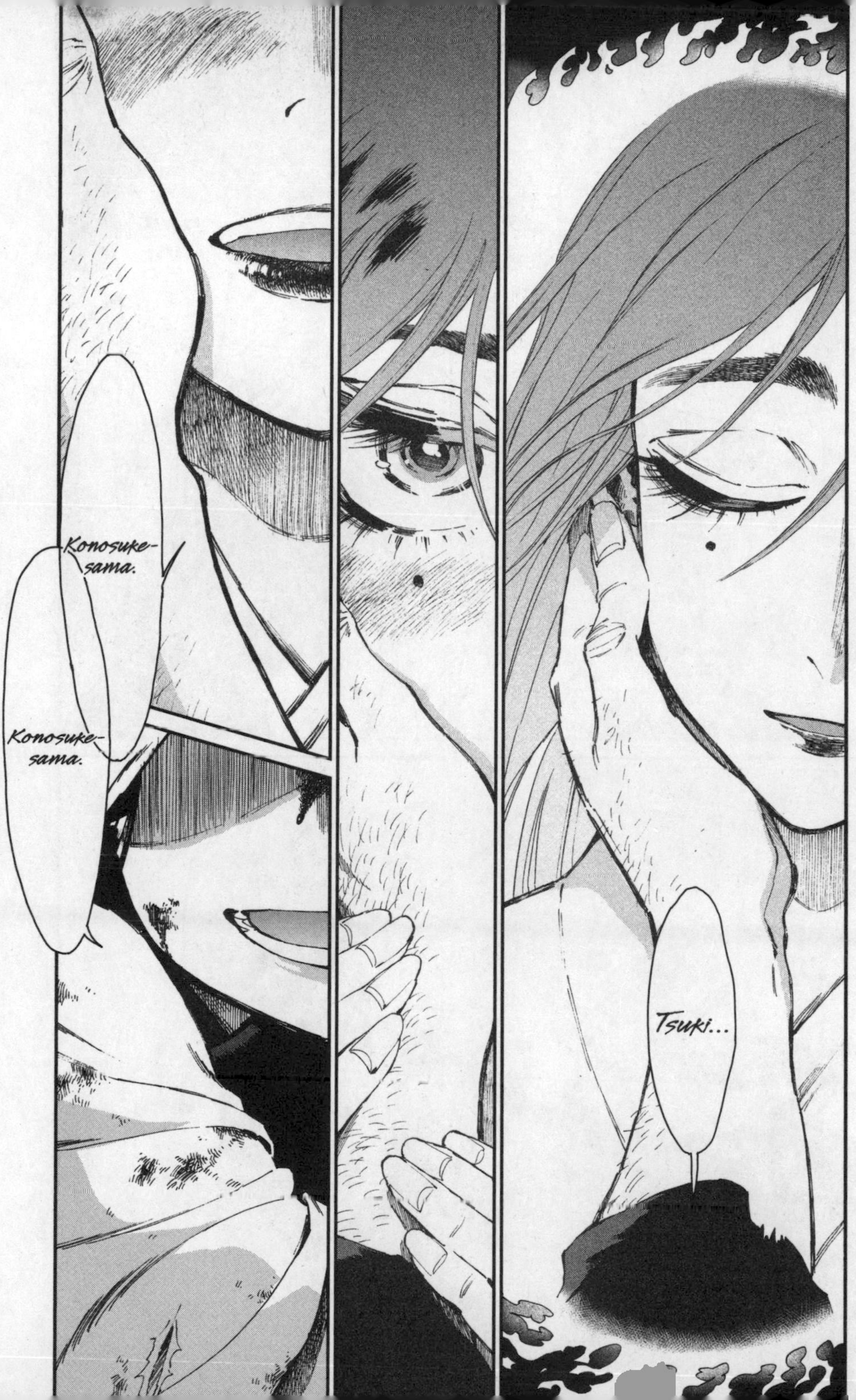
Tsuki...
Konosuke-sama.
Konosuke-sama.

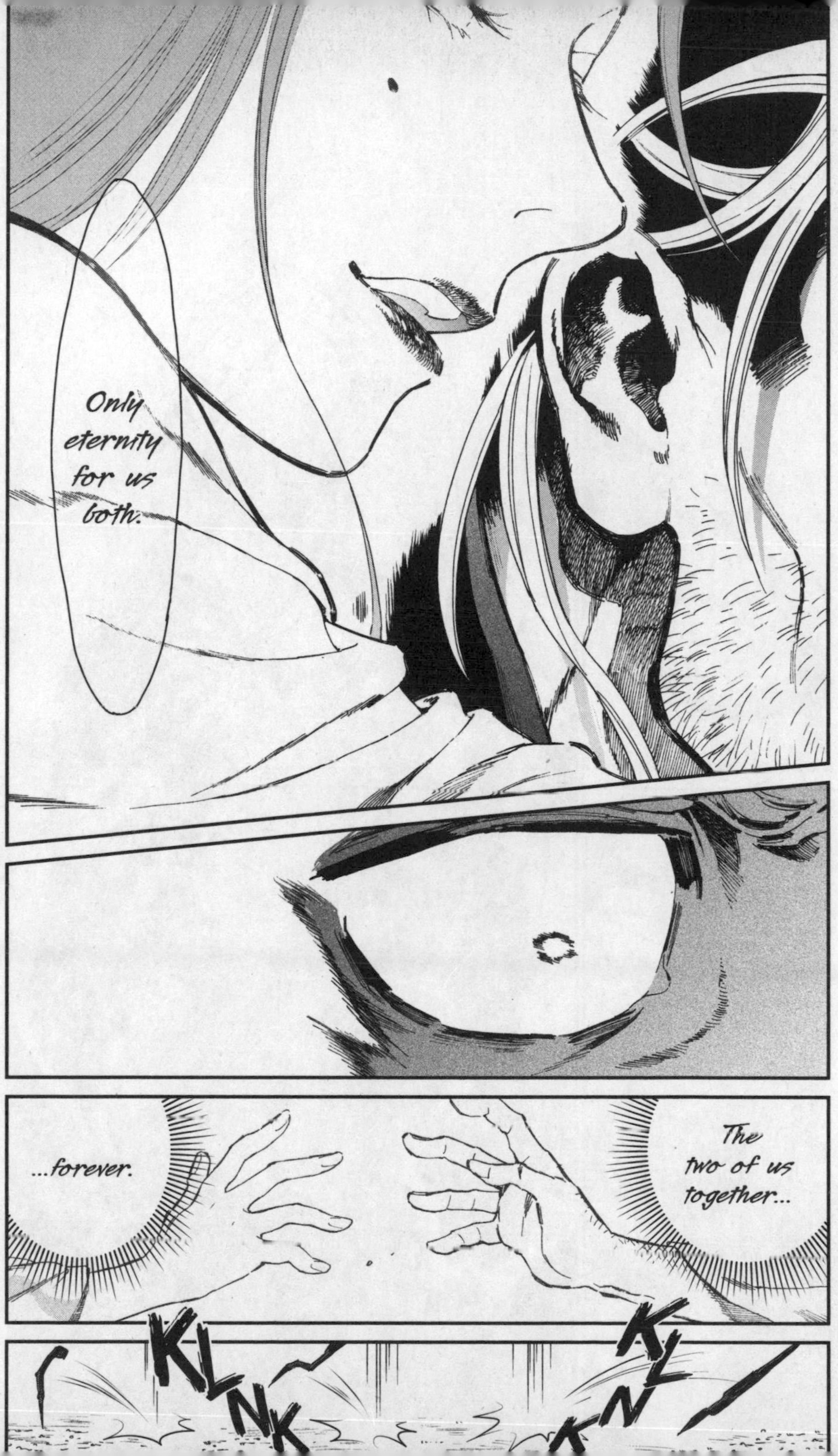
Only eternity for us both.
The two of us together...
...forever.
KLNK
KLNK

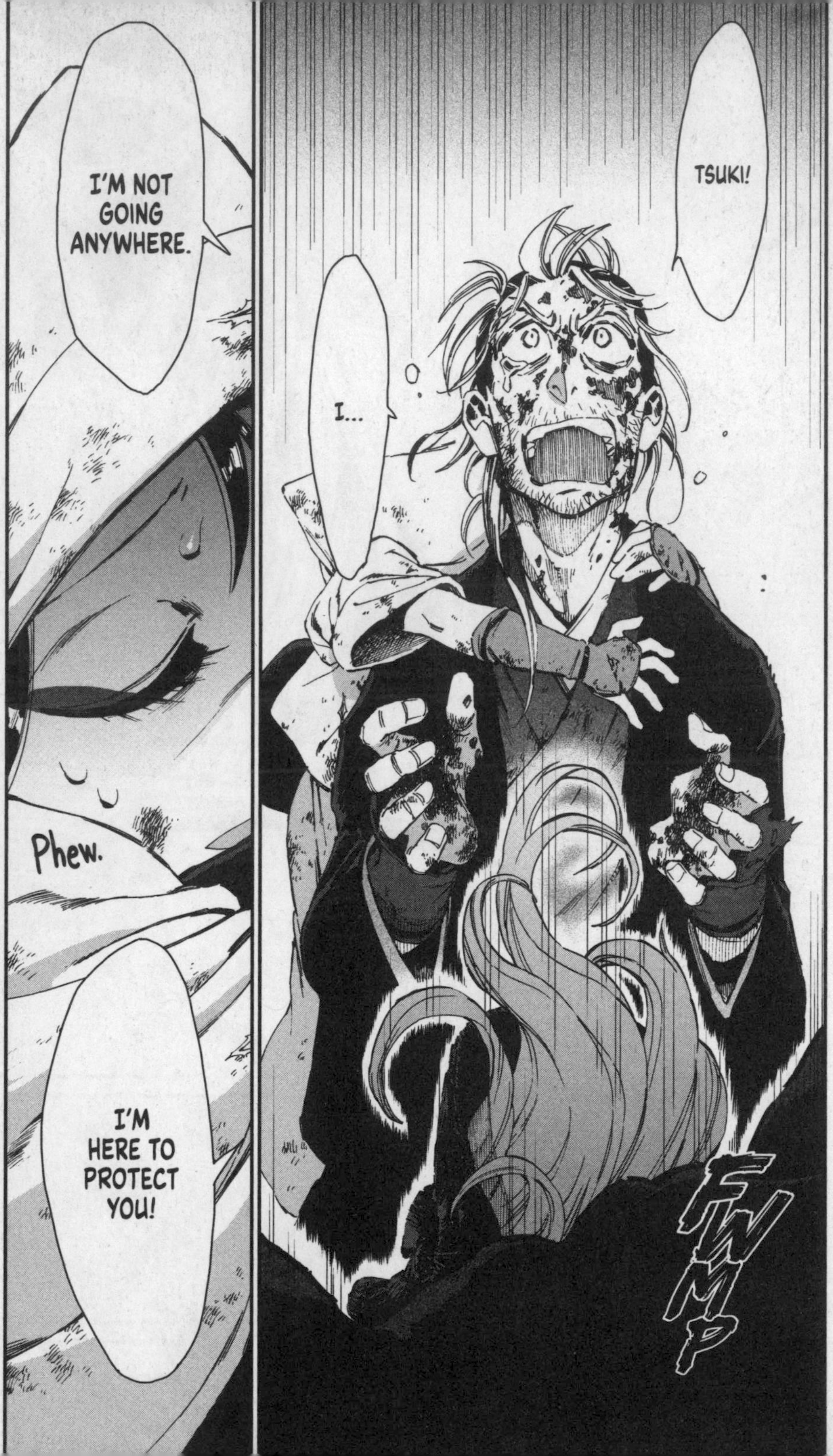
TSUKI!
I...
FWMP
I'M NOT GOING ANYWHERE.
Phew.
I'M HERE TO PROTECT YOU!

STEEL *of the* CELESTIAL SHADOWS

Trivia of the Celestial Shadows

#4 Ichiko Mediums

- A.K.A. *miko*. They were different in a number of ways from the miko maidens employed by shrines in modern times.
- There were also ichiko/miko who lived at specific shrines (as priests' wives, for instance), but plenty of ichiko traveled around making a living by performing seances or reading fortunes, like Aki. Another type worked as prostitutes.

Note
※There were also royal court ichiko, but I'm only writing about civilian ichiko here.

- The word differed from region to region. They were called azasamiko, *ichiko*, *itako*, *nonou* (in Shinano), *onakate* (in Yamagata), *shiroyumoji*, *itaka*, *kongarasate*, and so on.
- Many would carry around *gehobako* boxes full of tools.
- Ichiko never had a central organization, the way onmyoji and Shugendo practitioners did. They would defer to their husbands, fathers, or foster fathers.
- Many would end up marrying religious figures such as onmyoji or Shugendo practitioners.

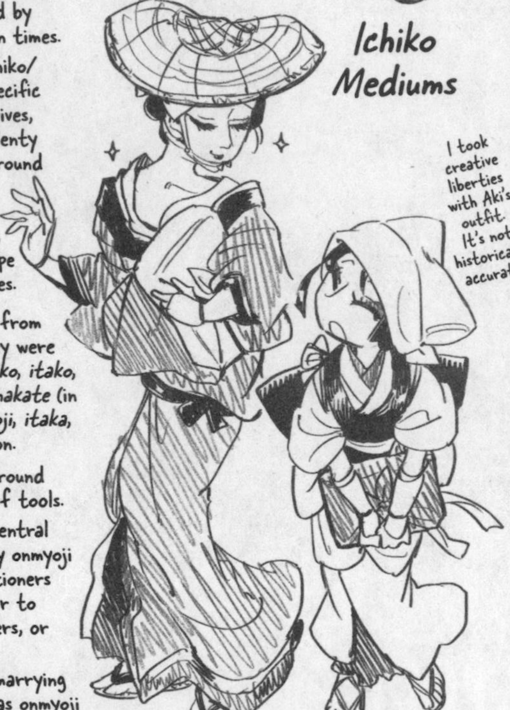

I took creative liberties with Aki's outfit. It's not historically accurate.

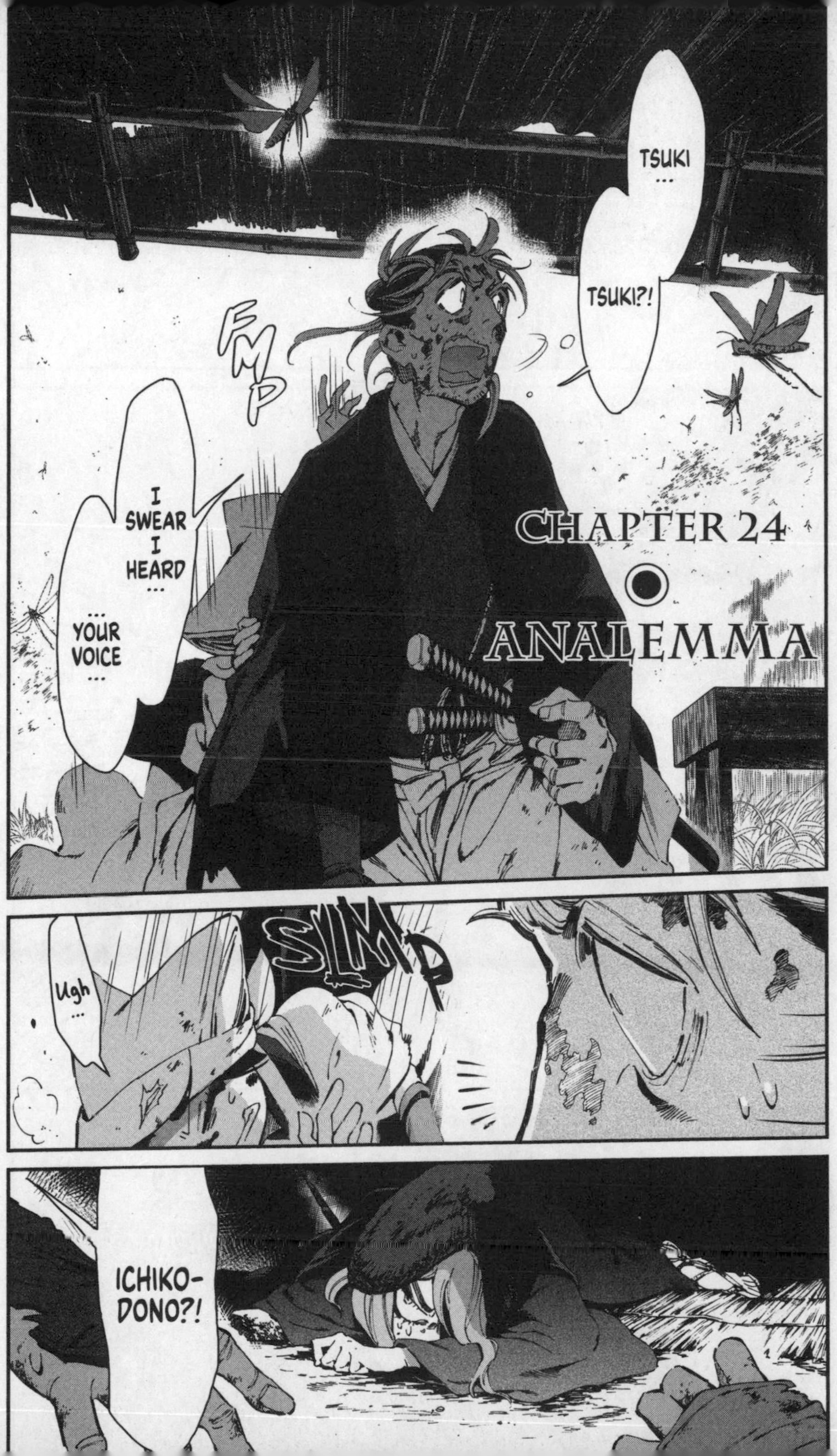
TSUKI ...
TSUKI?!
FMP
I SWEAR I HEARD ...
... YOUR VOICE ...
CHAPTER 24
ANALEMMA
SLMP
Ugh ...
ICHIKO-DONO?!

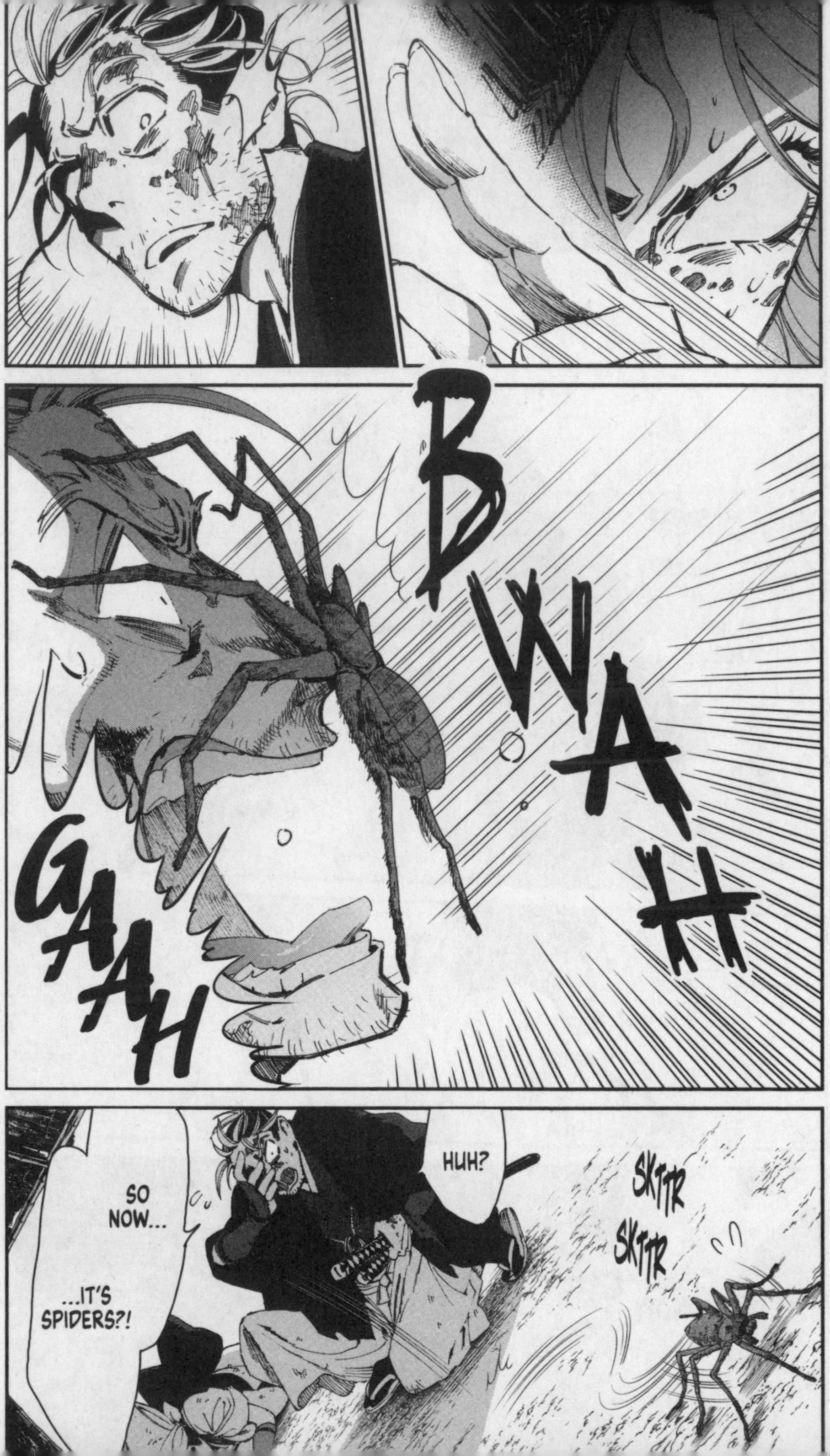
BWAH
GAAH
SKTTR
SKTTR
HUH?
SO NOW...
...IT'S SPIDERS?!

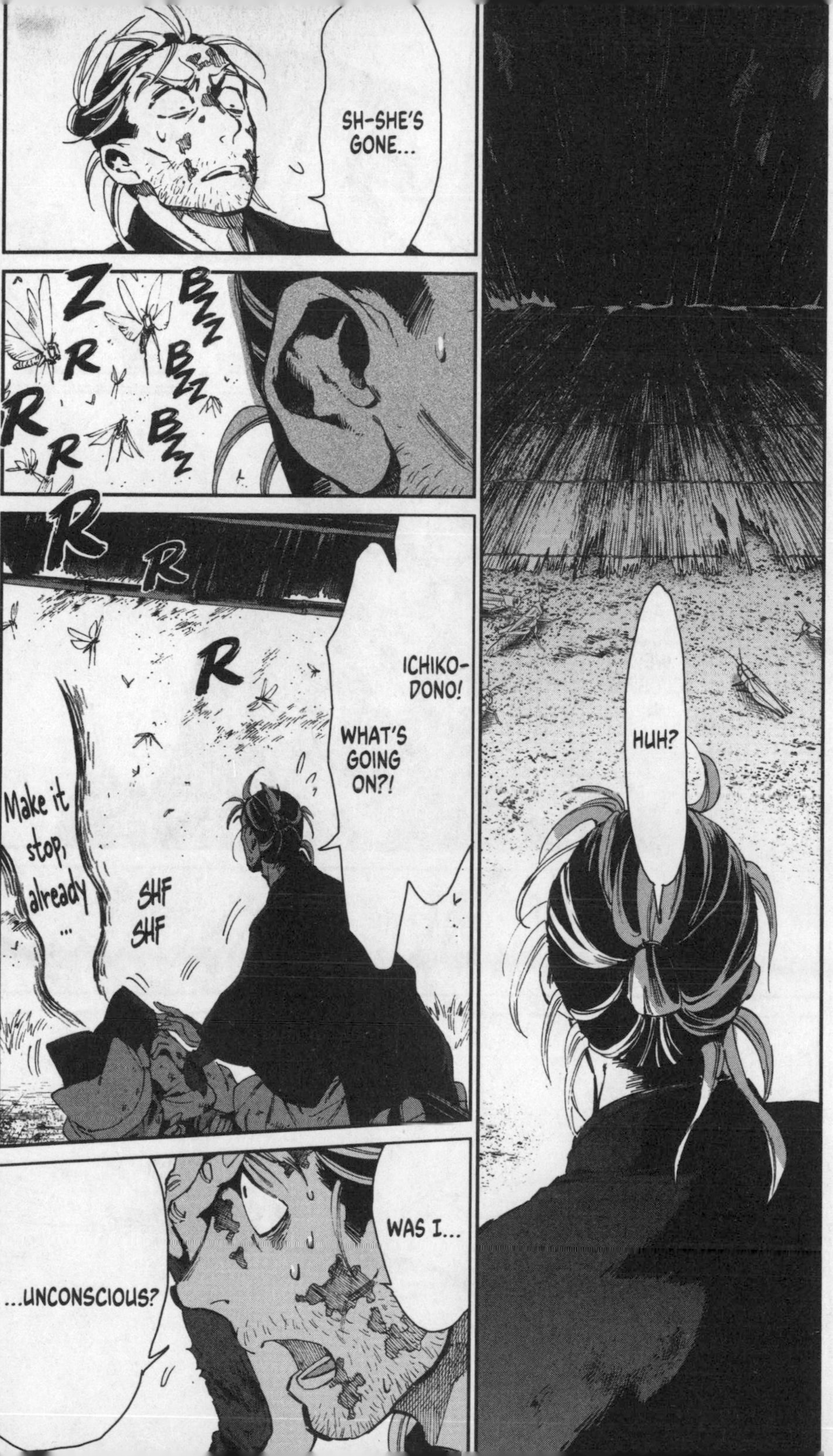
HUH?
SH-SHE'S GONE...
Z
BZZ
R
BZZ
R
BZZ
R
R
R
R
ICHIKO-DONO!
WHAT'S GOING ON?!
Make it stop, already ...
SHF SHF
WAS I...
...UNCONSCIOUS?

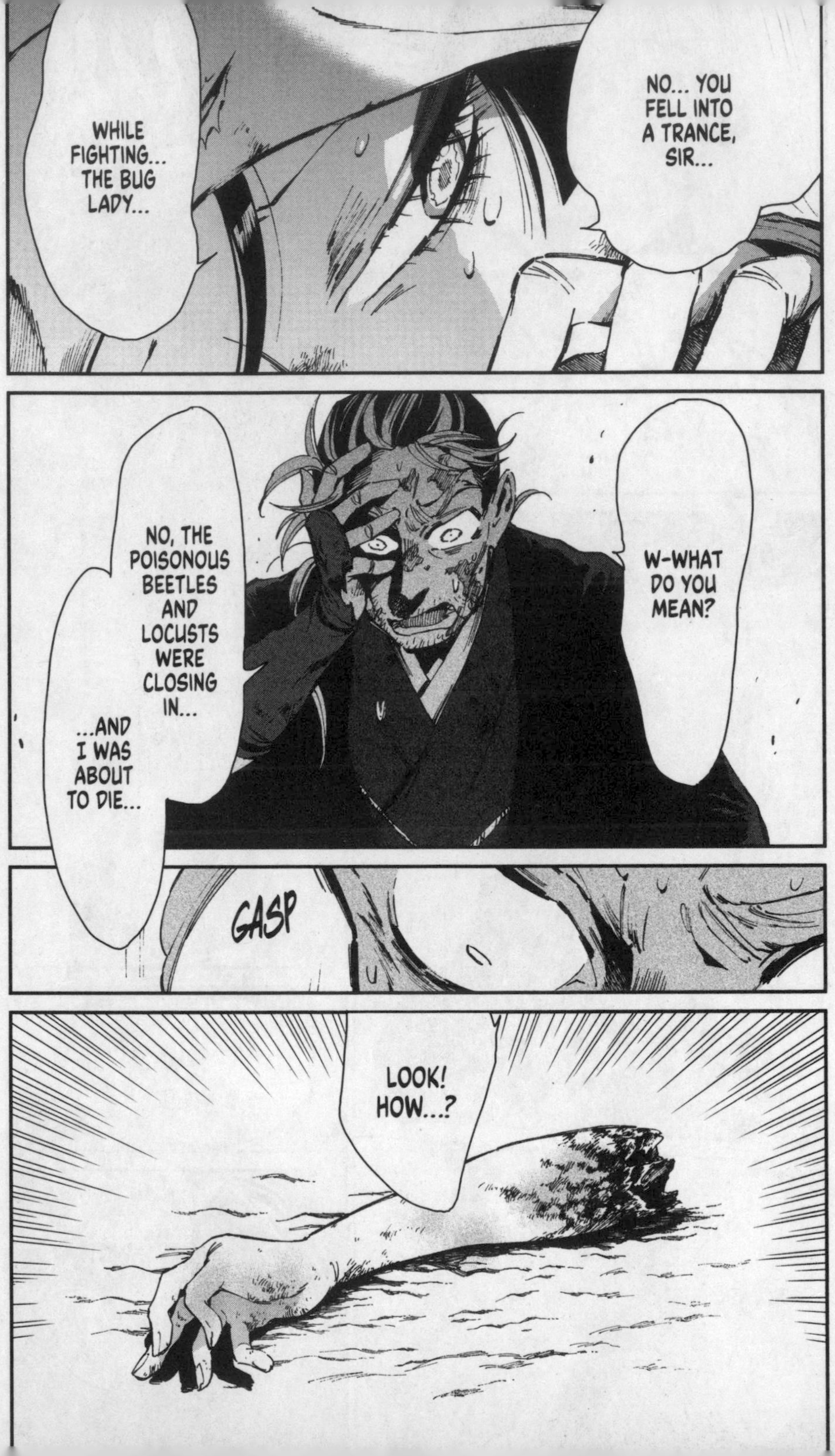
NO... YOU FELL INTO A TRANCE, SIR...
WHILE FIGHTING... THE BUG LADY...
W-WHAT DO YOU MEAN?
NO, THE POISONOUS BEETLES AND LOCUSTS WERE CLOSING IN...
...AND I WAS ABOUT TO DIE...
GASP
LOOK! HOW...?

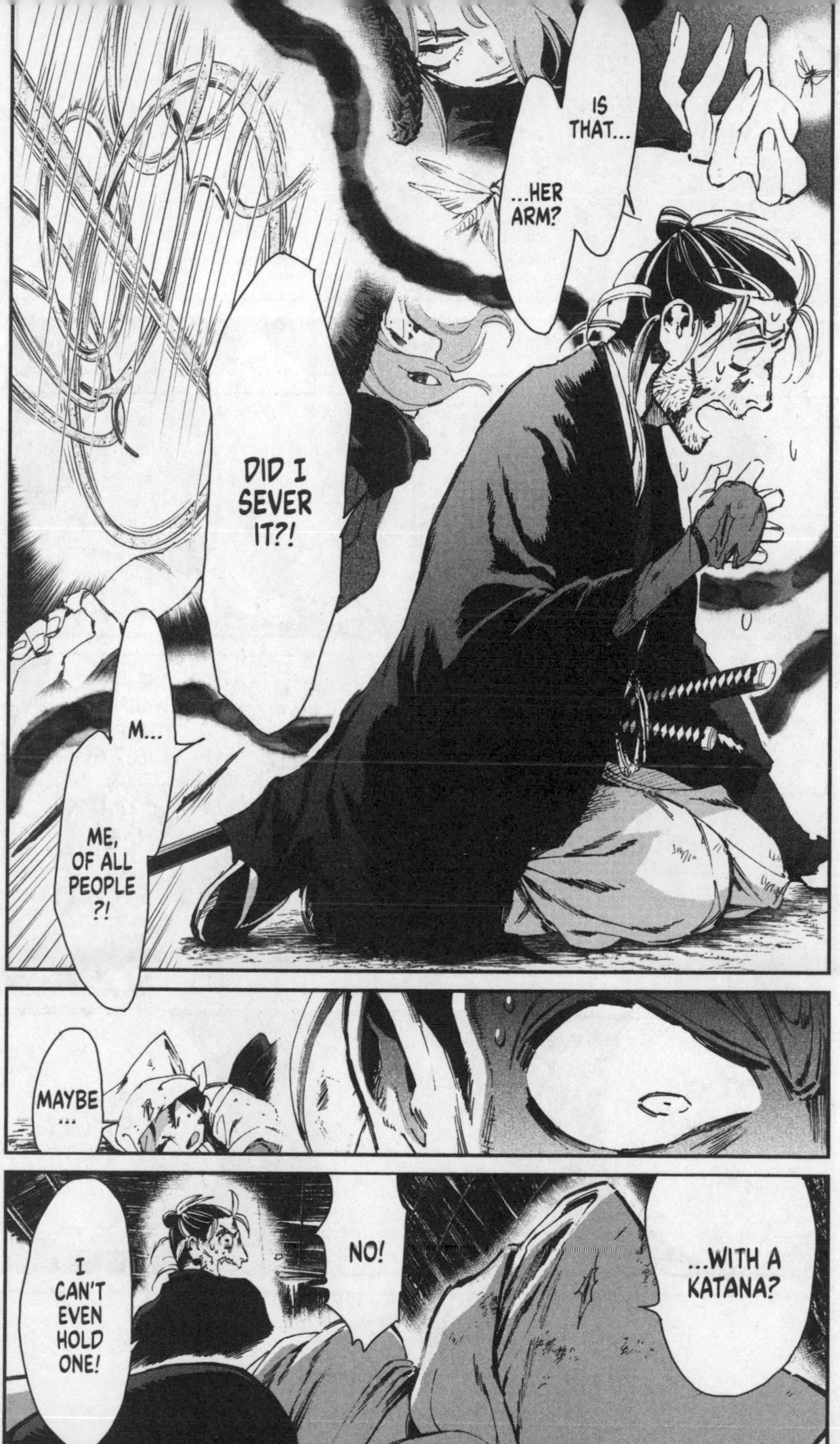
IS THAT...
...HER ARM?
DID I SEVER IT?!
M...
ME, OF ALL PEOPLE ?!
MAYBE ...
...WITH A KATANA?
NO!
I CAN'T EVEN HOLD ONE!

FROM BIRTH, I'VE NEVER BEEN ABLE...

...TO TOUCH A SWORD, NOR ANY METAL...

AND ANY ATTEMPT TO DO SO...

...ALWAYS ENDS WITH...

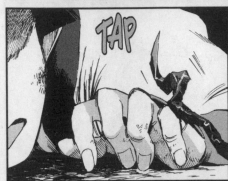

TAP

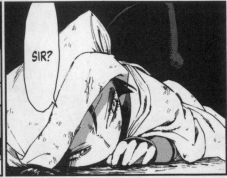

SIR?

...

MM, SURE...

MUCH LIKE THAT IRON NAIL YOU HOLD...

...THE METAL WARPING ITSELF TO REJECT ME.

CAN'T HAVE BEEN EASY FOR YOU, SIR.

A SAMURAI WITH A GIFT LIKE THAT?

A GIFT?

AND YOUR ABILITY...

A SPECIAL POWER, SIR.

YES.

WANNA TRY IT OUT?

...GIVES ME AN IDEA.

HE'S TOO MUCH...

DAMN...

...WITH A GIFT LIKE THAT...

...HE'LL THREATEN HARETAKE-SAMA'S ULTIMATE DREAM!

BUT IF I LET HIM GET AWAY...

...HARETAKE-SAMA!

I WON'T LET HIM SCREW IT ALL UP...

...BEATEN TO DEATH OR WORSE IN THAT BACKWATER SHITHOLE OF A TEMPLE!

...I WOULD'VE BEEN...

IF YOU HADN'T LIFTED ME OUT OF MY MISERABLE LIFE...

FWP

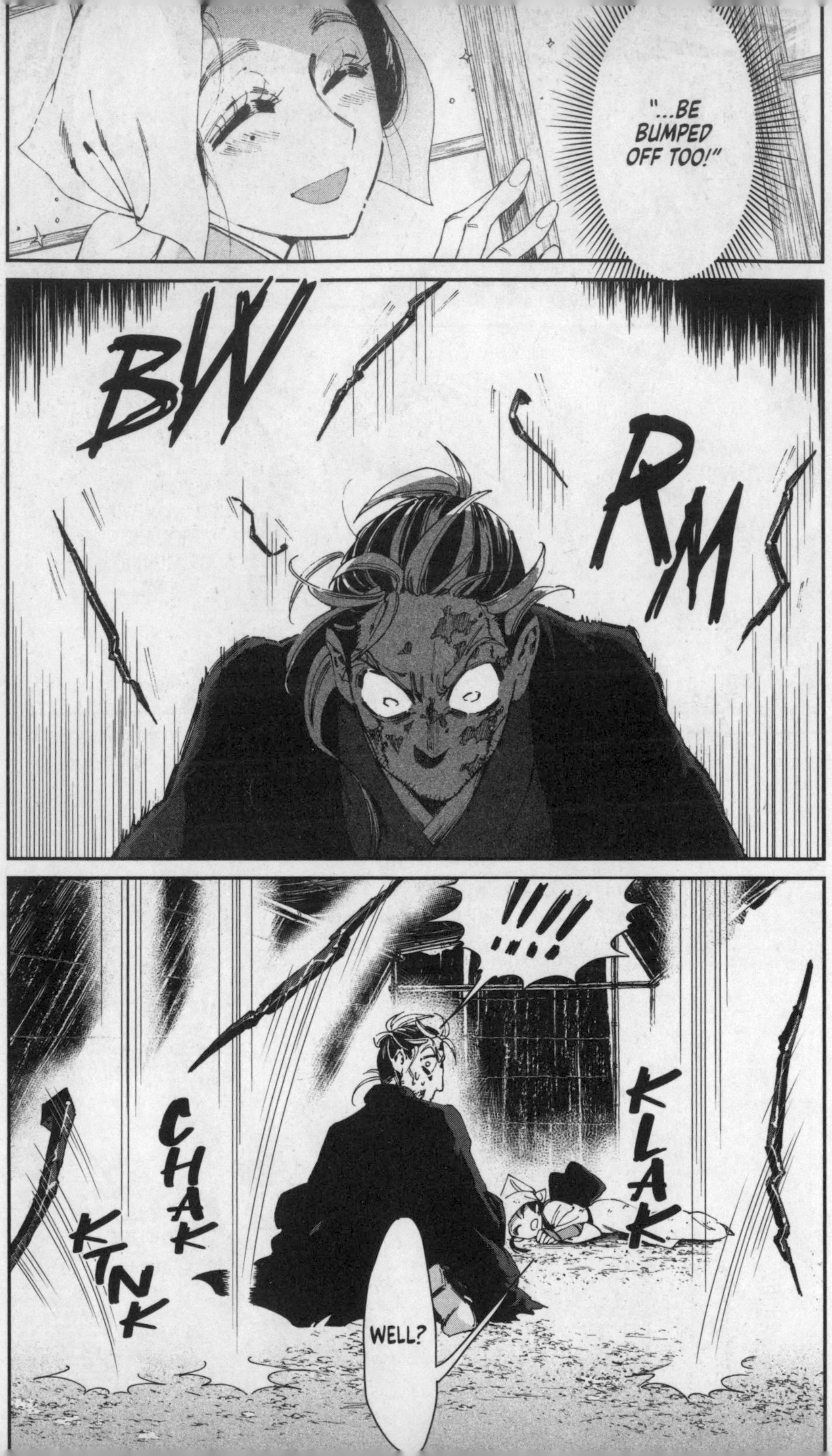
"...BE BUMPED OFF TOO!"
BW
RMS
!!!!
CHAK
KTNK
KLAK
WELL?

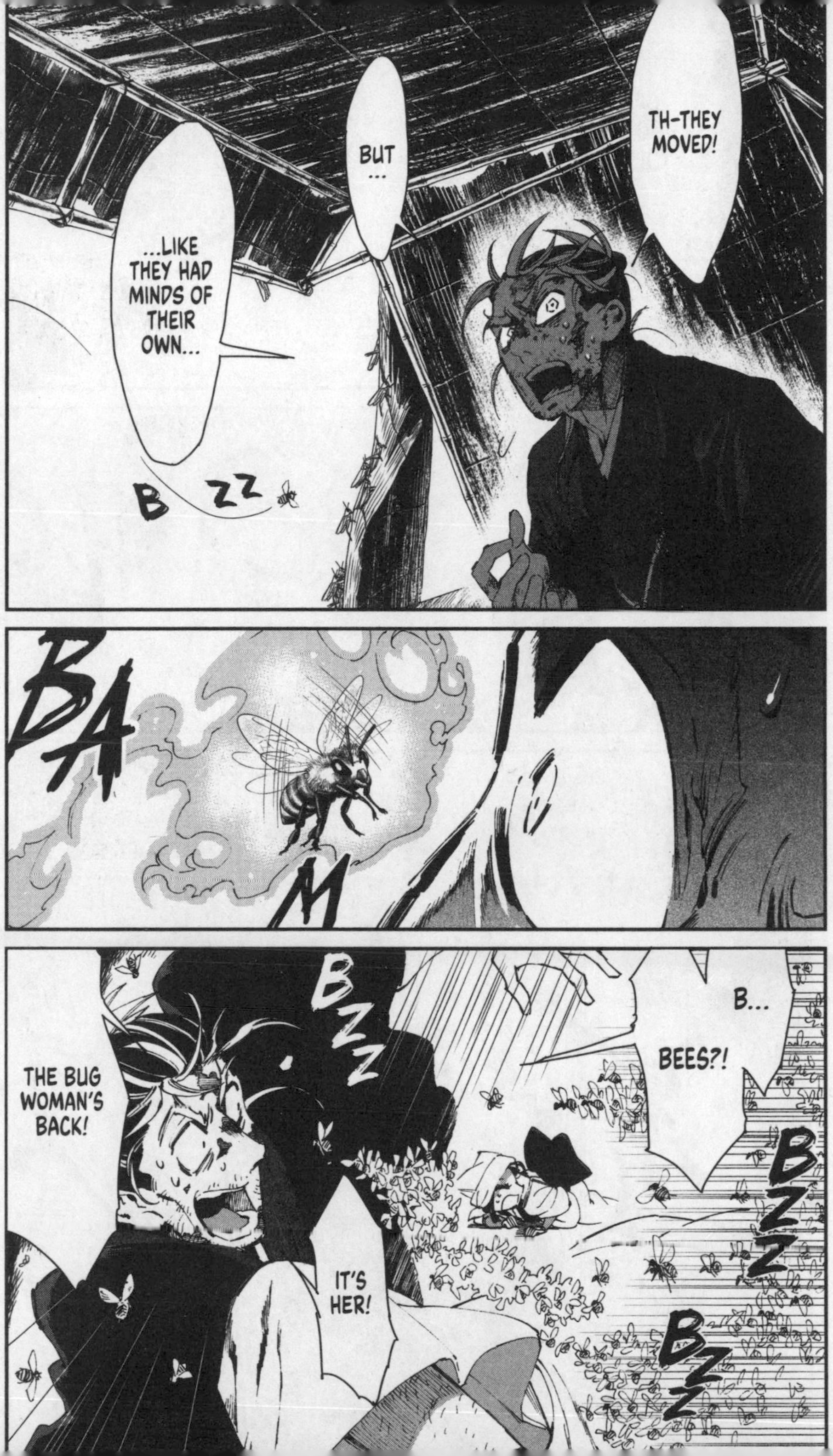
TH-THEY MOVED!
BUT ...
...LIKE THEY HAD MINDS OF THEIR OWN...
BZZ
BAM
B... BEES?!
BZZ
BZZ
BZZ
IT'S HER!
THE BUG WOMAN'S BACK!

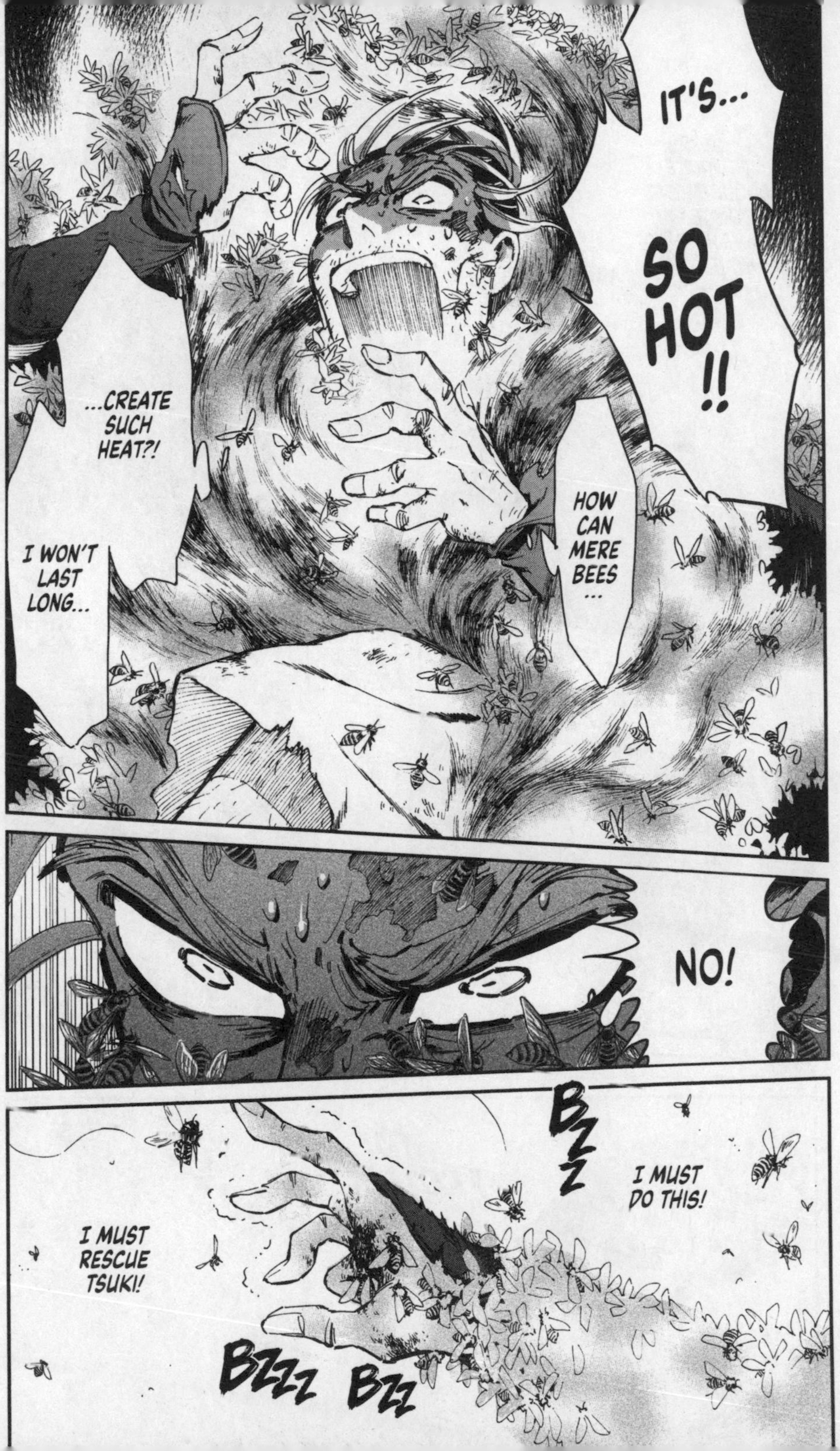
IT'S...
SO HOT!!
HOW CAN MERE BEES...
...CREATE SUCH HEAT?!
I WON'T LAST LONG...
NO!
BZZZ
I MUST DO THIS!
I MUST RESCUE TSUKI!
BZZZZ BZZZ

STEEL *of the* CELESTIAL SHADOWS

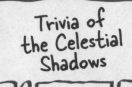

Trivia of the Celestial Shadows #⑤

Kozukappara Execution Grounds

> Even at night, it's a bright, clean train station area (I took a stroll)

- Located near Minami–Senju Station these days.

- Travelers entering Edo via Senju would have to pass by. This was intentional; they *had* to bear witness.

An *Enmei Jizo* statue was built here in memoriam of the condemned and executed. It still exists today, though it's known as the *Kubikiri Jizo* (decapitation Jizo).

- In the Bakumatsu period, samurai would casually suggest a visit to the execution grounds, as if on a dare.

- There was apparently a red–light district nearby. I'd expect there to be some spooky songs about the execution grounds from that period, but nothing turned up in my research. Maybe you'll have more luck searching?

Crucifix

Severed heads on display

Guard house

← To Sanya, Yoshiwara

Passing travelers

→ To Senjuohashi

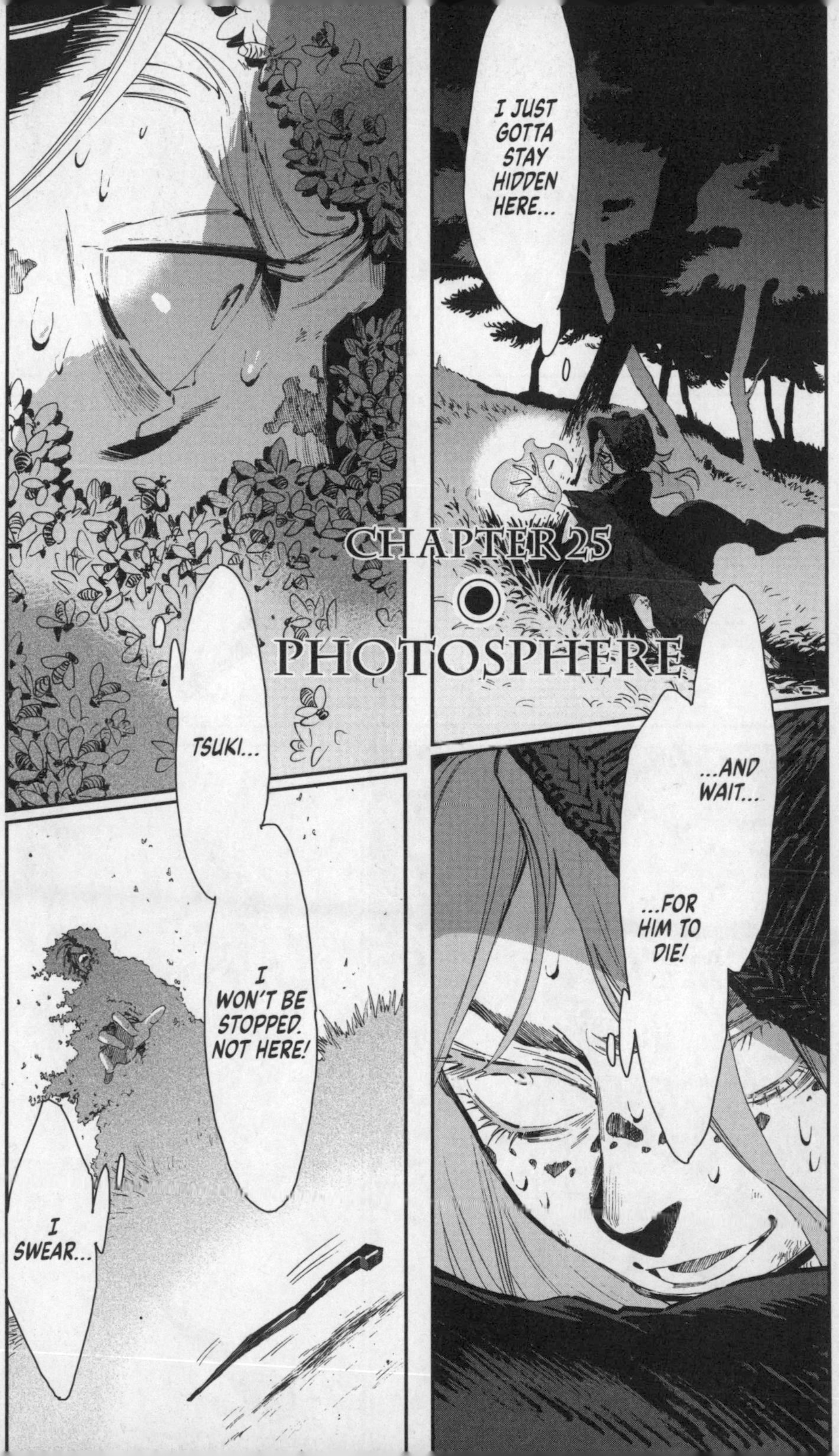
I JUST GOTTA STAY HIDDEN HERE...
CHAPTER 25
PHOTOSPHERE
TSUKI...
...AND WAIT...
...FOR HIM TO DIE!
I WON'T BE STOPPED. NOT HERE!
I SWEAR...

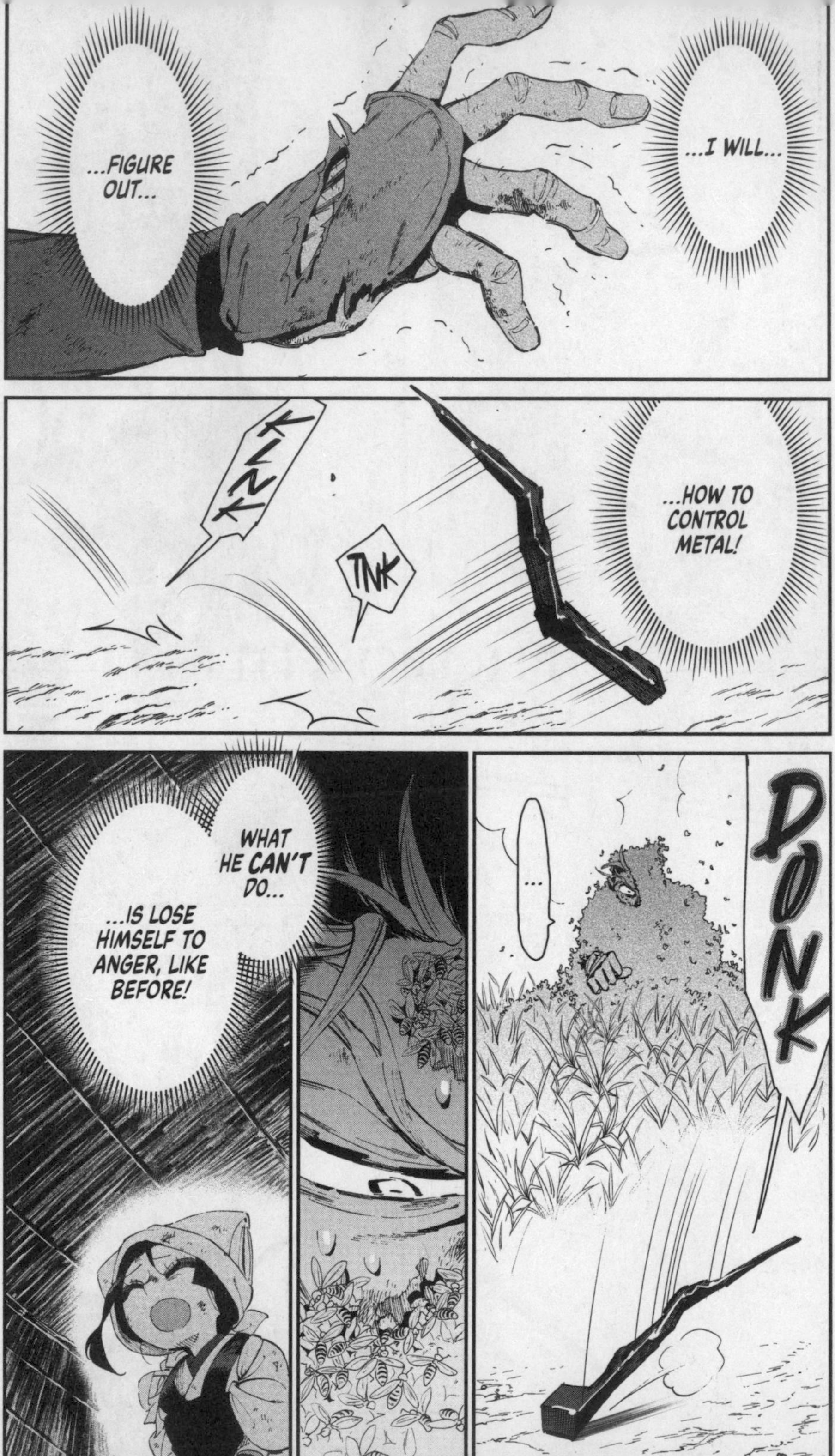
...I WILL...
...FIGURE OUT...
...HOW TO CONTROL METAL!
TNK
KLNK
DONK
...
WHAT HE CAN'T DO...
...IS LOSE HIMSELF TO ANGER, LIKE BEFORE!

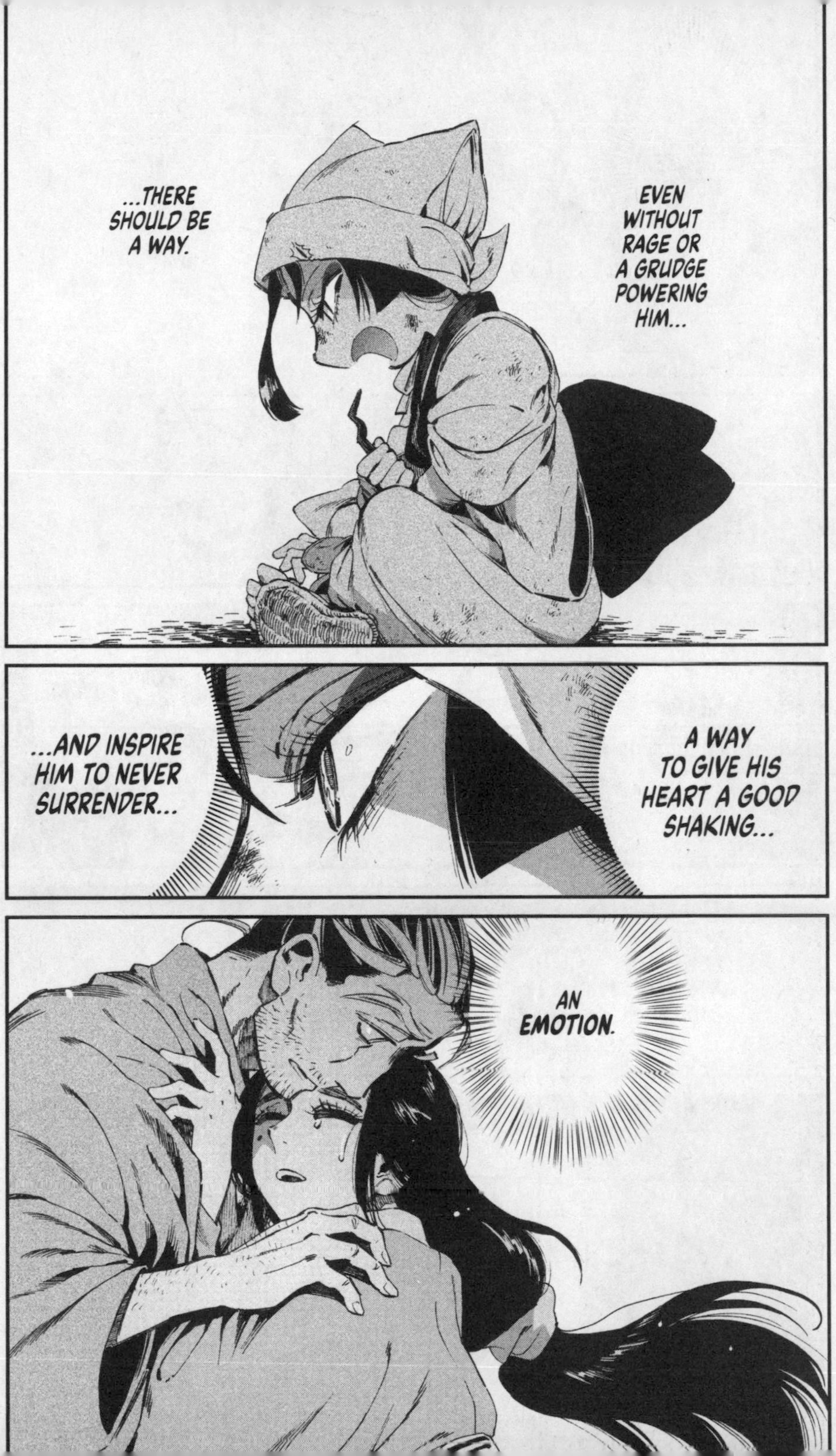
EVEN WITHOUT RAGE OR A GRUDGE POWERING HIM...
...THERE SHOULD BE A WAY.
A WAY TO GIVE HIS HEART A GOOD SHAKING...
...AND INSPIRE HIM TO NEVER SURRENDER...
AN EMOTION.

I YEARN TO FEEL YOU.

TSUKI...

THERE IS NO OTHER PATH.

...BY YOUR SIDE.

TO LIVE...

...LIGHT TO THE FUTURE.

YOU ARE MY ONE AND ONLY...

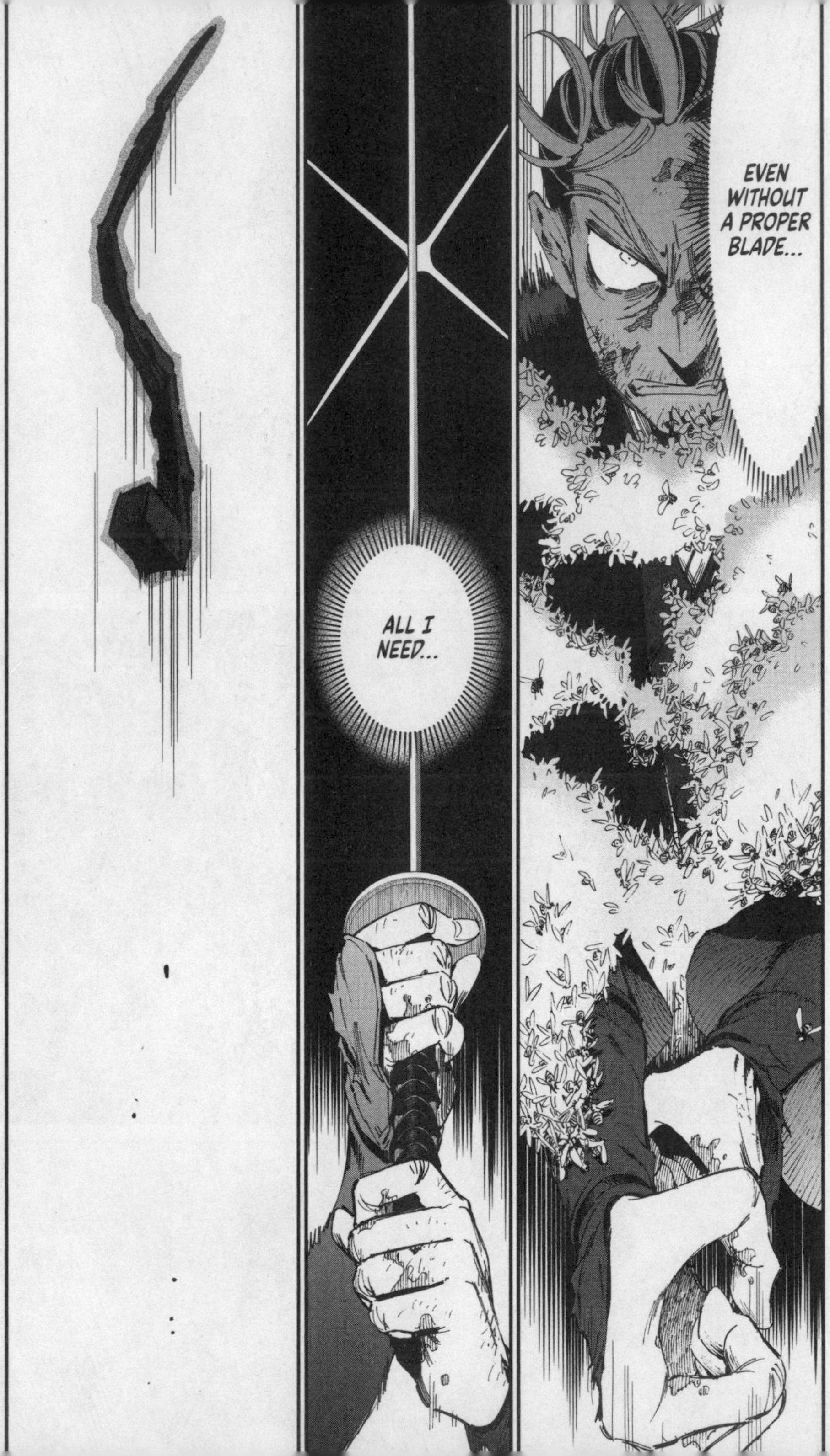
EVEN WITHOUT A PROPER BLADE...
ALL I NEED...

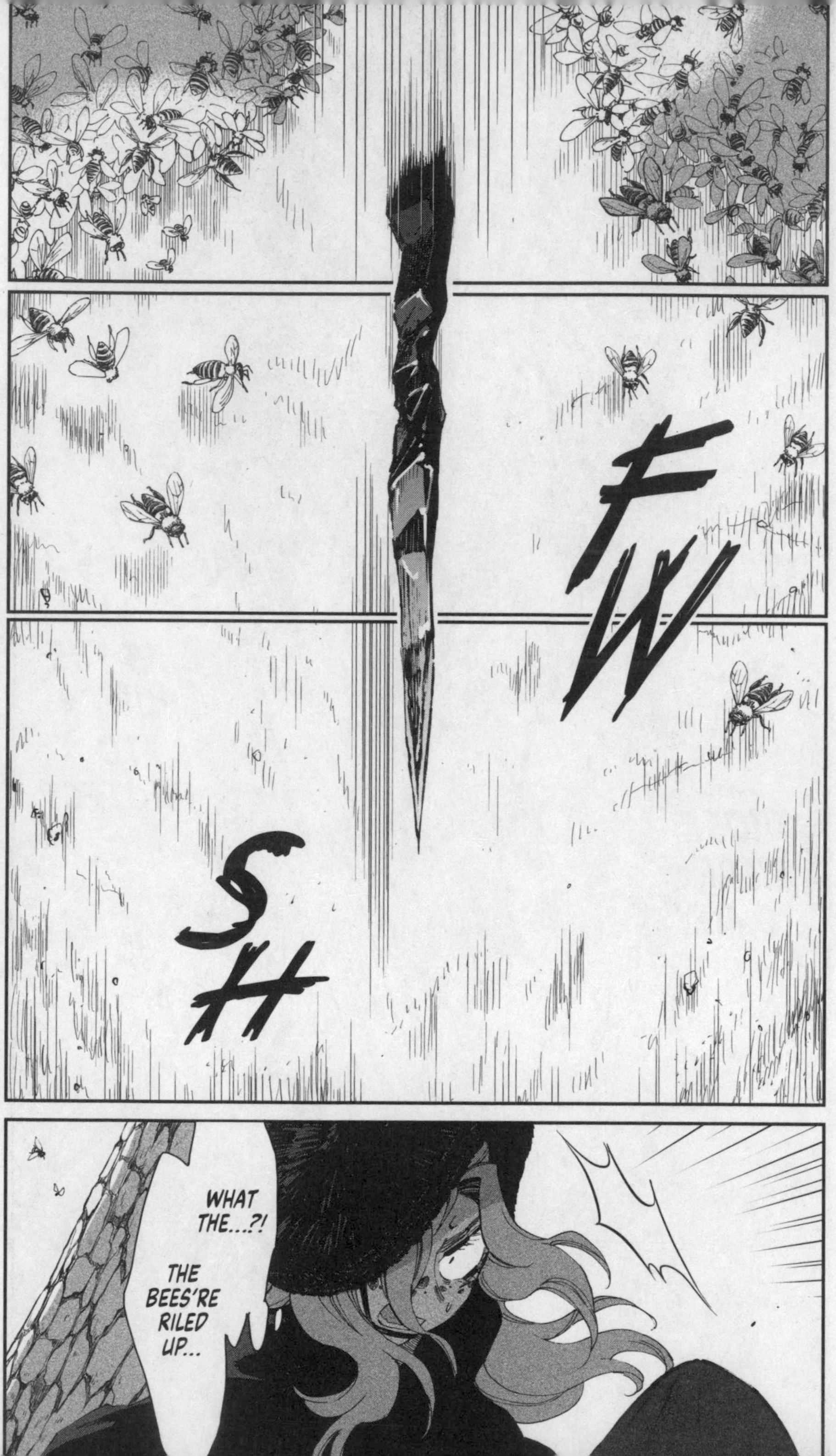
FW
SH
WHAT THE...?!
THE BEES'RE RILED UP...

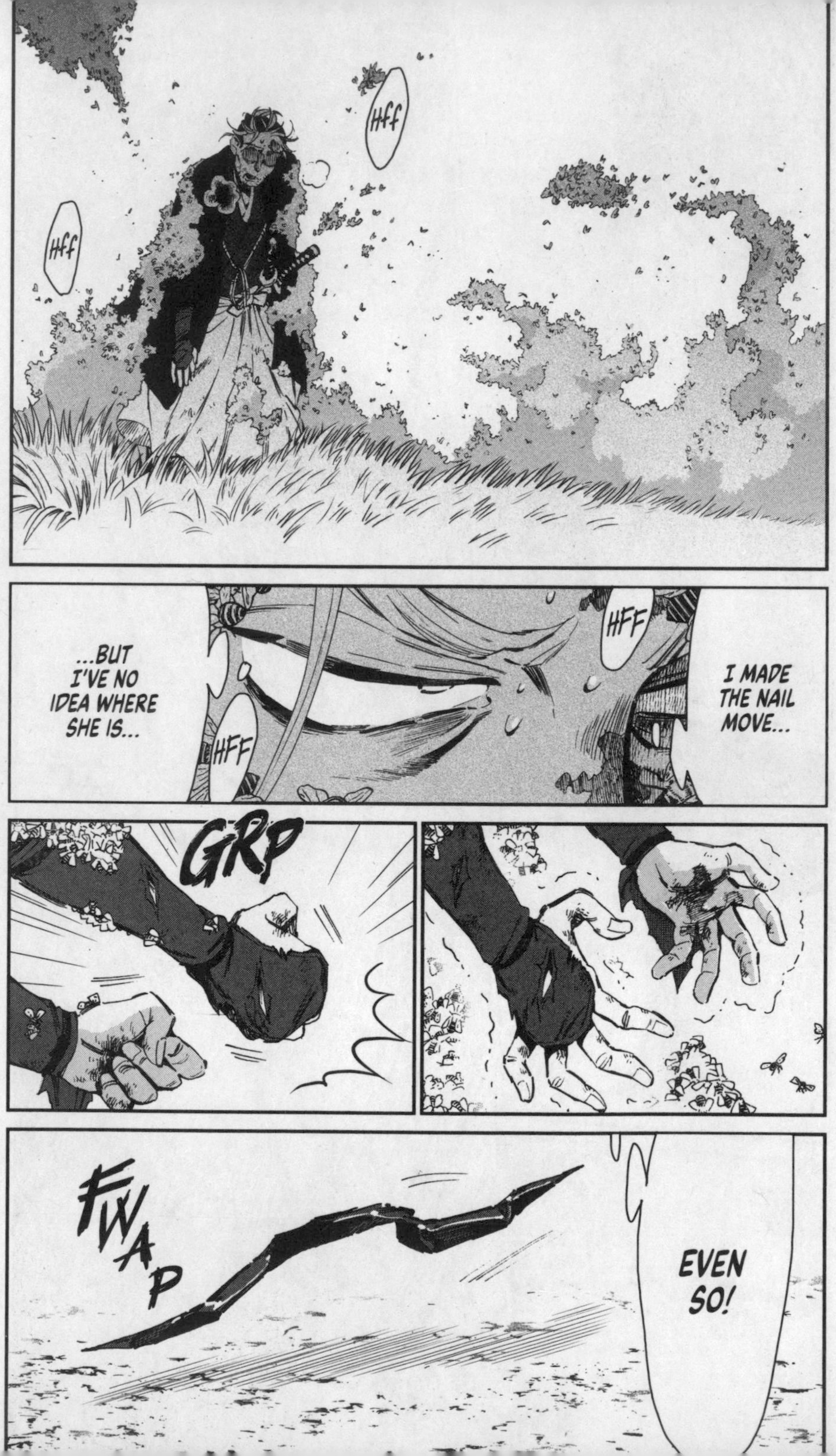
Hff
Hff
I MADE THE NAIL MOVE...
HFF
HFF
...BUT I'VE NO IDEA WHERE SHE IS...
GRP
FWAP
EVEN SO!

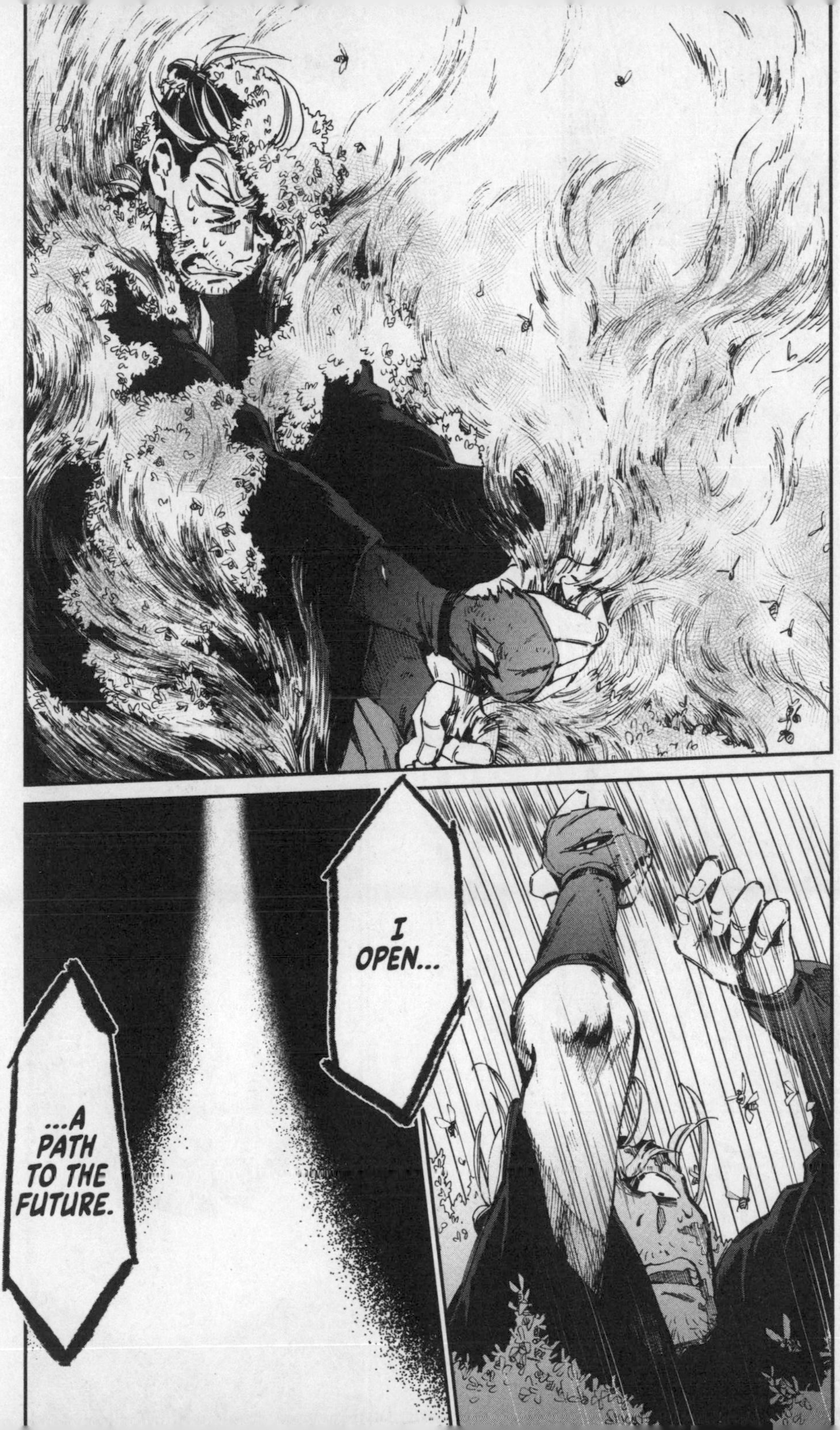
I OPEN...
...A PATH TO THE FUTURE.

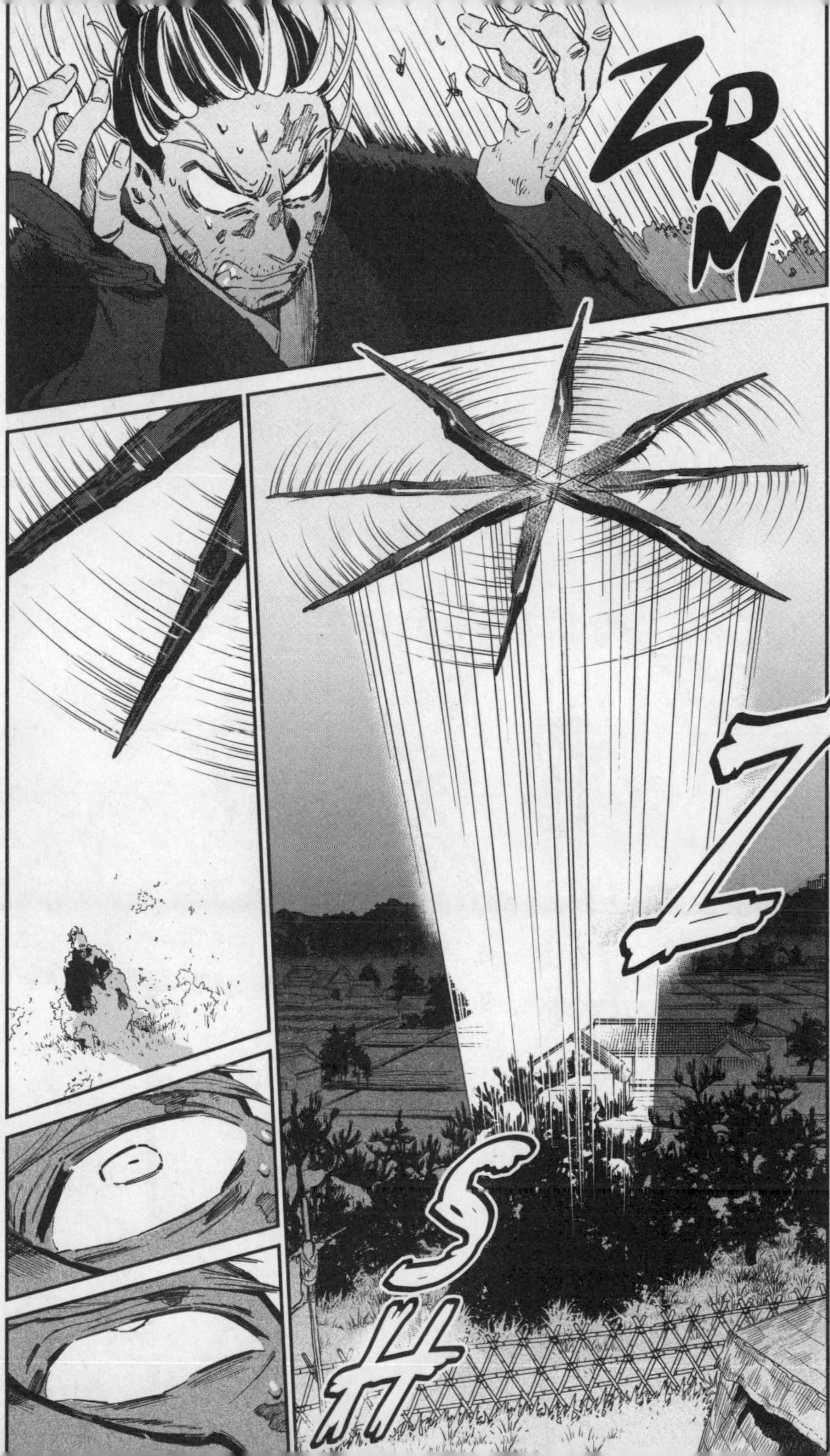
ZRM
ZSH

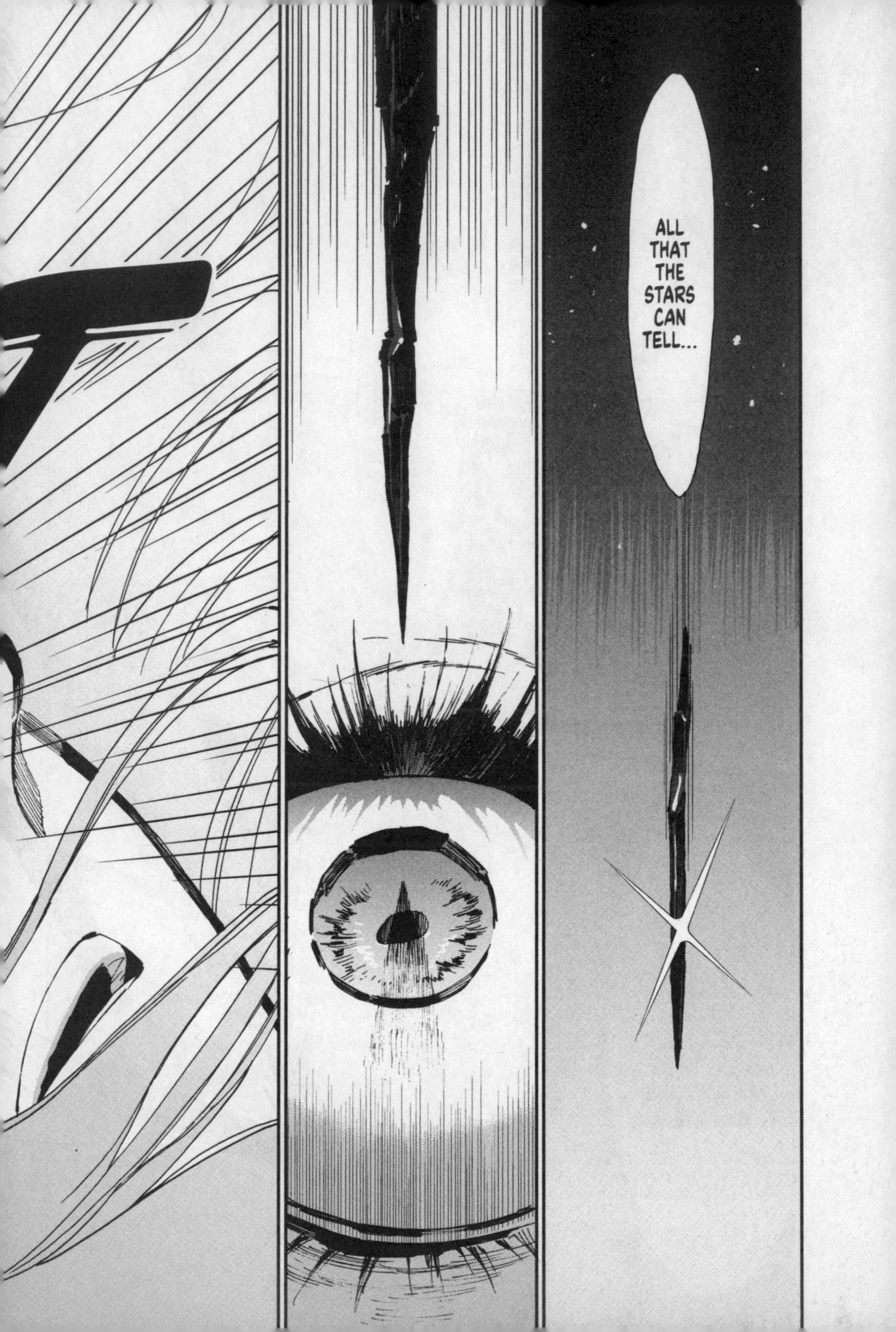
ALL THAT THE STARS CAN TELL...

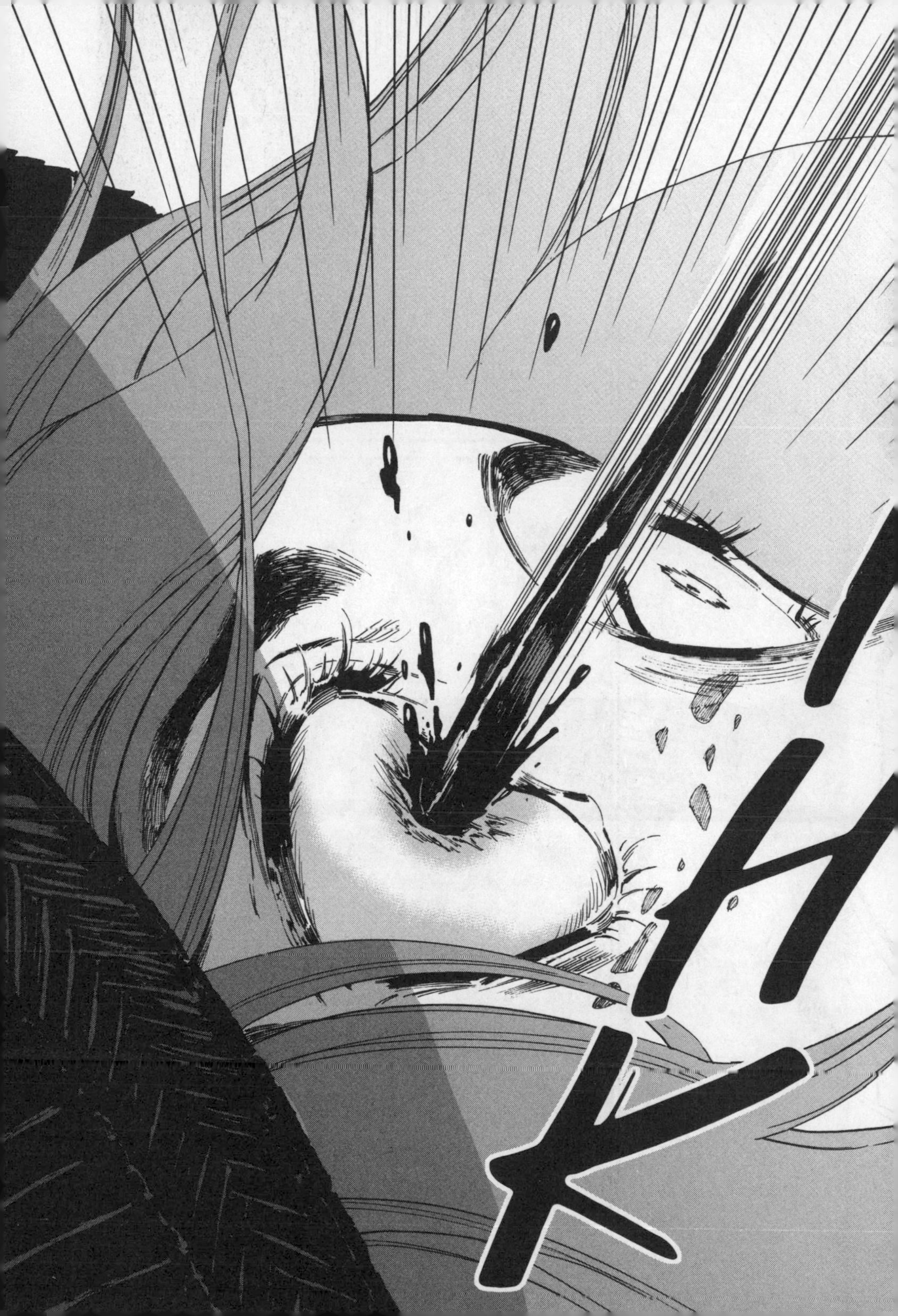

STEEL *of the* CELESTIAL SHADOWS

Madara Concept Art

Madara

Wields bugs. Strictly speaking, she summons them from else— where.

Views herself and the bugs as one and the same.

Born in a rural community, she emerged from her mother covered in insects. Later, a poor harvest (caused by leafhopper bugs) was blamed on her. The townsfolk decided to burn her, in the fashion of the traditional torch procession to purge crop-eating bugs. After barely escaping with her life, she was taken in by a temple. While assisting grave diggers on the temple grounds, she could avoid prying eyes.

Haretake made her aware of the value of her own life, and of the lives of bugs. She came to believe that bugs, humans, and all of nature are essential elements of the world. Because Haretake is such an absolute figure to her, she's more than willing to kill those who might threaten him. By viewing all life as being equally valuable (to an extreme extent), she doesn't think highly of any given individual life.

Insect aficionado, Shiba Kokan once said, "I feel that humans and insects are not so 'fundamentally different.'"

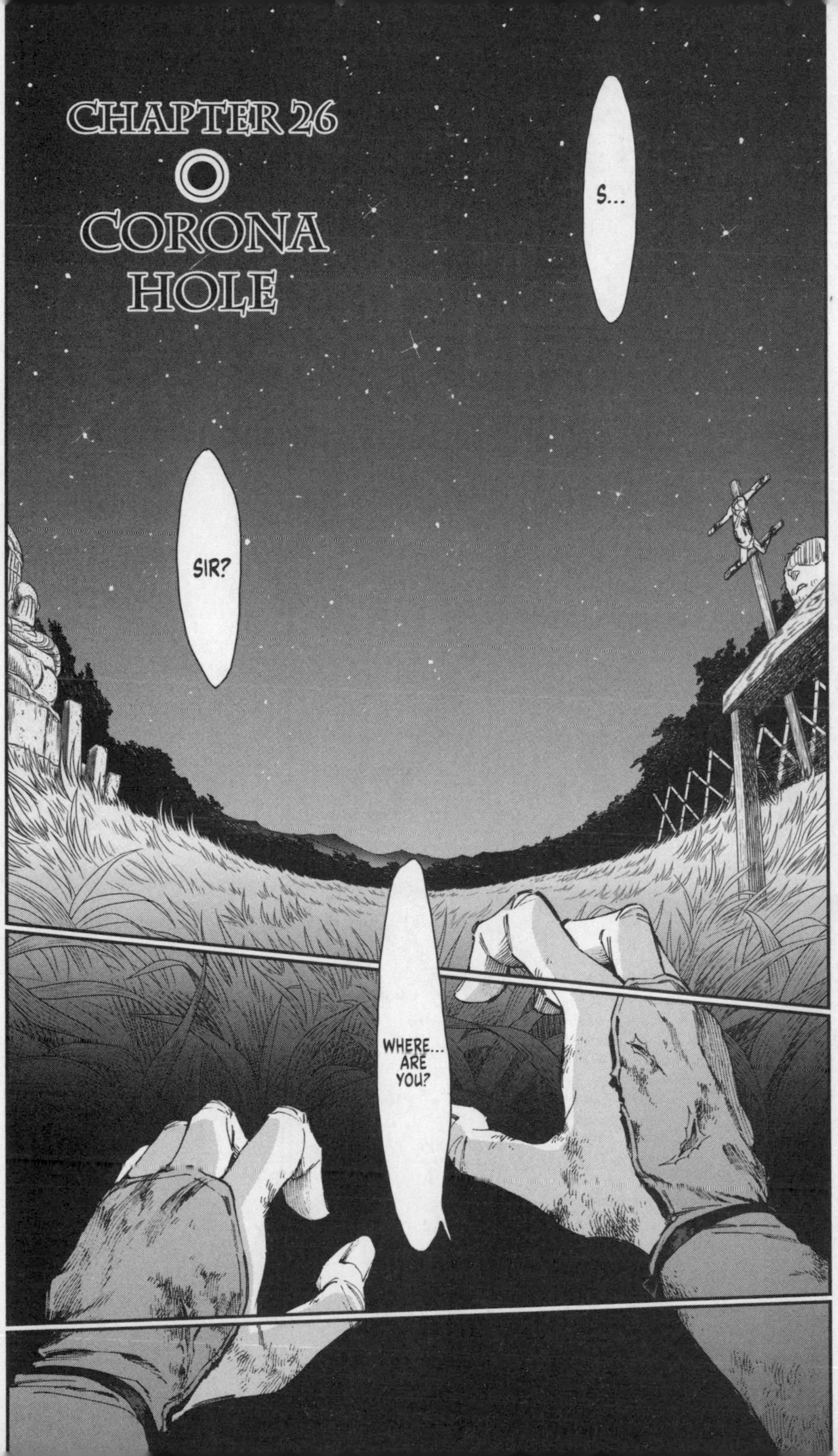
CHAPTER 26
CORONA HOLE
S...
SIR?
WHERE... ARE YOU?

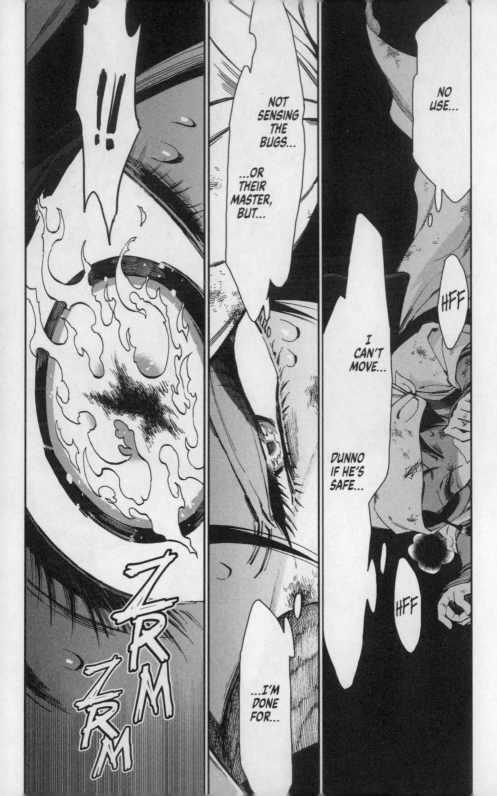

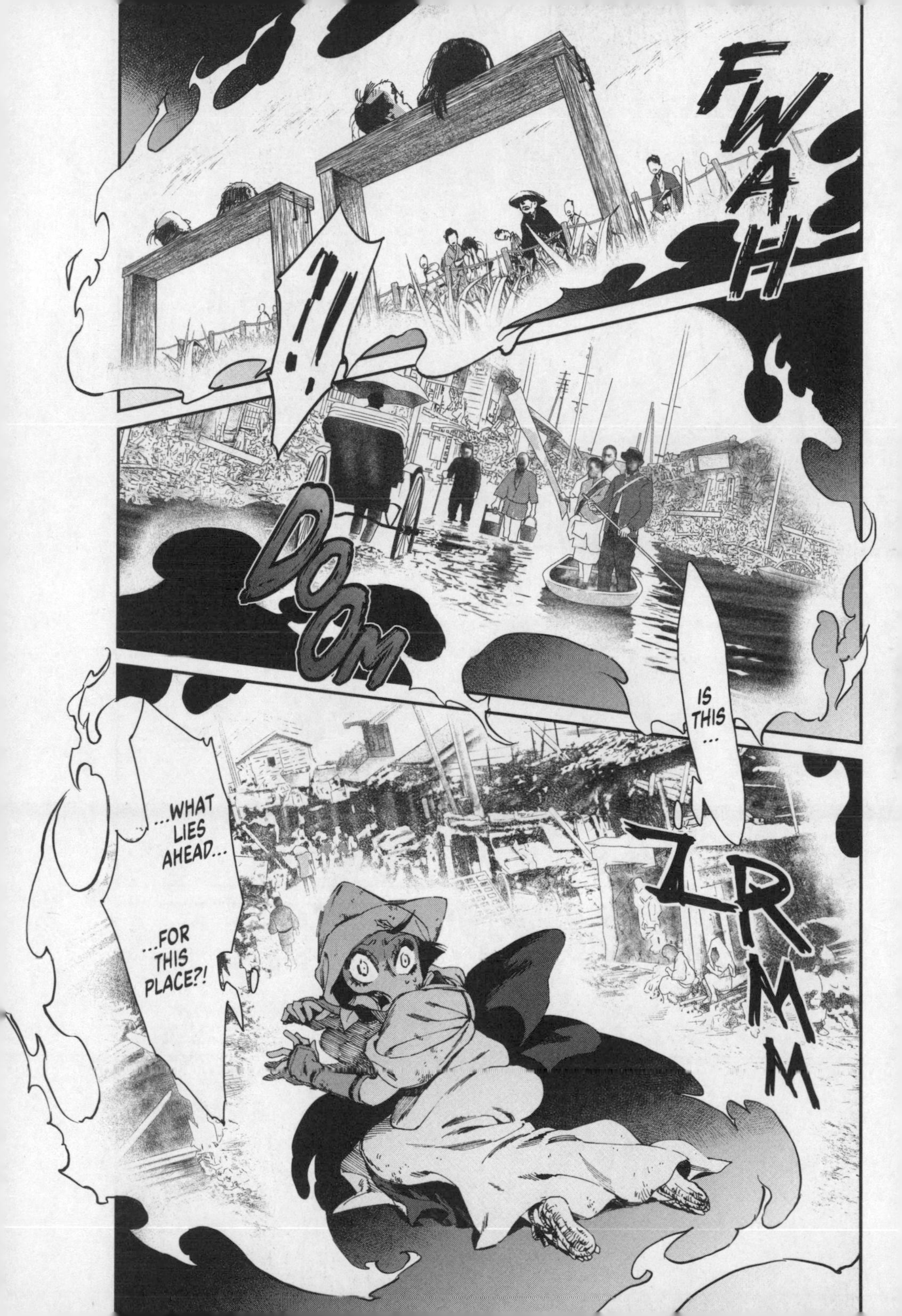
FWAH
?!
DOOM
IS THIS...
...WHAT LIES AHEAD...
...FOR THIS PLACE?!
ZRMM

CAN'T... SUPPRESS... MY POWER! IT'S TOO MUCH!

N-NO, STOP!

HAAA

HAAA

IF I GOT A READ ON A PERSON RIGHT NOW...

CAN'T... SHUT MY EYES!

TMP

Ack ...

Ah ...

...I'D SEE TOO MUCH! IT'D BREAK ME!

RELAX.

...AND OUT.

CALM DOWN.

HFFF

HAAH

FWOO

NICE AND SLOW. BREATHE IN...

CAN YOU GET UP? LEAN ON MY SHOULDER.

OL' RYUDO'S JUST FINE.

I'M BOKUTAKE!

WHO... ARE THESE PEOPLE?

AND OVER THERE'S MY PAL, ZANNEN.

YOU'LL WANNA CLEAR YOUR HEAD OF ALL THOUGHTS WHEN BOKUTAKE'S NEAR.

HOW'D HE KNOW MY NAME?

WE'RE NO STRANGERS TO OL' RYUDO.

Y'GOT THAT, AKI-SAN?

HE'S GOT A TALENT FOR READING MINDS.

A SHORTCUT, COURTESY OF A HEX.

EVERY INARI SHRINE ACROSS EDO CONNECTS TO THIS PASSAGE.

NOT ME. THIS'S COURTESY OF MY *MASTER*.

YUP!

...HIS GIFT'S NOT BEHIND THIS...

BUT...

TUG TUG

BOKU-TAKE!!

MY MASTER'S WAY MORE DASHING. SMARTER, TOO.

ZANNEN AIN'T MY MASTER, IF YOU'RE WONDERING.

AH.

...ARE ALL AGENTS OF THE TSUCHI-MIKADO.

...AND THAT MADARA GAL WHO YOUR PAL TOOK OUT...

SO ZANNEN, ME...

BUT...

TH-THEY'RE ALLIED WITH THE BUG LADY?!

TSUKI-SAN...

THIS FELLA'S WIFE SAVED MY HIDE ONCE.

...

K L A T

*THE SUMIDA RIVER

...AND WILL LEAVE EDO BY BOAT.

Y'KNOW THE OHASHI BRIDGE? WE CROSSED TO THE OTHER SHORE, TO HASHIDO INARI SHRINE.

NOW WE'VE HIT THE OKAWA*...

W-WHERE ARE WE?

KLAK TMP

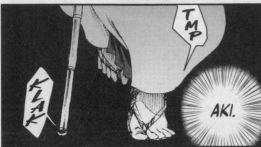

KLAK TMP

AKI.

SORRY I CAN'T HELP YA DOWN!

WATCH YOUR STEP!

"OUR EYES..."

"...MAY NOT SEE THE LIGHT."

"HOWEVER..."

CARE-FUL!

WOBBL

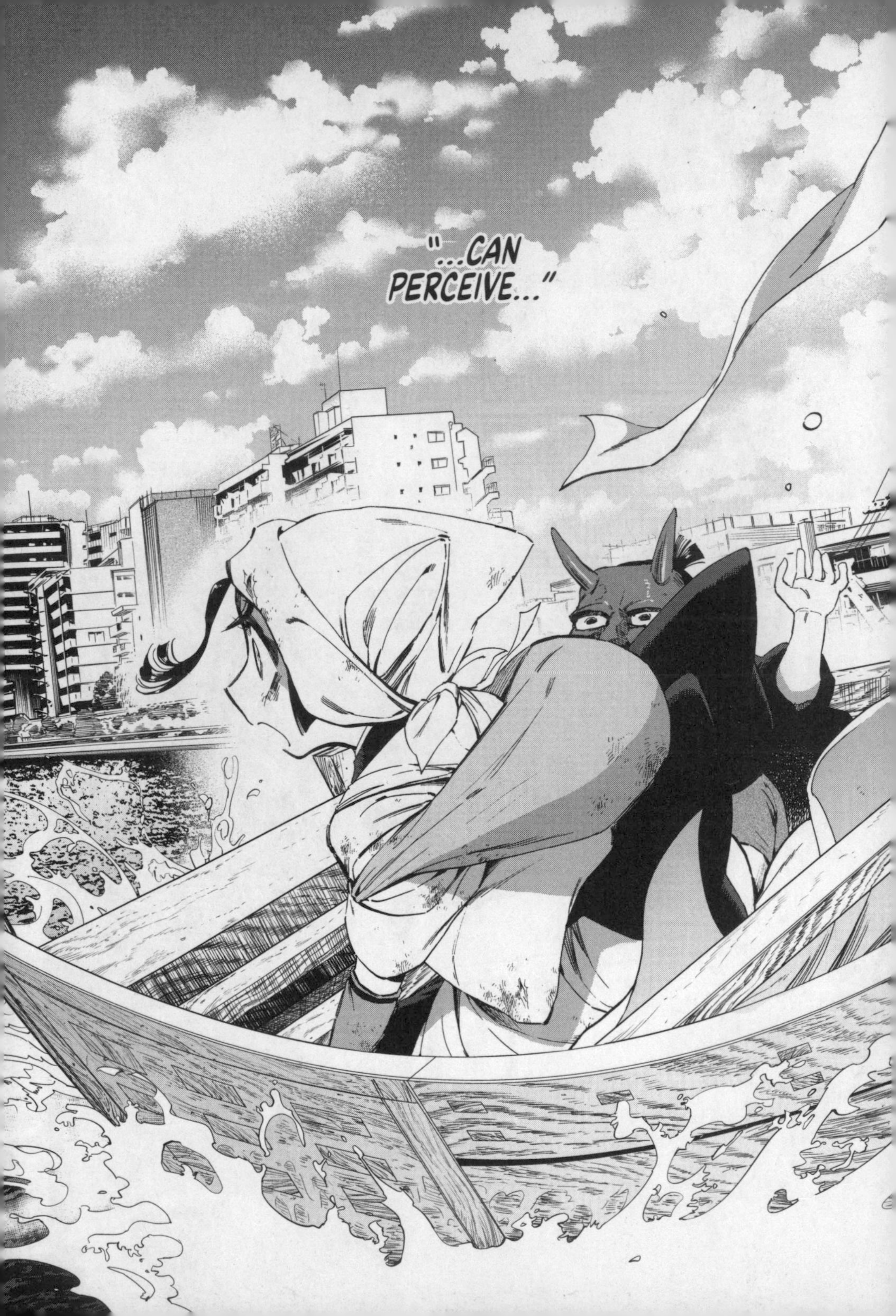
"...CAN PERCEIVE..."

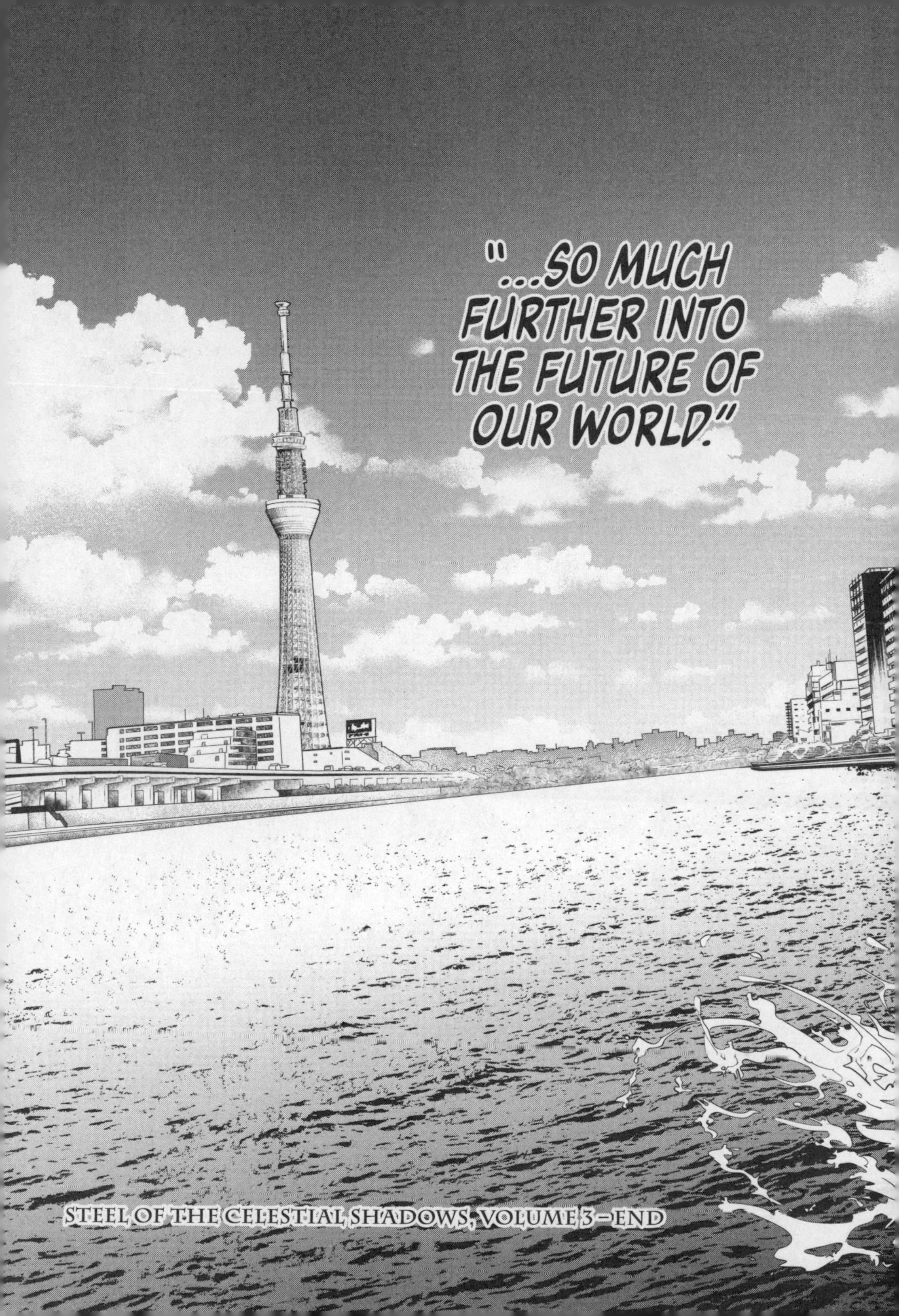
"...SO MUCH FURTHER INTO THE FUTURE OF OUR WORLD."
STEEL OF THE CELESTIAL SHADOWS, VOLUME 3—END

【 **WITH HELP FROM** 】 【 **CONSULTANTS** 】

(in no particular order,
and with titles omitted)

My Staff

Saburo Kirigakure

Doom Kobayashi

Masashi Motegi (Tadashi Sato)

Satoko Matsumoto

Hiroto Yokoyama

Subaru Niina

Takanashi

Fuki Hinohara

Saki Toda

Daichi Kawada

Noboru Hisayama

Toshiki Mizutani

【 **ORIGINAL DESIGN** 】

Kohei Nawata Design Office

【 **RESEARCH ASSISTANCE** 】

Kazuya Namiki
    [Jikishinkage-ryu Kuunkai]

Akira Takemoto

Bonus Comic

Thank you for reading *Steel of the Celestial Shadows!*

Meep, meep!

In a meeting, pre-COVID pandemic

KAGO KAKI
TAXI

It's said that fellow kagokaki operators would sometimes race each other, even while on the job, even if it meant that passengers would get jostled and fall out.

And so on, and so forth.

I recommend this book.

Mizu
Hisa

Too funny!

SPURT

Ed.

Ooh!

I really ought to thank my consultants, Noboru Hisayama Sensei, and Toshiki Mizutani Sensei, who performed meticulous checks on the work and helped patch up any holes.

My last series, Kasane, was set in modern times, but...

This one's a period piece!!

HA RA KI RI

I'm all kinds of nervous about tackling this challenge.

A fascinating and valuable collection, with (famous) reproductions of a tenement and a boat house!

Enough of that, please.

Saburo Kirigakure Sensei

Stick this on a long pole, and you'll be tempted to swing it around.

YAP YAP

Fukagawa Edo Archive Collection

I also have to thank my staff. Some of them even came with me on research trips (this was also pre-pandemic).